MW01701632

The Washington Post

DINING GUIDE

[*The definitive word on where to eat in and around the Nation's Capital*]

~REVISED AND UPDATED~

TOM SIETSEMA

FOOD CRITIC FOR THE WASHINGTON POST

The Washington Post Dining Guide
by Tom Sietsema

Published by

The Washington Post

1150 15th St. NW
Washington, D.C. 20071

The body copy is set in Filosofia, and the display typefaces are Trade Gothic Bold Condensed and Script MT Std.

Printed by Chroma Graphics, Largo, Md., in association with Alan Abrams.
ISBN: 1-930691-05-X

Publisher: Lionel Neptune
Editor: Janet Bennett Kelly
Book Design & Production: Brian Noyes
Copy Editor: Kathleen Stanley
Researcher: Terri Sapienza
Assistant: Karen Hill
Map illustration: Gene Thorp
Illustrations: Eric Hanson
Photographs: Allison Dinner

CONTENTS

INTRODUCTION

Pesce, Washington, DC

IT'S THE QUESTION EVERY FOOD CRITIC HEARS—and tries to beg off answering: What's your favorite restaurant? "Favorite restaurant for *what?*" is how I'm likely to respond. A date? Dinner with the kids? Something French, or Japanese? I could no more easily pick a single favorite venue out of the crowded field of contenders than I could prepare every recipe in "The Joy of Cooking" in a week. There's no *one* restaurant I'd want to eat in every day. On the other hand, there are plenty of places I admire for different reasons and for different occasions. After five years of table-hopping as The Washington Post's food critic, I want to share them with you in this, my second restaurant guide.

Keep in mind, this isn't a compilation of "bests" (though those restaurants are well-represented) and not all of the restaurants herein are winners (I eat bad food so you don't have to). Instead, consider this book a guide to places near and far, grand and plain, pricey and cheap, fun and serious, that represent the full scope of Washington eateries, from humble to haute and from fair to fabulous.

SINCE MY 2003 BOOK, the Washington restaurant scene has shifted, and mostly in exciting directions. Thai and Indian eateries are growing in number—and improving in quality. Little details here and there underscore raised standards: Fresh wasabi is the new norm in Japanese restaurants, and even unpretentious neighborhood spots are offering their customers an amuse-bouche (a bonus nibble from the chef) before dinner gets started. Red wine is still being served too warm, and vegetarians continue to have to hunt for good things to eat on too many menus, but bread baskets are more interesting and drinks are garnering headlines of their own. Plus, bursts of creative energy from high-profile chefs (Michel Richard, Jose Andres, Eric Ziebold) and lesser-known ones (Cathal Armstrong, Jerry Corso, Johnny Monis) are helping to keep Washington firmly on the national culinary map.

Ratings Guide

- ★ Satisfactory
- ★★ Good
- ★★★ Excellent
- ★★★★ Superlative

Restaurants that earn no stars are rated Poor. Ratings are based primarily on food quality but take into account service and ambience.

Helping you navigate the maze of possibilities, then, is this revamped restaurant guide, with star-rated reviews of 200 dining establishments and listings highlighting special features, including family-friendly venues, rooms with interesting views and places that forbid smoking.

IN MY RATING SYSTEM, zero stars reflects an overall experience that I think is poor. (However, this book contains no reviews that are rated as such.) One star stands for a satisfactory experience; two stars means good; three stars is excellent; and four stars is superlative. I base my ratings primarily on the quality of the food but also take into account service and ambience. Just keep in mind, a restaurant review is not an exact science, but rather, an educated opinion.

In the Washington area, restaurants run the gamut, from down-home to upscale, from French to Brazilian to Japanese. It's impossible to compare a pupusa with a curry. Yet those restaurants sharing the same ranking probably have a lot in common. Poor restaurants are generally disappointing on many levels. One-star restaurants are nice to know about if you live or work nearby; they may have only a handful of notable dishes or a single quality (a view, a scene) to distinguish them. Two-star restaurants have a few more frills and generally appealing cooking; they are worth driving across town for. Three-star establishments tend to be rewarding destinations, no matter where you're coming from; they typically blend high-quality cooking with environs and service to match.

To achieve four-star status, a restaurant doesn't have to spend a fortune on flowers or serve food on gold plates. It simply has to do what it does extraordinarily well—to the point of taking your breath away. No restaurant is perfect all the time, but a four-star venue is perfect more often than not. It adds up to an unsurpassed experience.

A FEW WORDS ABOUT HOW I WORK: I try to visit restaurants anonymously, making reservations under names other than my own, and my employer pays for all meals and services. A full review in The Washington Post Magazine is the distillation of multiple meals, a personal rule that allows me to see the restaurant at, say, a slow Monday lunch and a bustling Saturday dinner—and maybe again and again, sometimes over the course of several seasons.

As you use this book, remember that restaurants can—and often do—change. Chefs come and go, menus get rewritten, dining rooms get dressed up (or go drab). The silken pumpkin soup or homey chocolate cake that you read about in these pages may have been replaced by the time you visit their sources. So consider the reviews as jumping-off points rather than dictates engraved in stone.

On the job, I dine out an average of a dozen meals a week. This is not the way anyone but a food critic should eat. My advice to most of you is to collect a handful of restaurants you like, and to cultivate a relationship with them; when you get to know the menu, and the staff becomes familiar—when a place begins to feel like an extension of home—you can't help gaining more pleasure from the experience.

A BOOK IS A TEAM EFFORT, and I have had the privilege of working with a four-star stable of talent on this project. Here at The Washington Post, with the blessing of publisher Bo Jones, Lionel Neptune initiated and then shepherded the idea of an updated guide. He proved a diplomatic, attentive and tireless conductor. With the help of Karen Hill, Terri Sapienza, editorial aide in the Food section, cheerfully and valiantly oversaw fact-checking—no small task given that restaurants tend to be busy for much of the day and night (and more than a few of their staff don't speak English). Pals from my first tour of duty at this newspaper, design director Brian Noyes and copy editor Kathleen Stanley—two of the most professional and enthusiastic colleagues I've ever sweated deadlines with—went above and beyond the call of duty again to bring this book to fruition. Along with my top-notch chief editor, Janet Bennett, a friend and colleague from washingtonpost.com, their eyes for detail and helpful suggestions are evident all over these pages.

To all of you, thanks for squeezing this project into your busy lives.

I might not be writing these words if it weren't for Phyllis C. Richman, who gave a greenhorn his start as her assistant, or former Post food editor Jeanne McManus, who later hired me as a reporter. Over the years I've known them, both women have offered indispensable advice and bushels of support. And I've since been fortunate to count first Susannah Gardiner and later Lynda Robinson as editors for my weekly review in the Magazine. Every writer should be so lucky to have bosses who care about his work as much as they have—and to also remain upbeat and gracious in the process. A source of constant support, my parents, Elwin and Dorothy Sietsema, and my brother, John, remind me that nothing much matters if you don't have a loving family. (But, bro, would you please stop using our name when you make restaurant reservations?) And then there are the many friends and colleagues, too numerous to mention, who willingly go anywhere and everywhere to help me eat my way through the good, the bad and the ugly.

FINALLY, I'D LIKE TO THANK MY READERS. Your tips, your praise, your criticisms—I appreciate and encourage the dialogue. May this book help you to dine better, and may all your meals have stars in them.

Tom Sietsema

FOOD CRITIC FOR THE WASHINGTON POST

THE REVIEWS

Charlie Palmer Steak, Washington, DC

Critic's Pick

☆ ☆

A & J

1319-C ROCKVILLE PIKE, ROCKVILLE, MD
301-251-7878

THE ORIGINAL IS IN ROCKVILLE, the spinoff in Annandale. Both are small, both serve dim sum—and both always seem to be packed. It's not that people come here to be pampered: At the Rockville branch, I've watched servers shout back and forth to one another across the dining room, and in Annandale, my friends and I have waited shoulder to shoulder in a cramped entrance.

The food comes out fast, making the restaurants good choices for families, and the prices can't be beat.

And yet, there are plenty of reasons to seek out these snug Chinese restaurants. One of them is the succulent smoked chicken. A second is a salad of mustard greens tossed with soybeans and bean curd skin. And while you're ordering from the mile-long list, why not throw in some tart pickled cabbage, a restorative bowl of pork and radish soup, and "pan fried beef bun," which comes off like a juicy hamburger with an Asian accent? All are very good.

The food comes out fast, making the restaurants good choices for families, and the prices can't be beat: For less than $10, you feel as if you've feasted.

Open: M-F 11-9, SAT-SUN 10-9 ***Entrees:*** $1.55-$5.65 (SMALL DISHES)
Chinese Breakfast: SAT-SUN 10-12:30 ***Entrees:*** $1.25-$5.65 (SMALL DISHES)
Credit Cards: NO (CASH ONLY) ***Reservations:*** NO
Dress: CASUAL ***Cross Street:*** TEMPLETON PLACE
Parking: LOT ***Metro:*** TWINBROOK
Second Location: 4316-B MARKHAM ST., ANNANDALE, VA, 703-813-8181

★ ★

ACADIANA

901 NEW YORK AVE. NW, WASHINGTON, DC (DOWNTOWN) 202-408-8848
www.acadianarestaurant.com

HOT BISCUITS LAND ON THE TABLE as soon as we're seated, and turtle soup laced with sherry and barbecued shrimp with their heads on follow in due time. Once again, the owners behind downtown Washington's successful DC Coast, TenPenh and Ceiba are attempting to re-create a flavorful part of the world—in this instance, Louisiana—for the appreciative masses.

The business partners got a lot right. Those biscuits are terrific, fried green tomatoes crackle between the teeth and the aforementioned shrimp are lusty in their dark and brassy sauce, which comes with French bread for sopping up every luscious drop. A trio of deviled eggs—each sporting a different topping—is church supper fare gone upscale; a rosy fist of grilled beef gets a curtain of blue cheese sauce and onion rings that could pass for edible bracelets; and crepes stuffed with mellow bananas and garnished with candied orange peel proves a sweet nod to the classic bananas Foster. Some of the other flavors are timid, and the sorbets are a bust, but the winners outpace the clinkers on the menu.

A trio of deviled eggs—each sporting a different topping—is church supper fare gone upscale.

Like the other members of its family, Acadiana dishes up smiles and solicitousness. Unlike its nearby relatives, and despite the flowery fabrics and dangling chandeliers, the sibling is not especially attractive. If you want to feel transported to New Orleans, just close your eyes, sniff—and taste.

Lunch: M-F 11:30-2:30 *Entrees:* $12-$26
Dinner: M-TH 5:30-10:30 F-SAT 5:30-11 *Entrees:* $19-$27
Closed: SUN *Credit Cards:* ALL MAJOR *Reservations:* RECOMMENDED
Dress: BUSINESS CASUAL *Cross Street:* NINTH
Parking: $6 VALET BEGINNING AT 5:30 *Metro:* GALLERY PLACE-CHINATOWN

★ ★ 1/2

ADDIE'S

11120 ROCKVILLE PIKE, ROCKVILLE, MD 301-881-0081
www.blackrestaurantgroup.com

SET IN AN OLD BUNGALOW, Addie's still looks like someone's home. One room is a soft yellow, the other a soothing shade of green, and both wrap their customers in a warm embrace of comfort, with old food advertisements on the walls and easy, attentive service.

The food looks backward and forward at the same time: Homey roast chicken makes an appearance with fresh asparagus, tiny carrots—and a base of orzo made creamy with mascarpone. More straightforward, but equally inviting, is a grilled rib-eye steak with mashed potatoes, sauteed spinach and a top of lacy onion rings that quickly disappear as everyone at the table reaches over to try them while they're hot. Yellowfin tuna is edged with sesame seeds and then barely cooked, so that the fish resembles sashimi; sticky rice, cucumber salad and a glaze of wasabi and soy sauce give the dish an Asian accent.

Don't let your meal end until you've tried a sliver of the chocolate mint torte.

Don't let your meal end until you've tried a sliver of the chocolate mint torte. "It's like an after-dinner mint," our waitress said, and she was right. In all, the service and the food will make you happy you braved Rockville Pike during rush hour.

Lunch: M-F 11:30-2:30, SAT NOON-2:30 ***Entrees:*** $7.95-$13.95
Dinner: M-TH 5:30-9:30, F 5:30-10, SAT 5-10, SUN 5-9 ***Entrees:*** $18-$27
Credit Cards: ALL MAJOR ***Reservations:*** RECOMMENDED
Dress: BUSINESS CASUAL ***Cross Street:*** EDSON LANE
Parking: LOT ***Metro:*** WHITE FLINT

★ 1/2

AFGHAN

2700 JEFFERSON DAVIS HWY., ALEXANDRIA, VA
703-548-0022

THE VIEW FROM THE WINDOWS is mostly highway, and the service can be matter-of-fact. Yet this big restaurant—which almost triples in size when its folding doors are parted, revealing a satellite dining room—manages to conjure Afghanistan with evocative music on the sound system and food that speaks in a nurturing voice.

The flat bread alone warrants a visit. A ubiquitous sight in dining rooms and shop windows in Kabul, here in Alexandria it shows up on seemingly every table: flat ovals more than a foot long, crisp and chewy after doing some time in a clay oven.

At lunch, bargain hunters can round out the bread with a meal composed of a dozen or so chafing dishes on a buffet, all for $7.95. Imagine fried eggplant, chicken curry, and Basmati rice threaded with carrots and sweet with plump raisins. At any time, there are à la carte kebabs of deftly seasoned chicken, beef and ground lamb (my pick); luscious crescent-shaped dumplings stuffed with scallions and topped with a zesty yogurt and meat sauce; and vegetable pleasures extending to fried spinach and—one last Afghan touch—sauteed pumpkin.

At lunch, bargain hunters can round out the bread with a meal composed of a dozen or so chafing dishes on a buffet, all for $7.95.

Open: DAILY 11-10:30 *Entrees:* $8.95-$14.95
Lunch Buffet: M-F 11-3 $7.95
Credit Cards: ALL MAJOR *Reservations:* RECOMMENDED
Dress: CASUAL *Cross Street:* CALVERT AVENUE
Parking: LOT *Metro:* CRYSTAL CITY

★ 1/2

AL CROSTINO

1324 U ST. NW, WASHINGTON, DC (U STREET CORRIDOR)
202-797-0523

LIKE ITS SIBLING, Al Tiramisu in Dupont Circle, Al Crostino wraps you in a warm embrace. And as at Al Tiramisu, the two-level, lime-green and lemon-yellow space is pint-size. "I wonder if they have tables in the bathroom," a friend joked after she and I were seated in a narrow corridor behind the central dining area.

As a diner might expect, there are crostini on the menu. The selections are subject to change but have included toasted rounds of bread slathered with a mild chicken liver pâté and anchovy-laced mozzarella—my favorites—as well as more routine minced roasted vegetables and porcini mushrooms. Beyond those nibbles, the menu reads much like that of Al Tiramisu, offering skewered seafood, lamb chops with a glaze of honey and balsamic vinegar, and, irritatingly, specials whose prices don't get recited by the server but are outside the average price of the regular menu.

Pastas include pillowy hats stuffed with minced mushrooms and ricotta cheese gilded with a buttery, sage-scented moistener.

There have been some perfectly pleasant moments during my visits. Escolar is tiled in slices of zucchini so thin you can read through them and lapped with a creamy and delicate sauce of mascarpone and prosecco. Lovely. Pastas include pillowy hats stuffed with minced mushrooms and ricotta cheese gilded with a buttery, sage-scented moistener. And the aforementioned trio of tiny lamb chops gets a nice boost from its tart-sweet sauce—but not from the dull clump of chard that serves as an escort, along with ordinary roasted potatoes.

Other dishes taste as if they hail from a different kitchen. The squid and shrimp skewer I gravitate to at Al Tiramisu is offered here as just some ordinary seafood in a tasteless crumb coating. I ordered the sliced steak after a server praised it as "off the hook!"; what I got was juicy but surprisingly tame, despite a scattering of shredded arugula and rosemary needles on the beef.

Creme caramel makes me yawn, too, and "crunchy Italian cookies" turn out to be ordinary bite-size biscotti. Cheese—and another glass of vino—make for a stronger ending at what can only be summed up as Al Tiramisu Lite.

Open: SUN-TH 5-11, F-SAT 5-MIDNIGHT ***Entrees:*** $12-$30
Credit Cards: AE, DC, MC, V ***Reservations:*** RECOMMENDED
Dress: CASUAL ***Cross Street:*** 13TH
Parking: STREET ***Metro:*** U ST / AFRICAN-AMER CIVIL WAR MEMORIAL / CARDOZO

Critic's Pick

☆ ☆ 1/2

AL TIRAMISU

2014 P ST. NW, WASHINGTON, DC (DUPONT CIRCLE) 202-467-4466
www.altiramisu.com

A MAN WITH A STARCHED WHITE chef's jacket strolls through the dining room with an earthy harbinger of fall in Italy. "The season's truffles!" trumpets owner Luigi Diotaiuti. All smiles, he holds out a bowl of what looks like white rocks; their intoxicating perfume reminds you they're kitchen gold (and best indulged, shaved, over risotto).

Despite its cramped and sometimes noisy quarters, Al Tiramisu remains the city's most joyful Italian experience. Part of this mood is encouraged by the convivial and attentive staff up front, but the cooks play along, too. They grill a fabulous veal chop, treat flapping-fresh fish with care (look for treasures like turbot or Dover sole) and do pasta proud, be it ravioli filled with butternut squash and draped with a smooth walnut sauce or gnocchi, tender nuggets treated to an onion-sweetened tomato sauce.

Despite its cramped and sometimes noisy quarters, Al Tiramisu remains the city's most joyful Italian experience.

Dessert is a no-brainer: Just repeat the restaurant's name.

Lunch: M-F NOON-2 ***Entrees:*** $15.90-$18.90
Dinner: DAILY 5-11 ***Entrees:*** $15.90-$18.90
Credit Cards: AE, DC, MC, V ***Reservations:*** REQUIRED
Dress: BUSINESS CASUAL ***Cross Street:*** 20TH
Parking: $5 VALET AT DINNER ***Metro:*** DUPONT CIRCLE

Critic's Pick
★ ★ 1/2

AMICI MIEI

1093 SEVEN LOCKS RD., ROCKVILLE, MD
301-545-0966

DON'T LET ITS SHOPPING-MALL LOCATION or a provocative photograph of Sophia Loren at the front door scare you off. The cheese factor at Amici Miei ("My Friends") is limited to fresh mozzarella in the tomato salad and creamy ricotta (and spinach) inside delectable ravioli.

Brought to life in December 2004 by Davide Megna, the former chef of Washington's Arucola, and Roberto Deias, a one-time waiter at that establishment, the restaurant dishes up real Italian cooking with gusto and finesse: smoky baby octopus arranged on soft cubes of potato with herb sauce; a classic vitello tonnato (sheer slices of veal topped with a creamy sauce of tuna and capers); and pizza that leaves its wood-burning oven with a thin charred crust and a fresh-tasting tomato sauce.

Most of the pastas are made in-house, as are the breads, and the chicken is free-range.

Details add up. Most of the pastas are made in-house, as are the breads, and the chicken is free-range. If the dining room reminds you of a generic hotel, the setting gets a boost from an exposed kitchen and affable cruise director (host Deias).

Lunch: M-SAT 11:30-2:30 ***Entrees:*** $6.95-$10.95
Dinner: SUN-TH 5-10, F-SAT 5-10:30 ***Entrees:*** $8.95-$21.95
Credit Cards: ALL MAJOR ***Reservations:*** RECOMMENDED
Dress: CASUAL ***Cross Street:*** MONTROSE ROAD
Parking: LOT ***Metro:*** ROCKVILLE

★ 1/2

AMMA VEGETARIAN KITCHEN

344-A MAPLE AVE E., VIENNA, VA
703-938-5328

A MERE SHOEBOX, this combination carryout / eatery puts its energy into flavors, not frills. So the utensils are plastic, and the cooking packs some punch—enough to keep the dozen or so tables occupied during prime time. It's promising to see so many Indian faces in the mix, though it might help if the staff had a better command of English.

The main attractions on the brief roster are the thin, crisp pancakes called dosas. Their batter, made with rice and lentils, is allowed to ferment and is then fried into a pleasantly tangy round that can be broken off and dipped into coconut chutney or partnered with a filling and gently rolled up (picture an Indian burrito). At Amma, which has a dressier sibling of the same name in Georgetown, the filling choices include variations on potatoes mashed with onion and a bit of cumin. Sambar, a souplike accompaniment made of lentils, okra and other vegetables, is included in the price of each dosa, turning the snack into a meal.

The main attractions on the brief roster are the thin, crisp pancakes called dosas.

A display case next to the counter at the back tempts you with two-bite appetizers—greaseless turnovers stuffed with peas and potatoes, and minced-vegetable "cutlets" animated with black mustard seeds. Dip them into the accompanying sauce of mint and green chilies, and what was good zooms toward greatness. The same holds true for the hot lemon and mango pickles, which you can buy for an extra 59 to 79 cents to set off additional fireworks.

Aside from some soft Indian music and a few geometric prints on the walls, Amma puts the plain in Jane. For about the price of a movie ticket and a Big Gulp, though, it's bargain-priced entertainment.

Open: M-F 11:30-2:30 AND 5:30-9:30, SAT-SUN 11:30-10 ***Entrees:*** $3.99-$6.99
Credit Cards: D, MC, V ***Reservations:*** NO
Dress: CASUAL ***Cross Street:*** GLYNDON
Parking: LOT ***Metro:*** DUNN LORING-MERRIFIELD
Second Location: 3291-A M ST. NW, WASHINGTON, DC, 202-625-6625

★ 1/2

AMSTERDAM FALAFELSHOP

2425 18TH ST. NW, WASHINGTON, DC (ADAMS MORGAN) 202-234-1969
www.falafelshop.com

THIS TRIM EATERY takes its name from the Middle Eastern snack of mashed chickpeas, which are shaped into little balls and fried to a neat crunch before your eyes, then slipped into warm pita pockets and dressed up with a choice of nearly 20 toppings. Picture shredded beets, turmeric-tinged cabbage, a jalapeno-ignited herb sauce and garlicky roasted eggplant—everything arranged in a colorful salad bar and yours for the garnishing. (A sign warns you to be neat; there are no eating utensils.)

Picture shredded beets, turmeric-tinged cabbage, a jalapeno-ignited herb sauce and garlicky roasted eggplant—everything arranged in a colorful salad bar and yours for the garnishing.

That said, the fluffy-centered fritters are scrumptious on their own, liberally seasoned with garlic, cumin, parsley and coriander. A sandwich made with three of them costs $3.85; one with five goes for $5.50. Take your pick between white or whole-wheat pita. Don't bother with the french fries, which come from a bag and taste like it; the "virgin" brownies, on the other hand, are deliciously dense and chocolate-y. "No pot," the menu helpfully explains their title.

The room is narrow, simply outfitted with a few tables (I like the lone window perch) and some photos of Amsterdam. The guys behind the counter are as friendly as the hours of operation: This Adams Morgan pit stop is open daily for lunch and dinner, and until 4 a.m. on Friday and Saturday nights.

Open: SUN-M 11-MIDNIGHT, TU-W 11-2:30 AM, TH 11-3 AM, F-SAT 11-4 AM
Prices: $3.85-$5.50 *Credit Cards:* NO (CASH ONLY) *Reservations:* NO
Dress: CASUAL *Cross Street:* BELMONT *Parking:* STREET
Metro: WOODLEY PARK-ZOO / ADAMS MORGAN

★ ★

ANNANGOL

4215 ANNANDALE CENTER DR., ANNANDALE, VA
703-914-4600

TAKE YOUR CUE from the photo of the pig on the menu at Annangol. Pork is the specialty of this bustling Korean kitchen, which serves the protein in barbecue, in soups and as part of a stir-fry. One preparation in particular stands out: "marinated pork bellies," thick and rosy slices of meat edged in a band of fat and cooked before your eyes on either a small portable grill or one built into the table.

As the pork segues from deep to light pink, and from soft to gently crisp, much of its fat melts away, leaving diners with a succulent and fiery meal. Accompanied by a plate of chilled lettuce leaves, steamed rice and sweet fermented soybean paste, the dish is also interactive: Diners use the lettuce as a wrap to bundle the other ingredients and eat everything like a burrito.

Don't expect a lot of pampering at Annangol. You'll be greeted when one of the servers gets around to it, and the little parade of Korean snacks (panchan) that generally comes to the table, free, after you've placed your order sometimes shows up after your entrees. Yet without any prompting at one lunch, a waitress paused between customers to grill an order of meat for my companion and me. It was a welcome gesture. And those panchan—typically garlicky sprouts, pickled radish, seaweed salad, mashed eggplant and a dark-brown acorn custard—are replaced with fresh bowls as they're consumed.

Octopus stir-fried with green peppers and onions is a blast in every bite, literally, thanks to its searing red chili sauce.

There are lots of satisfying paths to pursue on the menu. Octopus stir-fried with green peppers and onions is a blast in every bite, literally, thanks to its searing red chili sauce. In another sweat-inducing main course, folds of pork and kimchi—Korea's famously hot fermented cabbage—are heaped on chalk-white slabs of creamy tofu.

Tables are separated by half-walls, and decoration is limited to half-roofs and overhead fans, which draw away any smoke from the busy table grills and whirl the perfume of chilies, garlic and sizzling meat about the room. Even if you're not hungry when you enter, you will be by the time you sit down. The aroma is enticing.

Open: M-SAT 11-2 AM, SUN 11-MIDNIGHT *Entrees:* $6.99-$18.99
Credit Cards: AE, MC, V *Reservations:* NO
Dress: CASUAL *Cross Street:* COLUMBIA PIKE
Parking: LOT *Metro:* NO

☆ ☆

APARTMENT 2G

206 S. ROYAL AVE., FRONT ROYAL, VA 540-636-7306
www.jsgourmet.com

IT'S NOT OFTEN that you have the chance to watch your dinner prepared as it is here, where two photogenic chefs—husband and wife David and Stacey Gedney—beam (and get beamed) from a slip of a kitchen in the rear of the building to a small screen near you. Far from being a distraction, the silent televised performance is a little bonus, much like the amuse-bouche that precedes a weekend dinner. "Our own reality TV," jokes a server.

Set above a food shop called J's Gourmet and carved from former living quarters, Apartment 2G counts a total of four TVs in its intimate dining rooms. The dining format is a little different, too: There's a budget-friendly menu of tapas to draw the locals on Wednesdays and Thursdays, and a more elaborate, four-course dinner to lure tourists and others on Fridays and Saturdays.

The mid-week collection of Spanish-inspired small plates relies on quality ingredients and simple arrangements. A saucer-size crab cake is almost all seafood, crisped on its surface and perched on a slaw of finely sliced fennel, red onion and sweet bell peppers. Chicken croquettes are full of flavor, rich with cream, garlic and fresh herbs. Chorizo draped with heat-softened onions, on the other hand, is surprisingly tame, and the cooks seem infatuated with mayonnaise, which they use, in one form or another, with abandon.

Chicken croquettes are full of flavor, rich with cream, garlic and fresh herbs.

Weekend dinners commence with a light snack from the kitchen—maybe a single shrimp garnished with bright minced mango and a drizzle of remoulade—and continue with a first course and a salad that remind you what season it is. There are usually only two entree choices, typically meat (picture beef with polenta) and fish (perhaps scallops with a pale green coulis of sweet peas). Desserts lean to the lovely; a favorite is the moist and fine-crumbed Mexican chocolate cake.

This is not food that will take your breath away. But, in combination with the warm service and unusual venue, it's food that will make you happy. Think of an evening at Apartment 2G as having dinner in the home of friends who are solid cooks—friends who also happen to keep the camera rolling while they're entertaining you.

Open: W-SAT 6:30-9 TAPAS: $4.75-$9.50, F-SAT ***Entrees:*** 4-COURSE PRIX FIXE MENU $45
Closed: SUN-TU ***Credit Cards:*** AE, MC, V ***Reservations:*** RECOMMENDED
Dress: CASUAL ***Cross Street:*** STONEWALL DRIVE
Parking: LOT ***Metro:*** NO

Critic's Pick
★★½

ARTIE'S

3260 OLD LEE HWY., FAIRFAX, VA 703-273-7600
www.greatamericanrestaurants.com

CORPORATE RESTAURANTS often get a bum rap—and frequently with good reason. In too many of them, the servers are tethered to a strict smile-and-sell routine, the cooks working off recipes dictated from some distant office.

There are exceptions, and Artie's, part of the Falls Church-based family of Great American Restaurants, is one of them. From the hostess who sees that you're promptly seated to the waitress who steers you to dishes that she's actually tasted, the service is as chipper and helpful as at Disney World. The dining rooms—one beneath beams and decorated with model boats, another outfitted with windows, a sloping roof and roomy red booths—prove similarly smart and upbeat.

Salads speak to the season; side dishes merit blue ribbons.

From Artie's kitchen come fresh takes on American favorites: a first-class crab cake shaped with little more than jumbo lump crab; sauteed trout scattered with pecans and bedded on glorious mashed potatoes; bites of tender filet mignon tossed with pasta, crisp red bell peppers and a lime-brightened tequila sauce; and hamburgers tickled with hickory smoke. Salads speak to the season; side dishes merit blue ribbons (dig that coleslaw); soups pulse with flavor.

The generous portions rule out ordering dessert—until you see your neighbors ooh and ahh over warm and nutty apple pie or custardy bread pudding made with white chocolate. Of *course* you'll make room.

Lunch: M-F 11:30-4 ***Entrees:*** $8-$19
Dinner: SUN-M 4-10, TU-TH 4-11, F-SAT 4-MIDNIGHT ***Entrees:*** $12-$24
Brunch: SAT 10:30-3, SUN 10-3 ***Entrees:*** $8-$15
Credit Cards: ALL MAJOR ***Reservations:*** RECOMMENDED
Dress: CASUAL ***Cross Street:*** LEE HIGHWAY
Parking: LOT ***Metro:*** VIENNA/FAIRFAX-GMU

★ ★ 1/2

ASTER

101 S. MADISON ST., MIDDLEBURG, VA 540-687-4080
www.asterrestaurant.com

CUBAN-BORN HUMP ASTORGA was an interior decorator before he became a chef, and there's plenty of evidence at Aster, his handsome five-room restaurant in Middleburg, that he still cares about presentation in his work.

Witness an amuse-bouche, one of several to come your way at dinner: Pickled carrots are threaded on a toothpick and set above a shot glass of cool, curry-scented soup. "Eat the carrots and knock back the shot," diners are told. An eye-catching first course of "deconstructed" clam chowder is staged on a plate divided into four parts: bite-size clam croquette, quarter-size corn custard, a couple tablespoons of corn, potato and bacon ragout and a small cup of clam foam.

Astorga can get carried away. "Cheeks and Bellies," pairing barbecued veal cheeks and "pulled Thai pork bellies," is both too sweet and too busy—the showy entree could easily lose one of its many garnishes, which run to slaw, potato salad and grilled watermelon.

Pickled carrots are threaded on a toothpick and set above a shot glass of cool, curry-scented soup.

That still leaves plenty to like. Consider hoisin-glazed ahi tuna, rosy-centered and arranged in upended pieces with a haystack of julienned vegetables and thin noodles, everything circled with a foamy carrot emulsion. Servers are as suave as any you'll find in the city, and desserts range from the precious (a miniature pineapple-carrot cake with orange-coconut panna cotta) to the amusing (a little root beer float composed with cherry-ginger ice cream and sassafras foam).

Open: TU-SUN 5:30-10 *Entrees:* $24-$35 *Closed:* M
Credit Cards: AE, D, MC, V *Reservations:* RECOMMENDED
Dress: BUSINESS CASUAL *Cross Street:* W. FEDERAL
Parking: LOT *Metro:* NO

Critic's Pick

★ ★ ★

BANGKOK 54

2919 COLUMBIA PIKE, ARLINGTON, VA 703-521-4070
www.bangkok54restaurant.com

NO SOONER DO YOU WALK in the door than you know you're in the right place. From the host stand, you can watch as the cooks chop and stir, the fresh ingredients for your meal on display in a visible kitchen. As you're led to a table, you'll observe that the owners have an eye for detail that extends to the setting.

Bangkok 54 represents the new breed of Thai restaurants, having moved beyond neon colors and laminated tables to banquettes made cozy with bright pillows and some serious art. Leave any hankering for satay or pad thai for your neighborhood standby and explore the spectrum of dishes that sets this place apart from the crowd. Pork belly stir-fried with fresh basil, and shredded catfish atop a salad of green mango, peanuts and cilantro make delicious stopping off points, as do cubes of beef and potato in a gently sweet curry—a massaman to remember—and tofu that's roasted then sauteed with chilies and garlic for wild effect.

Leave any hankering for satay or pad thai for your neighborhood standby.

Bangkok 54 is perfect for a first date, great for a group. But even soloists get the benefit of a caring staff and a party on their palates.

Lunch: M-F 11-3, SAT-SUN 11-5 ***Entrees:*** $5.95-$12.95
Dinner: SUN-TH 5-10, F-SAT 5-11 ***Entrees:*** $6.95-$12.95
Credit Cards: ALL MAJOR ***Reservations:*** RECOMMENDED
Dress: CASUAL ***Cross Street:*** S. WALTER REED DRIVE
Parking: LOT ***Metro:*** PENTAGON CITY

★ ½

BAR PILAR

1833 14TH ST. NW, WASHINGTON, DC (U STREET CORRIDOR) 202-265-1751
www.barpilar.com

WHO SAYS PUB GRUB HAS TO BE GRUBBY? One of the nicest sights for sore eyes—and taste buds—is the menu at Bar Pilar, which sits just a few storefronts away from its sister restaurant, the more senior Cafe Saint-Ex.

Both restaurants fall under the supervision of executive chef Barton Seaver who arrived in April 2005 from Jaleo, where he worked as a sous-chef. At Bar Pilar, the short list of possibilities includes hamburgers and chips and salsa, but they're joined by respectable vegetable fajitas, chicken-fried steak and even lomo saltado. The last—juicy strips of marinated beef in a tangle of onions, tomatoes, jalapeno and potatoes—is the idea of Pilar's chef, Clarysa Aguilar, a native of Guatemala and an alumna of Cafe Saint-Ex. The American twist: tater tots instead of the more traditional french fries.

There's more to explore: Campbell's has nothing on Aguilar's rich, roasted tomato soup, flanked with crisped cheese sandwiches, and while the meat loaf is underseasoned, its bed of mashed potatoes, punched up with garlic oil, helps divert your attention. If you like to sup late, this kitchen's for you: Dinner is served nightly until 1 a.m.

Pilar was the name of Ernest Hemingway's famed boat, which explains why you see pictures of him (and of him fishing) on the walls of this narrow watering hole.

Like its sibling, Bar Pilar embraces a literary theme. Pilar was the name of Ernest Hemingway's famed boat, which explains why you see pictures of him (and of him fishing) on the walls of this narrow watering hole. Despite having fewer than 40 seats, Bar Pilar packs in plenty of fun. Above the bar hangs a plasma-screen TV, which plays current flicks; in the rear is a photo booth, where $5 gets you a strip of four black-and-white photos.

Dinner: DAILY 5-1 AM ***Entrees:*** $8-$13
Brunch: SAT-SUN 11-4 ***Entrees:*** $7-$10
Credit Cards: AE, D, MC, V ***Reservations:*** NO
Dress: CASUAL ***Cross Street:*** T STREET NW
Parking: STREET ***Metro:*** U ST / AFRICAN AMER CIVIL WAR MEMORIAL / CARDOZO

★ 1/2

BELGA CAFE

514 EIGHTH ST. SE, WASHINGTON, DC (CAPITOL HILL) 202-544-0100
www.belgacafe.com

NO QUESTION, Le Mannequin Pis in Olney remains the best taste of Belgium around. This is not to suggest a diner can't get a nice pot of mussels and frites at Belga Cafe on the Hill—you can, and the roster of imported beer is amazing—but simply to say that visitors need a cheat sheet to avoid the pitfalls. Like Belga's "Euro-fusion," which mismatches traditional Belgian accents with uncomplimentary ingredients or forces them into tortured combinations. No one would expect to find "sushi" in a Belgian restaurant, but the chef feels the need to put his spin on the subject: Stubby rolls of Belgian endive and prosciutto dusted with sumac are ... weird.

Stick with stuff you're apt to find if you actually went to Brussels for dinner.

That unfortunate appetizer is one of several side shows—another is a dessert of asparagus fritters with same-flavored ice cream—that detract from a meal at this good-looking if often crowded hangout.

Stick with stuff you're apt to find if you actually went to Brussels for dinner: Crumb-coated cheese croquettes made with tiny gray shrimp, steamed mussels (served in a double-decker pot), maybe leg of rabbit prepared with what you should have in your glass: a good beer.

Lunch: TU-F 11:30-3 *Entrees:* $16.99-$23
Dinner: TU-TH 5:30-10, F-SAT 5:30-10:30, SUN 5-9:30 *Entrees:* $16.99-$25
Brunch: SAT-SUN 11-3:30 *Entrees:* $8.50-$21
Closed: M *Credit Cards:* AE, D, MC, V *Reservations:* RECOMMENDED
Dress: CASUAL *Cross Street:* E STREET SE
Parking: STREET *Metro:* EASTERN MARKET

★ ½

BISTRO D'OC

518 10TH ST. NW, WASHINGTON, DC (PENN QUARTER) 202-393-5444
www.bistrodoc.com

To put Bistro d'Oc in the context of other bistros around town, the deep orange dining room is neither as formal as Bistro Bis on the Hill nor as consistently delicious as Bistrot Lepic in Georgetown. Bistro d'Oc is more like a solid B student, likable and reliable and good to know about if you are in the neighborhood or in need of pre-theater sustenance (Ford's Theatre sits across the street).

The menu has its charms, too. From France, there are snails in garlic butter and a respectable pâté. Better than the French onion soup, though, is the very American bowl of chowder thick with sweet corn and rich bites of crab, punctuated with crisp bacon. Almost anything served with french fries is apt to please, be it the crisp-skinned roast chicken or beef ignited with pepper sauce. An appealing duck leg confit, rich and crisp, comes with more ordinary sauteed potatoes.

Some fish are more equal than others here. Sauteed salmon on a bed of cabbage with a thyme-laced red wine sauce is satisfying at dinner, as is a steamed salmon entree at lunch. But the bistro's take on bouillabaisse is a big disappointment, with less-than-prime fish and shellfish sitting in a watery broth vaguely seasoned with garlic and saffron.

Almost anything served with french fries is apt to please, be it the crisp-skinned roast chicken or beef ignited with pepper sauce.

Desserts lean toward Gallic crowd-pleasers. My favorite way to bid adieu is with crepes suzette. It's an old-fashioned splurge in a restaurant that wants to be more than a convenience and frequently hits that mark.

Lunch: M-SAT 11:30-2:30 *Entrees:* $11.95-$18.95
Dinner: M-TH 5:30-10, F-SAT 5:30-11, SUN 4-8:30 *Entrees:* $13.95-$21.95
Pre- and Post-Theater: DAILY 5:30-7, 9-10, 3-COURSE PRIX FIXE $21.95
Brunch: SUN 11:30-4 *Entrees:* $11.95-$17.95
Credit Cards: AE, DC, MC, V *Reservations:* RECOMMENDED
Dress: CASUAL *Cross Street:* E STREET NW
Parking: STREET *Metro:* METRO CENTER

★ ★

BISTRO FRANCAIS

3124-28 M ST. NW, WASHINGTON, DC (GEORGETOWN) 202-338-3830
www.bistrofrancaisdc.com

ALL DRESSED UP AND NO PLACE TO GO? That can be an obstacle when it's after midnight and you're hungry for something serious to eat. Cozy in dark wood and mirrors that exaggerate its size, this long-time Georgetown fixture comes to the rescue with all manner of appealing French fare: robust fish soup; avocado stuffed with crab; seafood pâté set off with a sharp horseradish sauce; thin-cut lamb steak topped with coins of melting herb butter; even steak tartare, punchy with mustard and served with a beet-flecked salad and a pile of skinny fries.

There is always a long list of specials, too, perhaps including cold poached salmon with a biting watercress sauce. Local chefs like to gather here after their own kitchens close, and you can taste why with a winner like that. Meanwhile, lunchtime yields a bargain: three courses for $14.95, a deal that includes a glass of wine.

The coq au vin may be dry and the desserts uninspired, but it's good to know about a spot that stays open until 3 on weeknights, 4 on weekends.

Onion soup? Of course. Eggs? You can pick from a number of omelets. The coq au vin may be dry and the desserts uninspired, but it's good to know about a spot that stays open until 3 on weeknights, 4 on weekends—long after official Washington has gone to bed.

Lunch: DAILY 11-4:30 *Entrees:* $7.50-$17.95
Dinner: SUN-TH 5-3 AM, F-SAT 5-4 AM *Entrees:* $14.95-$24.95
Pre-Theater: DAILY 5-7, 3-COURSE PRIX FIXE $19.95
Brunch: SAT-SUN 11-4 *Price:* $18.95
Credit Cards: AE, DC, MC, V *Reservations:* RECOMMENDED
Dress: CASUAL *Cross Street:* WISCONSIN AVENUE NW
Parking: STREET *Metro:* FOGGY BOTTOM-GWU

★ ★

BISTROT DU COIN

1738 CONNECTICUT AVE. NW, WASHINGTON, DC (DUPONT CIRCLE) 202-234-6969
www.bistrotducoin.com

ANYONE WHO'S SPENT TIME IN PARIS will recognize this people magnet. At night in particular, the yellow lighting, combined with like-colored walls, washes the high-ceilinged room in an eerie, nicotine-stained glow; a long, zinc-topped bar practically commands you to pull up for a kir while you're waiting for friends to arrive. And everything we've been told not to eat—organ meats, uncooked beef, french fries, creme brulee—shows up on a menu that celebrates the rich life. Some tiny type on the bill of fare adds to the decadence: "Cigarettes, Cigars: Oui!"

It can be fun to be bad at Bistrot du Coin. Baked snails provide an excuse to sop up more melted garlic butter than you should and steak tartare honors that meaty classic. ("How would you like that done?" a waiter jokes with us when we order it.) Along with big pots of steamed mussels (flavor mine with tomato and garlic, thanks), meat figures prominently on the menu. I'm partial to the thin, sinewy onglet (hanger steak), flanked by a pile of long golden french fries and sharpened with a thin sauce of shallots and peppercorns.

It can be fun to be bad at Bistrot du Coin.

Watch out for the trouble spots, like the watery onion soup, entombed in cheese, and the vapid duck confit served with mushy and bland sauteed potatoes. An apple tart is merely decent. Don't expect a lot of finesse from the staff, who can be abrupt: Our dishes were practically thrown at us one evening.

By meal's end, I'm exhausted. The feeling has nothing to do with the wine or the food but rather with the noise: At full throttle, which is almost always, Bistrot du Coin hums, throbs and booms with music and conversation. As I bid adieu, I feel as if I've just left a Metallica concert.

Open: SUN-W 11:30-11, TH-SAT 11:30-1 AM ***Entrees:*** $12.95-$21.95
Brunch: SAT-SUN 11-4 ***Entrees:*** $7.95-$8.95
Credit Cards: ALL MAJOR ***Reservations:*** RECOMMENDED
Dress: CASUAL ***Cross Street:*** FLORIDA AVENUE NW
Parking: STREET ***Metro:*** DUPONT CIRCLE

★ ½

BISTROT LAFAYETTE

1118 KING ST., ALEXANDRIA, VA 703-548-2525
www.bistrotlafayette.com

SMALL AND SPECIAL have always been a part of the repertoire of Keo Koumtakoun, whose work has been on display all over the Washington area for more than 15 years. Born in Laos and self-taught, the chef has cooked at Gallic restaurants in Gaithersburg, Vienna and the District. These days he's in Old Town Alexandria, turning out his French-accented food in a tiny dining room, appealing in shades of peach and snug with dark tables and people who appear pleased to be gathered around them.

For his latest tour of duty, Koumtakoun is offering bistro cooking that, except for a few daily specials, is for the most part familiar and comforting, things like French onion soup—a fine-tuned performance of light stock, soft onions and melted cheese on bread with a pleasant smoky char—and rack of lamb lightened with thyme jus.

For his latest tour of duty, Koumtakoun is offering bistro cooking that, except for a few daily specials, is for the most part familiar and comforting.

Not everything is a success: Squid sauteed with olives, peppers and garlic is an oily mess and chocolate "cake" is closer to a supersweet pudding.

Other dishes lead us into serious temptation, however. Koumtakoun's steak tartare, an entree, is first-rate: fine chopped raw beef ignited with mustard, capers and hot sauce and served with french fries (good ones, which also make an appearance with the steamed mussels). People who have sworn off escargots based on encounters with rubber bands posing as snails might reconsider after trying the tender, meaty and richly buttery and garlicky plate served as an appetizer at Bistrot Lafayette. Occasionally, a server might announce a dessert special of tarte Tatin; leap at the chance to try it, warm apple slices atop a buttery crust that melts on the tongue. Like a blue blazer, it comes off as a classic.

Lunch: M-SAT 11:30-2:30 ***Entrees:*** $7.95-$15.95
Dinner: M-SAT 5:30-10 ***Entrees:*** $18.95-$24.95
Closed: SUN ***Credit Cards:*** ALL MAJOR ***Reservations:*** RECOMMENDED
Dress: CASUAL ***Cross Street:*** FAYETTE
Parking: STREET ***Metro:*** KING STREET

Critic's Pick

★ ★ 1/2

BISTROT LEPIC

1736 WISCONSIN AVE. NW, WASHINGTON, DC (GEORGETOWN) 202-333-0111
www.bistrotlepic.com

IT'S SMALL AND SNUG and seemingly always busy, a gathering spot for ladies who lunch, dashing retired diplomats and the stray tourist lucky enough to find himself in this sunny dining room in upper Georgetown. The menu is varied, the cooking sure, the plates attractive. Delectable snails are tucked in a risotto stained black with truffles, which also lend their earthy appeal to the dish. A special of lobster bisque, served in a cast-iron crock, is as rich as it gets. And curry-fragrant chicken on Basmati rice reminds me that this kitchen knows its way around the spice cabinet. Look for boudin blanc, a mousse-like sausage that is one of my favorite dishes here, paired with sauteed apples and silky potato puree. There is food for light appetites—shrimp with whatever vegetables are in vogue—and food for people who want something more robust, maybe a special of nicely cooked lamb atop a risotto thick with potatoes.

Look for boudin blanc, a mousse-like sausage that is one of my favorite dishes here, paired with sauteed apples and silky potato puree.

Desserts aren't as tempting as they used to be—meringues are tough, a chocolate torte is dry—but a diner can still count on a loose French spirit to the service and fine, affordable wines by the glass.

Lunch: DAILY 11:30-2:30 ***Entrees:*** $12.95-$17.95
Dinner: M-TH 5:30-10, F-SAT 5:30-10:30, SUN 5:30-9:30 ***Entrees:*** $16.95-$26.95
Credit Cards: AE, D, MC, V ***Reservations:*** RECOMMENDED
Dress: BUSINESS CASUAL ***Cross Street:*** S STREET NW
Parking: STREET ***Metro:*** FOGGY BOTTOM-GWU

★ ★

BLACK MARKET BISTRO

4600 WAVERLY AVE., GARRETT PARK, MD 301-933-3000
www.blackrestaurantgroup.com

NESTLED IN A WOODED ENCLAVE, Black Market Bistro looks like something Norman Rockwell and Martha Stewart would have dreamed up had they ever worked together.

A friendly porch outside leads to a couple of cozy, high-ceilinged dining rooms, the most attractive of which peeks into the kitchen and includes a shiny bar with counter seating. All-American burgers and root beer floats share space on the menu with steak and shrimp, both made more fun with crushed herbs and garlic atop the ruddy beef and a barbecue accent and cheesy grits enhancing the seafood.

All-American burgers and root beer floats share space on the menu with steak and shrimp.

Black Market's pizza still needs work—the pale crust doesn't have much savor—but the endings are spot on. Crisps make lavish use of whatever fruit is in season and a dark slab of chocolate pâté sends forks flying.

Now and then, conversation is interrupted as a train rumbles by; rolling pins and worn-looking aprons help decorate the mint-colored walls. Life is good.

Lunch: TU-F 11-2:30, SAT 11-2 ***Entrees:*** $7-$14
Dinner: SUN 5-8, TU-TH 5-9, F-SAT 5-9:30 ***Entrees:*** $19-$25
Brunch: SUN 10-2 ***Entrees:*** $8-$14
Closed: M ***Credit Cards:*** ALL MAJOR ***Reservations:*** NO
Dress: CASUAL ***Cross Street:*** KENILWORTH AVENUE
Parking: STREET ***Metro:*** GROSVENOR-STRATHMORE

★ ★

BLUE GIN

1206 WISCONSIN AVE. NW, WASHINGTON, DC (GEORGETOWN) 202-965-5555
www.bluegindc.com

"ALL OUR DRINKS ARE REALLY GOOD," my server at Blue Gin announces as she sees a friend and me studying a long list of cocktails. "We make them with fresh fruit purees."

It's early on a Saturday night, which is the best time for someone who is more interested in refueling than in mating to land in this sleek, two-story lounge in Georgetown.

The ground floor, with its low ceilings and small dance floor, is pleasant enough, but upstairs is better. Here's where you'll find windows—a bank of them looking onto an exterior wall that doubles as a screen for movies projected from inside—and low leather couches that encourage you to slouch. The light fixtures look like fireworks sprays; the floor of a second, more intimate bar is paved in transparent glass blocks that allow patrons sitting there (voyeur alert!) to observe the flow of human traffic at Blue Gin's entrance.

Most of the food is threaded on skewers or served bite-size, perfect for sharing with friends and eating with your fingers.

This emphasis on looks does not take away from the quality of the small menu. Most of the food is threaded on skewers or served bite-size, perfect for sharing with friends and eating with your fingers. Greaseless spring rolls contain rich bites of lobster; a quick dip in the accompanying Thai chili sauce sets off a dance between sweet and hot, crisp and soft. Only slightly bigger than thimbles, crab cakes are capped in bread crumbs and pesto and presented with a puckery salad of shaved fennel. Skirt steak massaged with cumin and lime and wrapped around a thin skewer is one of a few dishes that come with fun, ribbonlike potato chips that don't last long.

A little research on the part of the kitchen could improve both the "lemon and garlic crusted" shrimp, which seems to be missing its garlic, and the tasty grilled lamb and onions in pita bread, which is too difficult to eat on Blue Gin's magazine-size tables. Slips such as those are somehow easier to digest when you've got a good drink in your hand (make mine Grey Goose vodka and passion fruit) and a woman who could pass for a model mixing it at the bar.

Dinner: M-SAT 6-MIDNIGHT *Entrees:* $10-$18
Closed: SUN *Credit Cards:* ALL MAJOR *Reservations:* RECOMMENDED
Dress: CASUAL *Cross Street:* M STREET NW
Parking: STREET *Metro:* FOGGY BOTTOM-GWU

Critic's Pick
★★½

BOB KINKEAD'S COLVIN RUN TAVERN

8045 LEESBURG PIKE, VIENNA, VA 703-356-9500
www.colvinrun.com

THE ONLY DANGER of hosting a business dinner at this sibling of Kinkead's, downtown Washington's bustling seafood emporium, is food that might upstage someone's pitch or presentation.

Take, for example, an order of she-crab soup, which a server spoons out of a big tureen into a smaller bowl of sweet crab set on a slender plate—a ceramic canvas that also includes a tiny crab sandwich and salad of pickled okra, tomatoes and corn. Similarly, sesame-edged squares of rare tuna over Chinese broccoli are presented with a steamer basket of spicy peanut noodles.

Such theatrics are followed by smiles of satisfaction as diners start eating; chef Jeff Gaetjen's plates are crowded but also quite flavorful. And there's much more than seafood to consider: Spring rolls filled with curry-laced pork and served with an herby salad make a tasty appetizer, and the best antidote to a nip in the air are meaty short ribs flanked with sauteed potatoes and bright green fava beans.

> ***The best antidote to a nip in the air are meaty short ribs flanked with sauteed potatoes and bright green fava beans.***

Where to huddle? For the sake of privacy, seek out a booth in the manly Shenandoah Room, all dark wood and gray stone; the brighter and more elegant Charleston Room; or the intimate Camden Room, with seating for up to a dozen, in the rear.

Lunch: M-F 11:30-2:30 ***Entrees:*** $14-$21
Dinner: SUN 5-9, M-TH 5:30-10, F-SAT 5:30-10:30 ***Entrees:*** $27-$41
Credit Cards: ALL MAJOR ***Reservations:*** RECOMMENDED
Dress: BUSINESS CASUAL ***Cross Street:*** TOWERS CRESCENT DRIVE
Parking: COMPLIMENTARY VALET ***Metro:*** WEST FALLS CHURCH-VT/UVA

Critic's Pick
★★½

BOMBAY CLUB

815 CONNECTICUT AVE. NW, WASHINGTON DC (DOWNTOWN)
202-659-3727

ROMANCE WITH AN INDIAN ACCENT—that's Bombay Club, the city's most sumptuous spot for shrimp with mango chutney and chicken tikka. You and your significant other will sit in broad chairs surrounded by pools of space in a large room dressed as if the British raj still held sway, an image reinforced by lazy circling fans, peachy lighting and piano music at dinner. And you don't have to drink alcohol to celebrate a special occasion, certainly not when there's bright pink watermelon juice on hand.

The food, both beautifully presented and refined in flavor, can be just as indulgent. Calamari is stir-fried with onion, tamarind, curry leaves and what tastes like fire. And every bite of the green-chili chicken is followed by delicious waves of coriander and mint. Among the recent additions to the script are a mildly seasoned shrimp masala and a dynamite side dish of green beans tossed with chilies, mustard seed and coconut. Anything from the tandoor is apt to please, be it ginger-laced lamb chops, whole trout or (even better) swordfish, the ultramoist and meaty slab enhanced with mint sauce. Breads show up hot and blistered from their time in the clay oven—I'm partial to the hot pockets filled with goat cheese—and desserts include first-rate versions of kulfi, the slightly chewy Indian ice cream, and carrot pudding, scented with cardamom. The ubiquitous molten chocken cake makes an appearance, too; this version is set off with aggressive spices.

Anything from the tandoor is apt to please, be it ginger-laced lamb chops, whole trout or (even better) swordfish.

Missteps are thankfully few: bland black-eyed peas, tough lamb rogan josh and well-intentioned service that sometimes goes overboard, with too much bowing and scraping.

Keep Bombay Club in mind for brunch: A buffet of Indian flavors, presented in silver chafing dishes and accompanied by free-flowing bubbly, is a ticket to India for less than $20.

Lunch: M-F 11:30-2:30 *Entrees:* $15-$22
Dinner: M-TH 5:30-10:30, F-SAT 5:30-11, SUN 5:30-9 *Entrees:* $15-$24
Pre-Theater: DAILY 5:30-7, 3-COURSE PRIX FIXE $26.50
Buffet Brunch: SUN 11:30-2:30 *Price:* $18.95
Credit Cards: ALL MAJOR *Reservations:* RECOMMENDED
Dress: BUSINESS CASUAL *Cross Street:* I STREET NW
Parking: COMPLIMENTARY VALET M-SAT AT DINNER *Metro:* FARRAGUT WEST

★ ★

BOMBAY TANDOOR

8603 WESTWOOD CENTER DR., VIENNA, VA 703-734-2202
www.bombaytandoor.com

BOMBAY TANDOOR, a spinoff of downtown Washington's Bombay Palace, delivers plenty of style for the price. Paintings of long-ago maharajahs stare down from the sand-colored walls, and acres of blue carpet cushion your walk from foyer to prettily set table. It's an enormous space warmed up with a rosewood bar and lilting Indian music that help you forget you're in a suburban business district.

Some of the cooking has that effect, too. Though the menu embraces all the familiar Indian restaurant staples, the kitchen distinguishes itself from the pack with a vindaloo of lamb or vegetables that should cheer the fire-eater with its blazing sauce of vinegar, chilies and ginger, as well as fluffy Basmati rice dishes (biryanis) with a choice of shrimp, lamb, vegetables or dried fruit.

Paintings of long-ago maharajahs stare down from the sand-colored walls, and acres of blue carpet cushion your walk from foyer to prettily set table.

Alas, the breads these days taste routine, the vegetable fritters ordinary. But lamb chops rubbed with the dusky spice blend known as masala and cooked in the tandoor are terrific, and butter chicken in a creamy tomato sauce lives up to its billing. Indian beer makes the best companion to this food, and it's poured into a frosted mug. Nice touch.

Lunch: M-F 11:30-2:30, SAT-SUN 12-3 ***Entrees:*** $7.95-$18.95
Buffet: M-F 11:30-3 ***Price:*** $9.95, SAT-SUN NOON-3 ***Price:*** $10.95
Dinner: SUN-TH 5:30-10, FRI-SAT 5:30-10:30 ***Entrees:*** $9.95-$18.95
Credit Cards: AE, DC, MC, V ***Reservations:*** RECOMMENDED
Dress: CASUAL ***Cross Street:*** LEESBURG PIKE
Parking: LOT ***Metro:*** DUNN LORING-MERRIFIELD

★ 1/2

BONEFISH GRILL

13005-J LEE JACKSON HWY., FAIRFAX, VA 703-378-4970
www.bonefishgrill.com

THE LURE AT EACH of these seafood restaurants is fresh fish in snazzy digs at prices that encourage you not to wait until your next birthday or promotion to return. The menu is mum about the restaurant's lineage, though a little digging reveals that Bonefish Grill is based in Florida and has almost 40 locations around the country. Do I detect a chain? Yep. It turns out that Bonefish Grill is primarily owned by none other than Outback Steakhouse.

The newcomer is at least a step or two above Outback, yet it retains a corporate flavor. So you can expect the background music to suggest Muzak, and your waiters to follow talking points from a script.

At a server's suggestion, I got acquainted with the signature appetizer, a hot mound of shrimp fried to a light crackle, piled high on a plate, dusted with chives and drizzled with a zippy cream sauce. It's a great guilty pleasure. The fried calamari is similar to what you'll find at a dozen other places—pretty good—served with two vibrant dipping sauces. But the chicken- and corn-stuffed Cajun egg rolls are no match for the zesty version served at Carlyle in Shirlington, and tuna sashimi is just thin slices of bland fish in desperate need of every one of its garnishes.

From a design standpoint, Bonefish Grill goes out of its way to make you forget it's a chain restaurant.

Grilled fish—take your pick from mahi-mahi, salmon, rainbow trout, grouper, swordfish and more—can be ordered plain or with one of several sauces and toppings, and each day brings a small list of specials to consider. One of the role models has been sauteed trout gilded with a Parmesan crust.

From a design standpoint, Bonefish Grill goes out of its way to make you forget it's a chain restaurant. Its lighting is subdued and the handsome fabric on the car-size booths looks like something the gang from "Queer Eye for the Straight Guy" might have picked out. It can take some casting before you find the best dishes, but if you avoid the restaurant's trouble spots, the fishing can be fine.

Dinner: M-TH 3-10, F 4-11, SAT 3-11, SUN 3-10 *Entrees:* $13.50- $32
Credit Cards: ALL MAJOR *Reservations:* RECOMMENDED
Dress: CASUAL *Cross Street:* MAJESTIC LANE *Parking:* LOT *Metro:* VIENNA / FAIRFAX-GMU
Other Locations: 6711 GOVERNOR RITCHIE HWY., GLEN BURNIE, MD, 410-553-0299; 10906 BOULEVARD CIR., OWINGS MILLS, MD, 410-654-5500; 82 MARKET ST., GAITHERSBURG, MD, 240-631-2401; 6315 MULTIPLEX DR., CENTREVILLE, VA, 703-815-7427; 1779 CARL D. SILVER PKWY., FREDERICKSBURG, VA, 540-548-1984; 7611 SOMERSET CROSSING DR., GAINESVILLE, VA, 703-753-2597; 43135 BROADLANDS CENTER PLAZA, ASHBURN, VA, 703-723-8246

Critic's Pick
★ ★ 1/2

BREADLINE

1751 PENNSYLVANIA AVE. NW, WASHINGTON, DC (DOWNTOWN)
202-822-8900

I TIME MY VISITS to this self-service bakery-cafe according to the day of the week, knowing that on Thursday, for instance, I can always find the best Cuban roast pork sandwich around (and knowing that mornings are less noisy and less crowded than just after noon). Tuesday, on the other hand, compels me to order a bowl of peanut soup, smooth with coconut milk and kicky with cayenne and ginger.

Actually, I always find something to admire here. The hefty BLT, made with tangy whole-wheat bread, thick smoky bacon and summery tomatoes, is a model of simplicity and good taste; the beef empanadas send me to Argentina with every bite; the french fries spoil me for any that aren't similarly hand-cut and twice-fried; and the chocolate cupcakes, fine-crumbed and frosted, hark back to kinder, gentler times. Recent research trips to Germany and Turkey by the chief baker are evident in Breadline's expanded menu: whole-grain breads reflect what you'd find in Munich and a "slim-line" of good-for-you flatbreads, one of which you could expect to see in Istanbul. (Think ground lamb kneaded into the crust, the top of which is scattered with yogurt and fresh mint.) And every day finds a different house-made sausage to explore.

The hefty BLT, made with tangy whole-wheat bread, thick smoky bacon and summery tomatoes, is a model of simplicity and good taste.

As always, I'll be up-front: Owner Mark Furstenberg, the occasionally cranky man behind the counter, is a longtime friend of mine. But he's a purist, with the noteworthy aim of serving you the very best fast food he can, in an industrial setting warmed up with old photos of bakeries on tangerine-colored walls.

Breakfast: M-F 7:30-11 ***Entrees:*** $1.50-$4
Lunch: M-F 11-3:30 ***Entrees:*** $3.75-$7.50
Closed: SAT-SUN ***Credit Cards:*** ALL MAJOR
Reservations: NO ***Dress:*** CASUAL
Cross Street: 17TH ***Parking:*** STREET
Metro: FARRAGUT WEST

Critic's Pick

★ ★ ★

BUCK'S FISHING AND CAMPING

5031 CONNECTICUT AVE. NW, WASHINGTON, DC (UPPER NW)
202-364-0777

I COULD EASILY EAT Carole Greenwood's food every night of the week. Her prime steak has no peer in town and her "world-class" mussels are not hyperbole, just exceedingly, incredibly luscious.

Knowing the chef's background—she trained as a sculptor—explains the arty setting, a room that's softly romantic and completely original: Blood red walls meet wild photographs meet a long communal table lit with handsome amber globes from on high. And yes, that's a canoe above your head, a prop in keeping with the small restaurant's subtle outdoorsy theme.

The menu is too small, which means you want to show up early so as not to miss the likes of a light salad of honeydew and country ham or a fabulous entree of crackling fried rabbit arranged on a bed of whatever vegetable or starch the chef was inspired by at the market.

The menu is too small, which means you want to show up early so as not to miss the likes of a light salad of honeydew and country ham.

At Buck's, the glory is in the many thoughtful details: a well-made cocktail from the effusive bartender; a few minutes of engaging conversation with James Alefantis, a host with the most; and a big slab of not-too-sweet chocolate cake with a drift of fresh whipped cream that begs for a glass of milk and sends you home on a sigh.

Dinner: TU-TH 5-9:30 F-SAT 5-10, SUN 5-9 ***Entrees:*** $15-$35
Closed: M ***Credit Cards:*** AE, MC, V ***Reservations:*** NO
Dress: CASUAL ***Cross Street:*** NEBRASKA AVENUE NW
Parking: LOT ***Metro:*** VAN NESS-UDC

★ ★

BUSBOYS AND POETS

2021 14TH ST. NW, WASHINGTON, DC (U STREET CORRIDOR)
202-387-7638

WHATEVER YOU THINK about Busboys and Poets, don't lump the project together with the fancy shops opening left and right on 14th Street NW. Owner Andy Shallal insists that his combination "progressive political" bookstore, restaurant and performance space "not become another gentrification marker" but rather "a part of the neighborhood that honors its past."

And another thing: While Busboys and Poets features a menu, Shallal says "it's not for foodies." After spending a year in the area, talking to residents about their preferences, the Washington restaurateur and social activist (he also owns Mimi's American Bistro in Dupont Circle) came up with a plan for simple food at cheap prices.

His listening tour seems to have paid off. Pizzas go for $5.95 to $8.95 a crackling round, and they're perfectly respectable. There's also a nice, juicy hamburger—so big it needs to be cut in half to eat—for $6.95, and a plate of crisp-moist catfish that challenges the soul-food competition with its tangy collard greens and spoonfuls of lemony caper sauce. A few Mediterranean accents crop up on the largely American script, including a great, garlicky puree of roasted eggplant served with warm folds of pita bread for scooping. Service comes off friendly—and sometimes forgetful.

The open and airy destination looks like a coffeehouse gone glam.

The open and airy destination looks like a coffeehouse gone glam. Picture chic couches and walls painted a soothing mint color, jazz on the soundtrack and an inviting group table. Adjacent to the central dining area—the space has room for 275 customers—is the Langston Room, replete with a professional sound system, lighting and stage for poetry readings and other events. Jam on!

Breakfast: M-F 8-11 *Entrees:* $3.95-$9.95
Lunch/Dinner: M-TH 11-MIDNIGHT, F 11-2 AM, SAT 3-2 AM, SUN 3-MIDNIGHT
Entrees: $6.95-$17.95
Brunch: SAT-SUN 10-3 *Entrees:* $3.95-$9.95
Credit Cards: ALL MAJOR *Reservations:* NO
Dress: CASUAL *Cross Street:* V STREET NW
Parking: STREET *Metro:* U ST / AFRICAN-AMER CIVIL WAR MEMORIAL / CARDOZO

☆ ☆

CAFE ATLANTICO

405 EIGHTH ST. NW, WASHINGTON, DC (PENN QUARTER) 202-393-0812
www.cafeatlantico.com

EVEN THE LIGHTS seem a little dimmer at this once-bright salute to South America. Smooth service and three floors of vibrant decor can't hide the reality that the kitchen seems to be cooking much the same menu it has for a long time now, and perhaps a touch less convincingly. Salmon belly beaded in quinoa? Duck confit with spinach and raisins? Been there, eaten that. Zzzzzzz.

Flank steak with a crumble of blue cheese, curly fried plantains and a puree of tropical tubers is as good—and busy—a plate as ever, as is the tail-on snapper enlivened with a sauce of olives, tomatoes and capers. What's new on the list is not necessarily habit-forming: Oysters on the half shell come jazzed up not just with ginger and jalapeno oil but also with passion fruit "air." Dropping the last accent would improve the dish.

Flank steak with a crumble of blue cheese, curly fried plantains and a puree of tropical tubers is as good—and busy—a plate as ever.

Cafe Atlantico remains an attractive pre-theater deal: Served between 5 and 6:30 nightly, the three-course dinner costs just under $25—but you better like candied pumpkin seeds and vanilla-papaya oil.

Lunch: M-F 11:30-2:30 ***Entrees:*** $9-$14
Dinner: SUN-TH 5-10, F-SAT 5-11 ***Entrees:*** $18-$26 ***Dim Sum:*** $1.95-$9
Pre-Theater: DAILY 5-6:30, 3-COURSE PRIX FIXE $24.95
Brunch: SAT-SUN 11:30-2:30 ***Credit Cards:*** ALL MAJOR ***Reservations:*** RECOMMENDED
Dress: BUSINESS CASUAL ***Cross Street:*** D STREET NW
Parking: $10 VALET AT DINNER ***Metro:*** ARCHIVES-NAVY MEMORIAL

★ 1/2

CAFE MILANO

3251 PROSPECT ST. NW, WASHINGTON, DC (GEORGETOWN) 202-333-6183
www.cafemilanodc.com

AUTHORS, ACTORS, socialites, pols—Cafe Milano attracts them all to its several stylish dining rooms (and one of the busiest outdoor patios in the city). Sometimes the Italian restaurant feeds them well, too. Tuna carpaccio makes a nice introduction, as does a racy salad of white anchovies and fennel. Spring delivers a fine asparagus puree, accessorized with thin shards of Parmesan that slowly melt into the hot green soup.

Moving deeper into the menu, diners can find a proper veal Milanese, pounded nearly as thin as paper and set off with a fluff of arugula, and whole sea bass, carefully cooked, deftly filleted at the table and arranged on the plate with glossy grilled vegetables. But gnocchi draped with a bland crumble of sausage and bitter rapini is a bust, and the pizza is decent, nothing more. The prices at Cafe Milano don't leave room for many slips.

The scene at this famous Georgetown address is always irresistible.

Does anyone care, though? As the lights go down at night, the energy level shoots up. The scene at this famous Georgetown address is always irresistible: Servers who look like they stepped out of an Armani ad, cute young things attached to their cell phones, a famous face or fat bank account at seemingly every other table all make for delicious stories tomorrow. Cafe Milano is as much a club as a place to refuel. You know where you stand here by where you're seated and what comes your way: Favorite guests might ease in with a complimentary fried squash blossom, while biscotti and a shot of something potent might precede your server's saying "ciao."

Lunch: DAILY 11:30-4 ***Dinner:*** 4-1 ***Entrees:*** $9-$42
Credit Cards: ALL MAJOR ***Reservations:*** RECOMMENDED
Dress: CASUAL ***Cross Street:*** WISCONSIN AVENUE NW
Parking: STREET ***Metro:*** FOGGY BOTTOM-GWU

★ ★

CAFE SAINT-EX

1847 14TH ST. NW, WASHINGTON, DC (U STREET CORRIDOR) 202-265-7839
www.saint-ex.com

CLOCKS ON THE WALL announce the time in five different cities, and black-and-white photographs of pilots expand on the flight theme in this snug dining room inspired by author-aviator Antoine de Saint-Exupery.

Chef Barton Seaver seems to know just what his audience wants to eat, giving a delicious twist or two to such standards as roast chicken (laced here with pistachio butter) and rib-eye steak (paired with sweet potato fries).

Chef Barton Seaver seems to know just what his audience wants to eat.

Bruschetta brings a clumsy heap of tuna and white bean puree, and potato gnocchi is dull and heavy. But my raves outnumber my rants. Beets, oranges and goat cheese add up to a fine salad, grilled tuna sits on a loose and creamy bed of risotto made interesting with cauliflower and encircled in black olive oil, and dessert includes an elegant goat-cheese cheesecake lightened with honey.

There's more at this corner address: patio seating in good weather and a cozy lounge—Gate 54—downstairs. And conveniently, Cafe Saint-Ex sits within a ticket's toss of the Studio Theatre.

Lunch: TU-F 11-5 *Entrees:* $8-$12
Dinner: DAILY 5-11 *Entrees:* $15-$22
Pre-Theater: DAILY 5-7, 3-COURSE PRIX FIXE $26
Brunch: SAT-SUN 11-4 *Entrees:* $7-$12
Credit Cards: AE, D, MC, V *Reservations:* NO
Dress: CASUAL *Cross Street:* T STREET NW
Parking: STREET *Metro:* U ST / AFRICAN AMER CIVIL WAR MEMORIAL / CARDOZO

★ ★

CANTLER'S RIVERSIDE INN

458 FOREST BEACH RD, ANNAPOLIS, MD 410-757-1311
www.cantlers.com

THERE REALLY IS A CANTLER behind this restaurant's name. He's Jimmy Cantler, and he lives near his scrappy namesake, which pulls in legions of crab eaters who don't mind tap-tap-tapping their way through a meal of hard-shells with wooden mallets. On a beautiful weekend afternoon, their Volkswagens and BMWs form a line that can stretch 20 cars long.

Fans will tell you that you want to show up early for the best seats (outside, overlooking lazy Mill Creek) and the biggest crabs (offered in five sizes, from small to super jumbo, and dumped before you on paper-covered tables).

Here's what else you should know: The potato salad and coleslaw take their cues from a Southern church social. The shell-on shrimp are good, the big crab cakes are even better. And a new chef has expanded the menu to include rockfish tacos, panko-crusted chicken, even hamburgers made with Kobe beef.

Cantler's big, dark dining room smells distinctly of sea and beer; the porch, heated in cool weather, brings you closer to the action on the water. After an hour or so of feasting, you may find yourself littered with bits of shell. Thank goodness for the tub-size wash basin out back.

Cantler's big, dark dining room smells distinctly of sea and beer; the porch, heated in cool weather, brings you closer to the action on the water.

Open: SUN-TH 11-10, F-SAT 11-11 ***Entrees:*** $4.99-$23.99
Credit Cards: ALL MAJOR ***Reservations:*** NO
Dress: CASUAL ***Cross Street:*** ST. MARGARET'S ROAD
Parking: LOT ***Metro:*** NO

Critic's Pick

★ ★ 1/2

CAPITAL GRILLE

601 PENNSYLVANIA AVE. NW, WASHINGTON, DC (PENN QUARTER) 202-737-6200
www.thecapitalgrille.com

TAKE A CUE from the restaurant's show window of dry-aging beef and pick a cut from within: If there's a better sirloin or porterhouse in town, I have yet to cut into it.

The Capital Grille is as manly a steakhouse as you can picture, from the dark wood to the stuffed animal heads to side dishes that arrive as small barges (nutmeg-laced creamed spinach) or as edible mountains (four hungry diners merely put a dent in a voluminous plate of onion strings and cottage fries).

If there's a better sirloin or porterhouse in town, I have yet to cut into it.

Still, it's a civilized oasis. When a patron at the bar asks for cigarettes, a server delivers a pack on a tray. At the table, courses might be punctuated by steaming, jasmine-scented towels.

To start, there are a bold French onion soup and bland crab and lobster cakes; to close, consider the decadent flourless chocolate espresso cake or dreamy coconut cream pie. From beginning to "check, please," the Capital Grille is a meat market of great appeal.

Lunch: M-SAT 11:30-3 ***Entrees:*** $10.95-$28.95
Dinner: SUN-TH 5-10, F-SAT 5-11 ***Entrees:*** $19.95-$36.95
Credit Cards: ALL MAJOR ***Reservations:*** RECOMMENDED
Dress: BUSINESS CASUAL ***Cross Street:*** SIXTH
Parking: COMPLIMENTARY VALET AFTER 5 ***Metro:*** ARCHIVES-NAVY MEMORIAL
Second Location: 500 E. PRATT ST., BALTIMORE, MD, 443-703-4064

★ ★

CARLYLE

4000 S. 28TH ST., ARLINGTON, VA 703-931-0777
www.greatamericanrestaurants.com

A $4 MILLION FACE-LIFT gives patrons fresh reasons to check out the Carlyle. Notice the expanded foyer? The new red-leather banquettes and globe-shaped lights fashioned from bronze and alabaster? The ground-floor bar is more handsome than ever, thanks to some mirrors and a soaring wall of frosted glass.

As always, the staff throws out a big welcome mat, and the American cooking is both familiar and interesting. Among just the appetizers, egg rolls adopt a Tex-Mex accent with their zesty fillings of smoked chicken, roast corn and black beans; creamy-centered crab fritters show up in spiky coats of shredded wheat; and each day gets a delicious soup of its own.

The kitchen acts as if it doesn't want any taste to feel left out. So it offers meaty beef ribs with a tangy barbecue sauce plus macaroni and cheese for the dedicated carnivore, and trout showered with spiced pecans and bedded on Parmesan potatoes for the fish fancier. The breads are baked right next door at the restaurant's own bakery (it even makes biscuits for your pooch), and from the bar comes a sidecar that reminds you of why the classic cocktail is back in vogue. Desserts run to old-fashioned comforts like deep-dish apple pie and, in season, a mile-high shortcake with a garden of fruit and a cloud of whipped cream.

Egg rolls adopt a Tex-Mex accent with their zesty fillings of smoked chicken, roast corn and black beans.

Not everything scores—one night's roast pork tenderloin is marred by an overdose of salt—but the hits far outnumber the misses. From the partylike atmosphere to the sleek design, the Carlyle is a model neighborhood restaurant.

Lunch: M-F 11-4 *Entrees:* $8-$19
Dinner: M-TH 4-11, F-SAT 4-MIDNIGHT *Entrees:* $9-$23
Brunch: SAT 10:30-3, SUN 9:30-3 *Entrees:* $8-$19
Credit Cards: AE, D, MC, V *Reservations:* LIMITED RESERVATIONS FOR PARTIES OF 6 OR MORE
Dress: CASUAL *Cross Street:* SOUTH QUINCY *Parking:* LOT *Metro:* NO

★ 1/2

CASA BLANCA

1014 VERMONT AVE. NW, WASHINGTON, DC (DOWNTOWN)
202-393-4430

IN THE WAKE OF SO MUCH that's new around Washington, it's easy for diners to overlook the tried and true—places like the veteran Casa Blanca, whose signage has it selling "Spanish food" but whose menu embraces Mexican, Salvadoran and Peruvian dishes.

The small storefront comes dressed with nothing but the basics: plain tables, plain chairs and a counter in the rear for carryout. Do yourself a favor and stick around. The rewards include a satisfying papa rellena—mashed potatoes wrapped around a core of beef, egg and olives, then fried—and crisp morsels of pork partnered with yuca and a sprightly salad. Spinach empanadas taste a little bland, but seviche proves plenty tangy with lime. Meanwhile, arroz con pollo—roast chicken with rice—is best for its fluffy yellow grains; veined with peas and pimento, the rice is good enough to star on its own.

The small storefront comes dressed with nothing but the basics: plain tables, plain chairs and a counter in the rear for carryout.

Owner Cesar Guzman is Peruvian, which explains some of Casa Blanca's flavors; his cooks come from Mexico and El Salvador, which explains the rest of the menu.

Open M-F 9-11, SAT 11-11, SUN NOON-9 ***Entrees:*** $5.50-$11.95
Credit Cards: NO (CASH ONLY) ***Reservations:*** NO
Dress: CASUAL ***Cross Street:*** K STREET NW
Parking: STREET ***Metro:*** MCPHERSON SQUARE

Critic's Pick

★ ★ ★

CASHION'S EAT PLACE

1819 COLUMBIA RD. NW, WASHINGTON, DC (ADAMS MORGAN) 202-797-1819
www.cashionseatplace.com

THE SCRIPT ON THE MENU is a telling detail: The choices are written in the fine hand of chef Ann Cashion. The black-and-white photos scattered throughout the softly lighted restaurant? Some of them capture moments from the lives of Cashion and her business partner, John Fulchino. And the wine list reflects a desire to enlighten diners as much as to ensure that they drink well.

Such personal touches suggest that someone is home and cares about your well-being. A few hit dishes on the French- and Mediterranean-inspired menu are frequently available, and thank goodness for that. I'd hate to miss the delicate leek-and-goat-cheese tart or the curried mussels with spinach. Yet there's always plenty to tempt regulars away from the tried and true. Pork is a sure bet; hope to find the meat shredded and cooked with orange, with salsa on the side and tortillas for wrapping. And the kitchen fries like a dream. If you think that's hyperbole, you haven't sampled Cashion's fried seafood—nubby oysters, golden scallops and crackling squid served with homemade tartar sauce and tangy pickles for balance. Service is casual and smart; dessert is worth sticking around for. Cornmeal pound cake sounds like Betty Crocker but tastes like Julia Child—not too sweet and gilded with maple whipped cream and fresh diced apple.

Pork is a sure bet; hope to find the meat shredded and cooked with orange, with salsa on the side and tortillas for wrapping.

Dinner: TU 5:30-10, W-SAT 5:30-11, SUN 5:30-10 ***Entrees:*** $19-$32
Brunch: SUN 11:30-2:30 ***Entrees:*** $8.95-$13.95
Closed: M ***Credit Cards:*** AE, MC, V ***Reservations:*** RECOMMENDED
Dress: BUSINESS CASUAL ***Cross Street:*** 18TH ***Parking:*** $5 VALET AT 6:30
Metro: WOODLEY PARK-ZOO / ADAMS MORGAN

★ ★ ½

CEIBA

701 14TH ST. NW, WASHINGTON, DC (DOWNTOWN) 202-393-3983
www.ceibarestaurant.com

ONE WAITER SHOWS UP with a stone bowl containing a bubbling mass of cheese, beef strips and velvety poblano peppers, trailed by another server with an earthenware dish of warm tortillas with which to eat the hearty appetizer. Curious diners on both sides of me lean in and ask what I've ordered.

"Queso fundido," I tell them as I dig into one of the many crowd-pleasers at Ceiba (pronounced SAY-bah). The fun in this whimsical tribute to Central and South America takes place in a series of rooms, some with pale blue "skies" overhead and big tropical plants in the windows, but my favorite claims a barrel-vaulted ceiling and sight of the busy kitchen. Launch with a tart margarita, continue with duck-stuffed empanadas or craggy crab fritters, and move on to the strapping pork feijoada, framed with a confetti of dark kale and lusty beans and rice, or shrimp threaded on skewers of sugar cane and brightened with pineapple salsa.

Not everything is great—striped bass seviche with corn nuts and sweet potato tastes flat—but enough is. Pastry chef David Guas practically dares us not to order dessert with seductions like dulce de leche cheesecake with tiny slices of pineapple poundcake and chocolate Cuban coffeecake ignited with a chili custard sauce. With your bill comes another sweet touch: caramel corn spilling out of a paper sleeve.

> ***Pastry chef David Guas practically dares us not to order dessert with seductions like dulce de leche cheesecake.***

Lunch: M-F 11:30-2:30 *Entrees:* $11-$17
Dinner: M-TH 5:30-10:30, F-SAT 5:30-11 *Entrees:* $18-$29
Closed: SUN *Credit Cards:* ALL MAJOR *Reservations:* RECOMMENDED
Dress: BUSINESS CASUAL *Cross Street:* G STREET NW
Parking: $5 VALET AT DINNER *Metro:* METRO CENTER

★ ★

CEVICHE

921-J ELLSWORTH DR., SILVER SPRING, MD 301-608-0081
www.latinconcepts.com

LONG BEFORE YOU SEE CEVICHE, you spot what's big, bland and soulless surrounding the South American restaurant: a Red Lobster to the left, a Potbelly to the right—a cornucopia of familiar corporate brands that can afford big rents and squeeze out local, independently owned shops and restaurants.

Climb the mosaic-tiled stairs to the upper reaches of the shopping complex next to the AFI Silver Theatre, though, and you'll find a handful of places to eat, huddled together like unwanted company, that aren't instantly recognizable. One of them is Ceviche, the latest in a collection of fashion-forward watering holes from restaurateur Mauricio Fraga-Rosenfeld, whose realm encompasses Chi-Cha Lounge, Gazuza and Mate in Washington and Gua-Rapo in Arlington.

With its hip setting and eclectic menu, Ceviche looks like a member of the family. The front of the venue offers a spacious and uncluttered lounge whose picture windows look onto the street action below. Clusters of low tables and smart red stools make for fun huddles, but equally inviting is a communal table and a long bar, tended to by congenial guys who help you make a pick from the cocktail list by serving a sample of whatever you're curious about.

Ask for your ceviche "Natural," and it comes dressed with cilantro, threads of peppers and plenty of lime.

Ask for your ceviche "Natural," and it comes dressed with cilantro, threads of peppers and plenty of lime. Hotter still is the "Peruano," fired up with hot peppers. The mildest ceviche, the "Hondureno," is creamy with coconut milk and faintly sweet.

Ceviche is a generous restaurant: Even the roast half-chicken looked as if it had stopped at Gold's Gym before it got to me. Marinated in cumin, oregano, bay leaf and beer, the big bird is seductively seasoned and cooked so that the flesh falls easily from the bones. Flank steak is fine, but my preference among the other meat entrees is pork, particularly pork rib made succulent with lime-braised onions. Finally, dinner is more delicious thanks to live guitar performances Wednesday through Saturday nights beginning about 8:30.

With any luck, Ceviche will start a chain reaction in its neighborhood that has nothing to do with the corporate logos that now dominate the block.

Open: M-TH 11:30-10, F-11:30-11, SAT 5-11, SUN 5-10 ***Entrees:*** $13-$21
Credit Cards: ALL MAJOR ***Reservations:*** NO
Dress: BUSINESS CASUAL ***Cross Street:*** GEORGIA AVENUE
Parking: LOT ***Metro:*** SILVER SPRING

Critic's Pick

★★

C.F. FOLKS

1225 19TH ST. NW, WASHINGTON, DC (DUPONT CIRCLE) 202-293-0162
www.cffolksrestaurant.com

"DID YOU PAINT?" a customer asks the owner. "The entry looks brighter." Art Carlson scans his tiny domain —11 green stools lined up at a Formica counter—in mock seriousness before delivering the punch line: "No, we must have mopped the floor."

While other restaurants bend like contortionists to please their patrons, Carlson lets his audience know it's his way or the highway, Bub. Newshounds (and there are plenty in this crowd of lawyers and journalists) have to settle for no TV; Carlson prefers opera and public radio. C.F. Folks is open only on weekdays and only for lunch because that's how much the owner wants to work—period.

As good as the almond chicken salad is, you'd miss the point of eating here if you didn't take your cue from the small blackboard on the wall.

The printed menu is mostly salads and sandwiches, and as good as the almond chicken salad is, you'd miss the point of eating here if you didn't take your cue from the small blackboard on the wall. That's where you'll find the five or so specials each day. Monday showcases Louisiana with red beans and rice and chunks of andouille, Wednesday detours to Italy (and maybe a fine pasta Bolognese) and India, and Friday it's a trip to the Middle East.

Who would expect to find a great slab of swordfish, colorful with a spunky tomato salsa and bedded on yellow rice, in a luncheonette? Regulars to C.F. Folks would.

Lunch: M-F 11:45-2:30 *Entrees:* $6.95-$11.75
Closed: SAT-SUN *Credit Cards:* ALL MAJOR *Reservations:* NO
Dress: CASUAL *Cross Street:* JEFFERSON PLACE NW
Parking: STREET *Metro:* DUPONT CIRCLE

Critic's Pick
★★★

CHARLESTON

1000 LANCASTER ST., BALTIMORE, MD 410-332-7373
www.charlestonrestaurant.com

FOR YEARS A SUNNY RESTAURANT known for its Southern-accented food, Charleston recently traded in its cheery trellis work, ceramic tile and palm frond sconces for walnut floors, silk-covered walls and persimmon-colored chairs. Chef Cindy Wolf revised her menu, too, sidestepping the traditional appetizer-entree-dessert format for something more flexible.

"Let me take a moment to explain our menu," a waiter begins one evening at the revamped Charleston. If it's your first visit here, you'll be grateful for the tour, because the stiff poster you've just been handed lists more than 30 dishes arranged in eight categories: "Hot," "Cool," "The Season" (featuring tomatoes in mid-August), plus "Fish & Shellfish," "Birds & Game," "Meats," "Cheese" and "Sweets." Diners basically compose their own tasting menu, picking anything from the collection for their three-, four- , five- or six-course meals.

Dewy salmon tartare presents another gem, capped with creme fraiche and a glistening dollop of caviar.

Experience has taught me to launch with something "Cool." The payoff might be raw wild rockfish sliced into rectangles, splashed with lemon and lime juice and further invigorated with minced jalapeno, red onion and cilantro. Dewy salmon tartare presents another gem, capped with creme fraiche and a glistening dollop of caviar. Lamb carpaccio comes to the table refrigerator-cold, but its charms reveal themselves as the sheer slices of uncooked meat warm up; fresh mint and flageolets (French kidney beans) add welcome breeziness and texture to the presentation.

The pacing is perfect. Nothing comes too fast, but you aren't glancing at your watch, either. Charleston is about leisurely and elegant dining, a philosophy matched in the servers' natty suits, deep knowledge of the menu and attention to detail.

Dinner is not a continuous joy ride—grilled lamb with a mere dot of pommes Anna is flat, and fattier than I would have preferred—yet the pleasures outpace the minor disappointments. Confit of pork with crisp fried green tomatoes and hoppin' john (black-eyed peas) hark back to Charleston's roots. The cheese course is more varied than I've seen in most Washington establishments and is handsomely staged: A cluster of juicy champagne grapes makes a fine garnish, and runnier cheeses are served in the bowls of spoons. The bottom line: A great restaurant has become even finer.

Dinner: M-SAT 5-10 ***Tasting Menus:*** 3-COURSE $64, 4-COURSE $78, 5-COURSE $90, 6-COURSE $102
Closed: SUN ***Credit Cards:*** AE, D, MC, V ***Reservations:*** RECOMMENDED
Dress: BUSINESS CASUAL ***Cross Street:*** S. EXETER ***Parking:*** COMPLIMENTARY VALET ***Metro:*** NO

Critic's Pick

☆ ☆ ☆

CHARLIE PALMER STEAK

101 CONSTITUTION AVE. NW (CAPITOL HILL) 202-547-8100
www.charliepalmer.com

CONVENIENT FOR LOBBYISTS and the people with whom they seek face time, this sleek, gray-and-blue destination on the Hill (notice the Capitol across the way?) is also a prime place to slice into steak, be it a thick rib-eye or pedigreed Wagyu sirloin with the texture of butter.

But meat is far from its only asset. The kitchen, under the eye of chef Bryan Voltaggio, also sends out fine oysters (nicely matched with beer sorbet), robust tuna tartare, buttery skate with an olive puree, and side dishes that go beyond the routine: Picture creamy goat cheese pasta, green beans with crunchy onions and fleshy chanterelle mushrooms.

With your steak comes a plate dotted with five different mustards.

No detail is too small. With your steak comes a plate dotted with five different mustards, and the suave servers wear suits that you wouldn't mind hanging in your own closet. Meanwhile, the rich American wine list means you will sip as well as you eat.

Lunch: M-F 11:30-2:30 ***Entrees:*** $13-$41
Dinner: M-F 5:30-10, SAT 5-10:30 ***Entrees:*** $23-$68
Closed: SUN ***Credit Cards:*** AE, DC, MC, V ***Reservations:*** RECOMMENDED
Dress: BUSINESS CASUAL ***Cross Street:*** FIRST
Parking: $5 VALET BEGINNING AT 5 ***Metro:*** UNION STATION

★ ★ ½

CIRCLE BISTRO

1 WASHINGTON CIRCLE NW, WASHINGTON, DC (FOGGY BOTTOM) 202-293-5390
www.circlebistro.com

BRENDAN COX seems to know just what many of us want to eat before we settle in elsewhere for a night of song, dance or drama at the nearby Kennedy Center: something light yet interesting.

Those adjectives certainly apply to the skilled chef's flaky tart of tomato and summer squash, and steamed mussels in a luxuriant broth of herbs and wine scattered with tiny croutons. Actually, there are a number of strong performances on his modern American menu. Hanger steak sliced into rosy rectangles and matched with a little cone of french fries is a fine display of meat; trout dusted with lemon zest and scattered with yellow and green beans, then finished with a butter sauce of herbs and almonds, is its equal from the water.

Hanger steak sliced into rosy rectangles and matched with a little cone of french fries is a fine display of meat.

Absent-minded service doesn't do justice to the quality of the cooking (you're apt to be kept waiting at the host stand and side dishes sometimes go AWOL). Stick around for dessert, however, where the reward for your patience might be a peach tartlet garnished with ginger ice cream, or delicate chocolate madeleines offered with a trio of dipping sauces.

Breakfast: M-F 7-10, SAT-SUN 8-10:30 ***Entrees:*** $8-$12
Lunch: M-SAT 11:30-2:30 ***Entrees:*** $12-$17
Dinner: SUN-TH 5-10, F-SAT 5-11 ***Entrees:*** $19-$26
Pre-Theater: DAILY 5-7:30, 3-COURSE PRIX FIXE $35
Brunch: SUN 11:30-2:30 ***Entrees:*** $7-$16
Credit Cards: ALL MAJOR ***Reservations:*** RECOMMENDED
Dress: BUSINESS CASUAL ***Cross Street:*** NEW HAMPSHIRE AVENUE NW
Parking: COMPLIMENTARY VALET ***Metro:*** FOGGY BOTTOM-GWU

★ 1/2

CITRUS CAFE

7075 INDIAN HEAD HWY., BRYANS ROAD, MD 301-375-6000
www.citruscafe-maryland.com

HEARING OUMAR SY discuss his résumé is like leafing through a memory book of Washington's recent-vintage French restaurants. There was the late, great Jean-Louis at the Watergate, under the revered Jean-Louis Palladin, where Senegalese native Sy got his start—as a dishwasher, in 1989. Then there was Provence, where Sy cooked for two years under another maestro, Yannick Cam. From 1996 to 2000, he was the head chef at Bistrot Lepic in Georgetown, a stint followed by several years at Petits Plats in Woodley Park.

These days, Sy is 35 minutes away from the action in Washington—"out in nowhere, if you look at it," he says—having been seduced by a good deal on a building, buoyed by development in Charles County and supported by his former sous chef at Petits Plats, Richard Morel. The two business partners have taken the former Stable, renamed it Citrus Cafe and turned the barnlike structure into something decidedly less so.

Open the menu, and you'll find French onion soup and coq au vin, but also familiar crab cakes and steak.

In their new roost, Sy and Morel have incorporated bits of their past with local preferences. Open the menu, and you'll find French onion soup and coq au vin, but also familiar crab cakes and steak. The restaurant's usual piped-in music gives way on Friday evenings to karaoke, a popular holdover from the Stable.

Your first taste from the kitchen is likely to be most reminiscent of the work the men did in their bistro days. A molten cap of cheese yields to sweet onions and beef broth in the French onion soup, while lobster bisque, subtle and creamy, gets dressed up with a pinch of sweet crab in the center of the bowl. The pâté is made in-house, too, and tastes like it. The most successful entrees involve fish and light sauces; my favorite is salmon, fashionably tiled in potatoes and napped with citrus beurre blanc.

Citrus Cafe provides a soupçon of sophistication along its stretch of Indian Head Highway, where the competition for dining dollars is pretty much limited to a few fast-food joints. While there's room for improvement, there are also enough draws to cheer its presence.

Lunch: SUN-TU 11:30-3 ***Entrees:*** $7.95-$12.95
Dinner: SUN-TU 4:30-10 ***Entrees:*** $9-$23.95 ***Closed:*** M
Brunch: SUN 11:30-3 ***Price:*** $15.95
Credit Cards: ALL MAJOR ***Reservations:*** RECOMMENDED
Dress: CASUAL ***Cross Street:*** ROUTE 210
Parking: LOT ***Metro:*** NO

Critic's Pick

☆ ☆ ☆

CITYZEN

MANDARIN ORIENTAL, 1330 MARYLAND AVE. SW, WASHINGTON, DC (SW WATERFRONT)
202-787-6006 www.cityzenrestaurant.com

STATUS-CONSCIOUS FOODIES cheered the news that a top chef from the revered French Laundry in Napa Valley was leaving that haute spot for the Nation's Capital. No sooner did Eric Ziebold arrive in Washington and settle in at the Mandarin Oriental hotel in the summer of 2004 than he began giving diners a taste of what he had learned from his acclaimed mentor, Thomas Keller, and from having cooked using only the finest and freshest ingredients.

Ziebold's handiwork also calls to mind the plates of some of the city's top toques. The young chef shares Frank Ruta's penchant for subtle, sensual flavors and Michel Richard's wittily luscious designs. One first course among many that exemplifies those styles: sheer pink ribbons of raw hiramasa (kingfish) supported on their plate by what look like miniature mushrooms but are actually crisp "stems" of water chestnuts wearing "caps" of slivered radish. Coriander and Japanese salt—grated tableside—tie the elements together in sublime fashion. In another heady appetizer, a ragout of beans is set off with crisped lamb tongue, zesty lamb sausage and a delicate sail of brioche for a most memorable "cassoulet."

A ragout of beans is set off with crisped lamb tongue, zesty lamb sausage and a delicate sail of brioche for a most memorable "cassoulet."

Deeper into the menu, wild duck gets an escort of artfully turned vegetables, spaetzle and smoky nubs of bacon, and rabbit is wrapped in a thin coat of potatoes and further accessorized with poached prunes and rabbit sausage. Divine. Entrees are preceded by a small wooden box lined with hot, single-bite Parker House rolls. Yeasty and lightly salted, with the option of sweet or salted butter, they disappear like Cuban cigars at a stag party. Save room for dessert: Tiny hazelnut pancakes with quince syrup and dried fruit is one of several endings that will make you glad you did.

Accompanied by fine wines—and an entertaining guide, Christopher Hile, to help you choose what to drink—this often extraordinary fare is delivered in a handsome, 70-seat dining room that bathes its patrons in warm lighting and soothing hues. It's a Champagne atmosphere for a meal that comes close to the gold standard.

Dinner: TU-TH 6-9:30, F-SAT 5:30-9:30 ***Entrees:*** 3-COURSE PRIX FIXE $75
Tasting Menus: 5-COURSE $95, 6-COURSE $110, 7-COURSE $125
Closed: SUN-M ***Credit Cards:*** ALL MAJOR ***Reservations:*** REQUIRED
Dress: BUSINESS CASUAL ***Cross Street:*** 12TH
Parking: COMPLIMENTARY VALET ***Metro:*** SMITHSONIAN

☆ ☆

CLAIRE'S AT THE DEPOT

65 S. THIRD ST., WARRENTON, VA 540-351-1616
www.clairesrestaurant.com

RESIDENTS OF WARRENTON knew the space simply as the Depot, a long-playing, family-run restaurant, before Claire Lamborne took over in February 2005. "I've wanted it for years," the local caterer says. One can understand the attraction. While the interior she inherited clearly had seen better days, the brick facade was a real looker. Lamborne spent $500,000 revamping the inside: New lights, fresh paint, different floors and redesigned bathrooms now make for a lovelier place to gather.

"Claire's Famous She Crab" soup merits the crowing. Thick with its namesake crab, the sherry-laced appetizer balances its expected richness with a bite from both cayenne and hot pepper sauce. Every spoonful delivers a pinprick of pleasure. Continuing the seafood theme are oysters in crunchy coats of cornmeal, served with a spirited dipping sauce, and, better yet, strips of seared, pepper-ignited ahi tuna paired with wonton crackers.

One draw is sliced flat-iron steak, striped with a kicky mustard sauce and teamed with onion-laced black beans.

There's plenty to like among the entrees. One draw is sliced flat-iron steak, striped with a kicky mustard sauce and teamed with onion-laced black beans and, as refreshing counterpoint, a light slaw of julienned carrot and jicama. Another treat brings together a trio of small but thick and meaty lamb chops with skin-on, "muddled" (read: smashed) red bliss potatoes and a cherry sauce that ricochets from sweet to tart in each drop. Dance around the puckish crab cakes, however, which would be evicted from most Washington seafood houses.

Where to sit? The brick-walled "fireplace room," with windows looking onto the street, is named for a hearth that is lighted when the weather turns cold. It's attractive and cozy, ideal for a small reunion of friends and family. The long and narrow "garden room" tugs at the romantic in me, however. As its name suggests, the tables look onto a patio and a patch of grass that includes a fountain; extending from a wall is a half-roof left over from the building's days as an actual depot.

Lunch: TU-F 11:30-2:30 ***Entrees:*** $9-$12
Dinner: T-TH 5:30-9, F-SAT 5:30-10 ***Entrees:*** $14-$29
Brunch: SUN 10:30-2 ***Entrees:*** $9-$12
Closed: M ***Credit Cards:*** AE, MC, V ***Reservations:*** RECOMMENDED
Dress: BUSINESS CASUAL ***Cross Street:*** LEE
Parking: LOT ***Metro:*** NO

★ ½

CLOUD DINING LOUNGE

1 DUPONT CIRCLE NW, WASHINGTON, DC (DUPONT CIRCLE) 202-872-1122
www.clouddining.com

TO EAT AND DRINK at Cloud on Dupont Circle is to be reminded of how many trends have rolled onto the dining landscape in recent years. For his latest venture, restaurateur Savino Recine, who closed Savino's Cafe & Lounge to redesign the space as a hip vision in white, packs in more fashions than the September issue of *Vogue*.

See the communal table? Notice the epic tapas menu? The roster of cocktails is up to the minute, too, with litchi martinis and blood orange cosmos. Now and then, Recine entertains his guests with card tricks and other magic. Beyond the main bar and dining room awaits a sunken lounge with white leather "beds" for really unwinding.

Beyond the main bar and dining room awaits a sunken lounge with white leather "beds" for really unwinding.

Those who have come to Cloud to graze as well as gaze will find a world of choices. From Spain come serrano ham and manchego cheese. Thailand is represented, quite respectably, by an assertive green curry chicken. Fried plantains with cilantro-garlic dip is an idea plucked from south of the border. Altogether, the kitchen offers about 50 hot and cold small plates.

There are some really pleasant moments. Lamb threaded on skewers proves nice and moist, enhanced by a dark tamarind sauce and sweet onions. Velvety roasted red piquillo peppers release a rivulet of warm goat cheese at the touch of a fork; the smoke of the vegetable and the tang of the cheese contrast nicely with sweet white raisins.

But Cloud is no Jaleo or Zaytinya, the city's first-class purveyors of small plates. Cloud's barbecued shrimp are good by themselves, but they're served with an avocado dip that tastes as if it had been poured from a jar. A Caesar salad has zero anchovy flavor and what smacks of Miracle Whip in its overthick dressing. Foil-wrapped butter looks out of place in this clubby venue, and the selection of wines by the glass approaches that of your typical frat party.

Recine is a dapper, hospitable and ubiquitous host, eager to know what you think of his playground and to show off its charms, which are multiple. I only wish the cooking got as much attention as all the gimmicks.

Open: TU-SAT 4:30-10:30 *Entrees:* $17.95-$18.95 *Tapas:* $3.50-$15.95
Closed: SUN-M *Credit Cards:* ALL MAJOR *Reservations:* RECOMMENDED
Dress: CASUAL *Cross Street:* NEW HAMPSHIRE AVENUE NW
Parking: STREET *Metro:* DUPONT CIRCLE

☆ ☆

COASTAL FLATS

11901 GRAND COMMONS AVE., FAIRFAX, VA 571-522-6300
www.greatamericanrestaurants.com

THE GREETING ON THE PHONE sounds familiar, in part because, if I call Coastal Flats at a particularly busy time, the voice on the other end of the line always asks me politely if I would mind holding. Nice gesture. And when my waitress looks as if there's no place she'd rather be than at my table—and she's able to rattle off every ingredient in an entree without referring to notes—that leaves me with a sense of deja vu, too. The warm bread basket, the rich lobster bisque—some of the cooking at this restaurant also stirs not-so-distant memories.

Coastal Flats has Great American Restaurant stamped all over it. The local mini-chain that brought us Artie's, Carlyle, Mike's American Grill, Silverado and several Sweetwater Taverns—seven good American restaurants scattered around Northern Virginia—is making a splash in Fairfax with a whale of a casual seafood restaurant. (The original was joined in September 2005 by a second location in Tysons Corner.)

Rock shrimp find themselves in the center of spiky fritters sprinkled with roasted-corn salsa and gilded with a teasing butter sauce.

The food at Coastal Flats brims with as much personality as the staff that works there, and the kitchen swims around for inspiration. Rock shrimp find themselves in the center of spiky fritters sprinkled with roasted-corn salsa and gilded with a teasing butter sauce. On the other hand, "sweet and spicy" calamari is far too much of the former and only a glimmer of the latter.

The restaurant's take on fish and chips partners grouper with a light, golden beer batter that keeps the fish moist; an assertive and fresh-tasting tartar sauce punches up the eating. Heed the server's recitation of specials, which in my experience have included expertly grilled swordfish with a mash of sweet potatoes, everything circled by a zingy sauce of lime and coconut.

The menu isn't all about surf, however. Indeed, one of the best items on it is the "Key lime" roast half-chicken. Rubbed with thyme, fennel, rosemary and paprika, it's as succulent a bird as I've had in the D.C. suburbs and served with a fluffy cous-cous jazzed up with almonds. It's haute stuff.

Lunch: DAILY 11-4 *Entrees:* $8-$19
Dinner: SUN-M 4-10, TU-TH 4-11, F-SAT 4-MIDNIGHT *Entrees:* $9-$29
Credit Cards: ALL MAJOR *Reservations:* LIMITED
Dress: CASUAL *Cross Street:* MONUMENT DRIVE
Parking: LOT *Metro:* VIENNA / FAIRFAX-GMU
Second Location: 7860 TYSONS CORNER CENTER, MCLEAN, VA, 703-356-1440

Critic's Pick

★ ★

COLORADO KITCHEN

5515 COLORADO AVE. NW, WASHINGTON, DC (BRIGHTWOOD)
202-545-8280

NAME A MIDDLE-CLASS American comfort food and Gillian Clark probably makes it—and makes it well.

Meat loaf? You bet. Fried chicken? Yep (even though it's Cornish hen standing in for the lead). Except for the saucer-sized potato chip waving from it, tuna noodle casserole resembles something Mom used to make and the pork chop is crunchy with a coat of golden corn flakes—and nicely turned out with cabbage and tender spaetzle.

But the menu isn't all Betty Crocker. The chef also acknowledges the 2000s with hake fried to a delicate crisp and served with elegant turned potatoes and a chocolate cake that's gooey and warm inside, and better than the typical, trendy molten dessert.

Except for the saucer-sized potato chip waving from it, tuna noodle casserole resembles something Mom used to make.

This often soothing fare comes in a sweet package of red chairs, diner-style tables and framed vintage food advertisements. The storefront is not too good to be true: Biscuits were dry on my last visit, as was lemon-coconut cake, and service can be memorable or not depending on your waiter. On the other hand, Colorado Kitchen also now pours beer and wine and must surely be the only restaurant within a mile to greet its guests with an amuse-bouche.

Lunch: F 11:30-2:30 *Entrees:* $7.50-$10
Dinner: W-SAT 5-10, SUN 5-9 *Entrees:* $13.50-$19.50
Brunch: SAT-SUN 11-2:30 *Entrees:* $5.50-$18.50
Closed: M-TU *Credit Cards:* AE, D, MC, V *Reservations:* NO
Dress: CASUAL *Cross Street:* 14TH
Parking: STREET *Metro:* COLUMBIA HEIGHTS

Critic's Pick
★★½

CORDUROY

FOUR POINTS BY SHERATON HOTEL, 1201 K ST. NW, WASHINGTON, DC (DOWNTOWN)
202-589-0699

TOM POWER is probably the least famous of Washington's culinary heroes, a situation exacerbated by a dining room that's removed from the downtown action, on the second floor of a minor hotel.

Take advantage of that. If you want peace and quiet, you're likely to find it here, where the previously stark space has been jazzed up with shimmering metal curtains, mirrors and warmer lighting. Power once worked for the demanding Michel Richard, and the tutelage is evident everywhere on Corduroy's menu, a focused collection of dishes that revel in good ingredients and simple execution.

Power's plump steak (it could be bison) offers heft, chew and real savor, and comes with delicious pan juices and a stack of thin french fries dusted with parsley flecks—a steak frites a French chef would be happy to call his own. Crisp-skinned striped bass rests on a sushi rice cake redolent of fresh ginger. It's a beautiful marriage between East and West. There are also light salads, lovely single-size pizzas, sometimes a fluffy omelet built around whatever mushrooms are in season and soups that sound plain but never are.

Power's plump steak (it could be bison) offers heft, chew and real savor.

The glory is in the details: good bread, nice wines by the (elegant) glass and a chef who never seems to be away from his stove.

Lunch: M-F NOON-2:30 ***Entrees:*** $10-$17
Dinner: M-F 5:30-10:30, SAT 5-11 ***Entrees:*** $18-$29
Closed: SUN ***Credit Cards:*** ALL MAJOR ***Reservations:*** RECOMMENDED
Dress: BUSINESS CASUAL ***Cross Street:*** 12TH
Parking: HOTEL PARKING VALIDATED (WHEN AVAILABLE) ***Metro:*** METRO CENTER

★ ★

COSTA VERDE

946 N. JACKSON ST., ARLINGTON, VA 703-522-6976
www.costaverderestaurant.com

LESS THAN FIVE MILES from downtown Washington, this Peruvian restaurant whisks its guests to another continent faster than you can say, "Make mine a pisco sour." (And you should: The cocktail is at once refreshing with whipped egg white and bracing with brandy, a nice companion to the crunchy corn nuts that show up as you're seated, along with a violent green dip.)

Spanish is the language of choice, salsa music provides a festive backdrop, and potatoes—boiled, roasted, fried—show up in more guises than Mike Myers in an Austin Powers flick.

Soft chunks of sweet potato round out a big platter of squid, octopus, shrimp, fish and mussels, garnished with lime and red onion, while fried potatoes make an appearance with the mixed grill of pork, chicken and beef. No mere sidekicks, tubers star on their own in such appetizers as papa rellena—mashed potatoes stuffed with chopped meat and fried.

Whole fried trout is delicious, as are the seviche (colorful with sweet potatoes) and the shrimp chowder.

The menu is half seafood, half meat, thoroughly homey and generous. I prefer the surf side: Whole fried trout is delicious, as are the seviche (colorful with sweet potatoes) and the shrimp chowder.

The open room isn't much to look at, though frilly curtains help dress up the place, and Saturday night is enlivened by musicians.

Open: M-TH 11-10, F 11-11, SAT 10-11, SUN 9-9 ***Entrees:*** $9.95-$16.95
Credit Cards: AE, D, MC, V ***Reservations:*** NO
Dress: CASUAL ***Cross Street:*** WILSON BOULEVARD
Parking: LOT ***Metro:*** VIRGINIA SQUARE-GMU

★ 1/2

COUSCOUS CAFE & CATERING

1195 20TH ST. NW, WASHINGTON, DC (DOWNTOWN) 202-689-1233
www.couscouscatering.com

JUST WHEN YOU THINK every decent location downtown has been gobbled up by a Starbucks, a Cosi or a Potbelly, along comes a place like Couscous Cafe & Catering to prove you wrong—and make your lunch hour a little sunnier.

A cup of tomato soup thick with cracked wheat, chickpeas and lamb, and phyllo-wrapped chicken with crushed almonds are the sort of dishes co-owner Aziz Benassou says he was raised on back in his native Algeria. Now he offers them in the 30-seat eatery he runs with the help of his mother and sister, Hadda and Ranu Benassou.

"Couscous is to us what pasta is for Italians," says the restaurateur, who features the processed wheat (semolina) in a stew of root vegetables and as an accompaniment to broiled salmon. A cold day calls for a bowl of homey lentil soup with carrots and bay leaves; a scorcher demands a glass of lemonade treated to fresh mint. And if a server recommends the daily special, pay heed: light and mildly spiced lamb meatballs might be your payoff.

A cup of tomato soup thick with cracked wheat, chickpeas and lamb, and phyllo-wrapped chicken with crushed almonds are the sort of dishes co-owner Aziz Benassou says he was raised on back in his native Algeria.

Meanwhile, North African music and walls painted in soothing yellow, green and burnt orange offer patrons a welcome break from the same old, same old at noon.

Breakfast: M-F 7:30-10:30 *Entrees:* $2.99-$5.99
Lunch: M-F 11-7 *Entrees:* $4.99-$9.99
Closed: SAT-SUN *Credit Cards:* AE, D, MC, V
Reservations: NO *Dress:* CASUAL *Cross Street:* M STREET NW
Parking: STREET *Metro:* DUPONT CIRCLE

★ ★

CRISP & JUICY

4540 LEE HWY., ARLINGTON, VA
703-243-4222

TRUE TO ITS TITLE, this Latin American rotisserie-chicken chain turns out birds of distinction, their meat always succulent and their skin always crisp (and nicely smoky from time spent in a wood-fired cooker). Sauce seems unnecessary, though Crisp & Juicy's tingling pink and garlicky green moisteners make irresistible additions to any order.

There's more to applaud: lusty black beans, crunchy yuca fries, soothing plantains. While the flan is stolid, the white cookies sandwiched with soft caramel nearly melt on the tongue. Some chicken and some sides add up to a memorable Latino picnic; indeed, a lot of the faces in the inevitable lines that snake out of one of Crisp & Juicy's five area locations appear to be people looking for a taste of home. And finding it, of course.

Carryout is the way to go, for the settings are small and spare.

Carryout is the way to go, for the settings are small and spare. (The narrow Arlington branch offers a brick-paved porch enclosed in glass whose tables go fast at peak hours.) But you've come to Crisp & Juicy to eat great chicken, not drink in the scenery, right?

Open: M-SAT 11-9:30, SUN 11-9 *Entrees:* $3.80-$9.35 (PLATTERS $5.35-$26.99)
Credit Cards: NO (CASH ONLY) *Reservations:* NO
Dress: CASUAL *Cross Street:* N. UPTON
Parking: LOT *Metro:* BALLSTON-MU
Other Locations: 913 W. BROAD ST., FALLS CHURCH, VA, 703-241-9091
3800 INTERNATIONAL DR., SILVER SPRING, MD, 301-598-3333
1331-G ROCKVILLE PIKE, ROCKVILLE, MD, 301-251-8833
1314 EAST-WEST HWY., SILVER SPRING, MD, 301-563-6666

★ ★

CRYSTAL THAI

4819 FIRST ST. N., ARLINGTON, VA 703-522-1311
www.crystalthai.com

EVEN AFTER 15 YEARS, Crystal Thai seems eager to please. The servers, dressed in traditional silk costumes, welcome strangers as if they were regulars. And unlike so much of the competition, this Thai restaurant eschews bright colors and splashy neon for a style that is more sedate. The dark mahogany bar would look at home in a steakhouse, chandeliers illuminate the crowd below, and white linens grace the tabletops. It was reassuring to see, more than once, tables full of people who probably grew up on Thai cooking.

Including specials, the number of menu possibilities reaches the triple digits, so allow me to cut to some highlights. Scallion-veined fish cakes (No. 2) are nice and light, though spirals of ground shrimp and crisp seaweed (No. 8) are more interesting, like seafood sausage served with a gently teasing sauce that's red with bell peppers. No. 28 (pok tak) is a superior soup, its golden broth sharpened with lemon grass, dressed with fresh herbs and brimming with tender squid and scallops. Of the main dishes, I'm partial to pork chops marinated in green curry (No. 78), singed by the grill and enhanced at the table with a vinegary cucumber-and-onion sauce, as well as a truly spicy and crispy "spicy crispy catfish" (No. 55). Pieces of the fish are mixed with Thai basil, fresh ginger and red chilies; eating the dish feels like a hundred tiny firecrackers going off on your tongue.

It was reassuring to see, more than once, tables full of people who probably grew up on Thai cooking.

While the kitchen is a reliable flame-thrower, it also displays an unfortunate sweet tooth. Basically, any recipe that is supposed to have a touch of sugar in its seasoning tends to have a shower of it here, be it the brown dipping sauce, apparently auditioning to be a dessert topping, served with the "Crystal rolls" stuffed with chicken, egg, carrot and mint, or the pad thai, the familiar mix of rice noodles and vegetables that practically gets candy-coated here.

The CliffsNotes version of the place would read something like this: Ease into a booth if you can, enjoy the solicitous staff, gravitate to what's hot—or the chef's specials—and ask the kitchen to go easy on the sweet stuff.

Lunch: M-F 11:30-3 ***Entrees:*** $7.25-$15.95
Dinner: M-TH 3-10, F 3-10:30, SAT-SUN NOON-10:30 ***Entrees:*** $8.25-$15.95
Credit Cards: ALL MAJOR ***Reservations:*** RECOMMENDED ***Dress:*** CASUAL
Cross Street: PARK DRIVE ***Parking:*** LOT ***Metro:*** BALLSTON-MU

☆ ☆

CUBAN CORNER

825 HUNGERFORD DR., ROCKVILLE, MD
301-279-0310

IS IT A PLACE TO EAT OR A SHRINE? At first glance, it's hard to tell. One wall is tiled with a who's who of Cuban Americans and their achievements; another displays the namesake island outlined in colorful neon and surrounded by painted palm trees and travel posters. Salsa music—and more conversations in Spanish than English—underscores the community-center feel.

The aroma of garlic, beef and onions wafting from the tiny kitchen of this small storefront reveals the Cuban Corner's real mission: to deliver a taste of the old country to the masses. This goal is accomplished with thin braided empanadas lined with onion-laced ground beef, fried green plantains stuffed with shrimp, red snapper in tomato-y vinaigrette, and my favorite entree, morsels of pork sauteed with green olives and pimentos ("montuno cubano" on the menu). Add some oiled white rice, inky black beans and soft, sweet plantains and you've got a meal to remember.

The aroma of garlic, beef and onions wafting from the tiny kitchen of this small storefront reveals the Cuban Corner's real mission: to deliver a taste of the old country to the masses.

Don't come here expecting a group hug: Your food is apt to come out quickly, and your interaction with the staff will probably lean toward the matter-of-fact, unless you're a regular. Most of the passion comes to the table by way of the upbeat music and the cooking. Even so, lunch finds a steady stream of office workers stopping in to refuel; as afternoon fades to black, the clientele shifts to couples and families. (Note to parental units: There's a children's menu for kids 10 and younger.)

The well-documented Cuban sweet tooth surfaces at dessert, most winningly with a slice of tres leches, or three-milk cake. Out comes a square of white cake drenched in a syrup of sweetened condensed milk, whole milk and evaporated milk. If I could vote to expand the honor roll at this mom-and-pop eatery, that cake would get a tile of its own on the wall listing Cuban wonders.

Open: M-TH 11-9, F-SAT 11-10, SUN NOON-8 ***Entrees:*** $6.69-$14.99
Credit Cards: AE, D, MC, V ***Reservations:*** RECOMMENDED
Dress: CASUAL ***Cross Street:*** MANAKEE
Parking: STREET ***Metro:*** ROCKVILLE

★ ★ ½

DAHLIA

4849 MASSACHUSETTS AVE. NW, WASHINGTON, DC (SPRING VALLEY)
202-364-1004

IS DAHLIA A PUBLIC RESTAURANT or a private club? One visit to the shopping center venue in Spring Valley finds so much air-kissing and hand-waving, I imagine myself at a fancy block party where everyone knows everyone else; another occasion, I spot chef-owner David Scribner ensconced at a table, chatting up diners who are obviously familiar to him. "I'm one person removed from every person in the dining room," Scribner, a native Washingtonian says, and he's semi-serious.

An alumnus of the jazzy Felix in Adams Morgan, Scribner most recently cooked at Smith Point in Georgetown, a solid American restaurant that eventually became a watering hole frequented by the Bush twins. Acccording to Scribner, both Felix and Smith Point were recognized primarily as night spots. "I was completely overshadowed by the bar scene," he says. That's definitely not the case at Dahlia, where what used to be the bar has been turned into a nonsmoking dining area and wine orders outpace anything that might get shaken or stirred behind a counter. "Food is what's driving this place."

I'll second the chef's claim. No one would come here for the modest design, but a lot of people would go out of their way for Dahlia's roast chicken. Bathed in fresh herbs, garlic, olive oil and a splash of soy sauce, the chicken is seared on the stove top, where it takes on a golden crust, then finished in a super-hot pizza oven. The result is unabashed succulence, with crisp bits of garlic clinging to the skin and flesh that remains utterly moist from bite to bite. Pizzas are terrific, as are the crab cakes, and Scribner nods to the wishes of longtime fans with signatures like seared scallops atop grits made luscious with pink folds of prosciutto and a ring of apple cider vinaigrette.

No one would come here for the modest design, but a lot of people would go out of their way for Dahlia's roast chicken.

Lunch: M-SAT 11:30-4 *Entrees:* $9-$16
Dinner: M-SAT 5:30-9:30 *Entrees:* $18-$30
Closed: SUN *Credit Cards:* AE, MC, V *Reservations:* RECOMMENDED
Dress: CASUAL *Cross Street:* 49TH
Parking: LOT *Metro:* TENLEYTOWN-AU

☆ ☆

DC COAST

1401 K ST. NW, WASHINGTON, DC (DOWNTOWN) 202-216-5988
www.dccoast.com

YOU DON'T HAVE TO BE A FISH EATER to appreciate this titanic ode to the bounty of the sea. Indeed, one of the best dishes I found on a recent visit was a mighty pork chop flanked by sweet potato puree and crisp green beans.

Of course, you're in (mostly) fine hands if you *do* eat seafood. Tender mussels in a heavy pot of sweet broth make for an appetizer of distinction, and the "tower of crab"—built from a soft-shell crab, a crab cake and spunky corn relish—is a delicious whimsy. The kitchen also has fun with fried oysters, treating them as if they were Buffalo chicken wings, which means the oysters are fried and accompanied by a "dip" of crumbled blue cheese and butter spiked with hot sauce. I tried, and failed, to restrain myself. Striped bass swims to the table fried, and whole. "Would you like me to show you?" a waitress asks. Nod "yes," and she expertly separates flesh from bone, and even spears a bite of fish for you to taste. A dunk in the garlic-and-soy dipping sauce adds zip.

Tender mussels in a heavy pot of sweet broth make for an appetizer of distinction.

Lesser moments—an oily lobster bisque, sludgy fruit sorbets—sometimes surface. But such bumps tend to be smoothed over by the likes of a hot chocolate souffle or a tangy lemon meringue "pie," cleverly contained (in a small Mason jar) with thin cookies and a dab of blueberry sauce.

All this in a two-story room with a stage set of an open kitchen and a crowd of people who look pleased to be on board.

Note: A new chef, James Clark, formerly of Palette in the Madison Hotel, took over the kitchen shortly before this guide went to press. Expect him to put his own stamp on the menu.

Lunch: M-F 11:30-2:30 ***Entrees:*** $14-$18
Dinner: M-TH 5:30-10:30, F-SAT 5:30-11 ***Entrees:*** $19-$29
Closed: SUN ***Credit Cards:*** ALL MAJOR ***Reservations:*** RECOMMENDED
Dress: BUSINESS CASUAL ***Cross Street:*** 14TH
Parking: $5 VALET M-SAT DINNER ***Metro:*** MCPHERSON SQUARE

Critic's Pick
☆ ☆ 1/2

DELHI CLUB

1135 N. HIGHLAND ST., ARLINGTON, VA 703-527-5666
www.delhiclub.com

FROM THE STREET, it looks like Just Another Restaurant in a neighborhood full of choices. Step inside, though, and you'll find a dash of style with your samosas: pretty green tables, decorative scarves on the walls and Indian music to lend a sense of the faraway.

Starters average just over $4 a plate, but show care and attention. Chicken wings are meaty and succulent, garnished with fresh herbs and zippy from their red seasoning. Spinach, potato and onion find their way into light and spiky fritters, and if you think all crab cakes come from the same mold, the chili- and ginger-ignited version here will change your mind.

If you think all crab cakes come from the same mold, the chili- and ginger-ignited version here will change your mind.

The long and tempting menu has something for every appetite. Carnivores should gravitate to anything made with lamb. Vegetarians should head in the direction of bhuna bharta, a smoky mush of eggplant, tomatoes and fragrant spices. Both camps can come together for the tandoor-baked breads, which are stuffed with cottage cheese, scattered with mint or topped with garlic and butter—and simply divine.

Lunch: DAILY 11:30-2:30 ***Entrees:*** $6.50-$8.50
Dinner: SUN-TH 5-10, F-SAT 5-10:30 ***Entrees:*** $8.50-$19.50
Brunch: SAT-SUN 11:30-2:30 ***Buffet:*** $9.95
Credit Cards: ALL MAJOR ***Reservations:*** NO
Dress: CASUAL ***Cross Street:*** CLARENDON BOULEVARD
Parking: STREET ***Metro:*** CLARENDON

Critic's Pick
☆ ☆

DEL MEREI GRILLE

3106 MOUNT VERNON AVE., ALEXANDRIA, VA 703-739-4335
www.delmereigrille.com

THE MENU OF THIS SMALL, friends-and-family-run restaurant is a little bit country and a little bit rock-and-roll, at once old-fashioned and up to date. If I need some cheering up, a heaping plate of lightly battered butter pickles, or "frickles," served with cool remoulade is where I might head. They're hot, crunchy, salty and "best with beer," as a waiter pointed out to me. In the same vein are a pinkish scoop of horseradish-spiked beer cheese dip dusted with cayenne and circled in crackers.

The appetizers don't all hark back to "Happy Days," though. There are also grill-singed shrimp with a small teepee of shoestring fries and a zesty cocktail sauce, and spinach salad enhanced by creamy avocado and toasted pine nuts as well as a basil-bright dressing.

And so it goes with the entrees, where a diner can opt for a messy and nostalgia-inducing sloppy joe—or a thick cut of salmon topped with tomato-onion chutney and supported on a thin raft of grilled asparagus. "Free range tarragon roasted" half-chicken, though, reads better on paper than it tastes; the chicken is overcooked. There's plenty to like about the braised beef ribs—the meat falls easily from the bone, and it comes with a pleasantly sweet barbecue sauce—flanked by cheesy mashed potatoes and tangy collard greens.

Eric Reid—whose childhood pal Mary Abraham watches over the dining room—is a generous cook, doling out portions as if he were feeding hungry teenagers. So his roster of gently priced steaks comes with a choice of two side dishes (head for the green beans with bacon, and macaroni and cheese) and an optional sauce. Of the seven meats, I'm partial to the bison strip steak, deep red in color and offering some nice chew, and the lean but flavorful flank steak.

Eric Reed is a generous cook, doling out portions as if he were feeding hungry teenagers.

Squeezed into a modest shopping strip, Del Merei Grille doesn't look like much from the street. And the small dining room, which adjoins a more handsome bar, relies mostly on red and gold paint for flair. If given the choice, however, most of us would probably forgo style for steak, and fashion for frickles.

Lunch: M-F 11:30-2:30 *Entrees:* $7-$15
Dinner: SUN-TH 5-10, F-SAT 5-11 *Entrees:* $16-$28
Credit Cards: AE, MC, V *Reservations:* RECOMMENDED
Dress: CASUAL *Cross Street:* GLEBE ROAD
Parking: LOT *Metro:* BRADDOCK ROAD

★ 1/2

THE DINER

2453 18TH ST. NW, WASHINGTON, DC (ADAMS MORGAN) 202-232-8800
www.trystdc.com/diner

HERE'S A WASHINGTON RESTAURANT that stays open not only after "news, weather and sports," but 24 / 7. There are too few kitchens that do so, and fewer still that offer the range that the Diner does; here, it's no problem if one of you wants French toast with a side of corned beef hash and someone else wants penne pasta or a turkey sandwich.

Carved from the former J&O Auto Parts, the Diner looks like what you'd expect of a place with that title, only bigger and more Restoration Hardware than Route 1. (Notice the flower stencils on the wall?) The pressed-tin ceiling hovers 15 feet above the white-and-black tile floor, and there are two counters to accommodate customers who like that option.

Omelets in the a.m. are fine, but I prefer the Diner later in the day, for grazing. The onion rings are a bit greasy, but chances are you won't leave one sweet, golden slice uneaten. A Caesar salad shows spunk in its creamy dressing, and the spicy chicken wings are tamed by a plunge into their cool dip, invigorated with mint and cilantro. Chili is likewise zippy, and thick with several kinds of beans. If you spring for the cheese and bacon, a hamburger goes from plain to satisfying, and the fries that come with it are hot, crisp and habit-forming. Pass on the shrimp-and-crab dip, though, which tastes mostly of creamy binder. Among the entrees billed as "homemade dinners" you can find a big, soft slab of meat loaf shored up with a small mountain of very good mashed potatoes. But a pork chop is both rigid and flavorless, despite its fruity glaze.

If you spring for the cheese and bacon, a hamburger goes from plain to satisfying, and the fries that come with it are hot, crisp and habit-forming.

If you want something sweet, splurge on a shake or a malt in the comforting flavors of chocolate, strawberry or vanilla (my pick). Any extra is served next to your glass in a tall metal container. If you're anything like me, you won't stop until you've hit bottom.

Open: DAILY 24 HR. ***Entrees:*** $1.99-$14.99 ***Credit Cards:*** MC, V
Reservations: NO ***Dress:*** CASUAL ***Cross Street:*** COLUMBIA ROAD NW
Parking: STREET ***Metro:*** WOODLEY PARK-ZOO / ADAMS MORGAN

DON LOBO'S MEXICAN GRILL

2811 M ST. NW, WASHINGTON, DC (GEORGETOWN)
202-333-0137

PAINTED IN GREEN, WHITE AND RED—the colors of the Mexican flag—decorated with sombreros and watched over by an efficient staff, Don Lobo's makes a tasty pit stop in Georgetown.

Its sangria brims with fruit, the taquitos are fat with shredded chicken, and an order of mussels shows up as a starburst of tender bivalves ignited with jalapenos in its cilantro-laced broth. If the black beans are a little bland and the sauteed shrimp prove merely decent, there's enough to keep diners entertained, including some tasty beef fajitas; the meat, marinated in pineapple juice, is rosy and succulent, and the thick, piping-hot tortillas that come with the dish are obviously made from scratch. And lunch yields some attractive bargains, like a combination plate of eggy chile relleno and chicken or beef taco with oiled yellow rice for less than $8.

Its sangria brims with fruit, the taquitos are fat with shredded chicken, and an order of mussels shows up as a starburst of tender bivalves ignited with jalapenos in its cilantro-laced broth.

The small and narrow restaurant doesn't approach the color of Rosa Mexicano in Penn Quarter or the flavor of Guajillo in Arlington, but what it lacks in style and variety it makes up for in cost and service (your water glass will never dip below full).

Lunch: M-F 11-3 ***Entrees:*** $6.95-$8.95
Dinner: DAILY 11-11 ***Entrees:*** $8.95-$15.95
Credit Cards: AE, MC, V ***Reservations:*** NO
Dress: CASUAL ***Cross Street:*** 28TH
Parking: STREET ***Metro:*** FOGGY BOTTOM-GWU

★ ½

DUKEM

1114-8 U ST. NW, WASHINGTON, DC (U STREET CORRIDOR) 202-667-8735
www.dukemrestaurant.com

YOU DON'T GET FORKS OR KNIVES; as is typical of Ethiopian dining, the food at Dukem is eaten with fingers and pieces of injera, the slightly sour crepe that also stands in for a plate.

If you're a novice, be advised: No staff member I encountered at this corner dining room spoke much English, if any. But pointing and enlisting the help of native Ethiopian customers, who seem to treat this as a gathering spot as much as a place to eat, can land you some pleasant memories to take back home.

One signature is kitfo, a mound of raw ground beef blended with house-made cottage cheese, herbed butter and hot red pepper. Imagine steak tartare mixed with fire. You don't have to be a carnivore to eat well, though. Follow the lead of seemingly every other table and request the vegetable combination: Out comes a floppy round of injera, dolloped with a variety of earth-toned selections, from chopped greens and yellow lentils to a tomato salad sparked with jalapenos.

One signature is kitfo, a mound of raw ground beef blended with house-made cottage cheese, herbed butter and hot red pepper.

Afternoon soap operas and CNN on TV yield to live Ethiopian music and dance onstage Monday and Wednesday evenings.

Open: SUN-TH 9 AM-1 AM, F-SAT 9 AM-2 AM *Entrees:* $5-$18.95
Credit Cards: ALL MAJOR *Reservations:* RECOMMENDED
Dress: CASUAL *Cross Street:* 12TH *Parking:* STREET
Metro: U STREET / AFRICAN AMER CIVIL WAR MEMORIAL / CARDOZO
Second Location: 1100 MARYLAND AVE., BALTIMORE, MD, 410-385-0318

★ ★

EAT FIRST

609 H ST. NW, WASHINGTON, DC (CHINATOWN)
202-289-1703

THIS SPARSELY-DRESSED Cantonese restaurant is not much to look at. Pink table tops seem to be its lone attempt at decor. But what the dining room lacks in flair is more than made up for by much of what you get from the kitchen, and a staff that is eager to help you locate the goods.

An active fish tank and a flock of roast ducks hanging near the kitchen window should be your cue to sample Eat First's fresh shrimp, fried whole flounder and crisp-skinned duck. The menu descriptions frequently underplay the options; an order of "sauteed oyster in shell with black bean sauce," for instance, brings six fresh, brick-size bivalves to the table—plump giants that will leave your fellow diners wide-eyed.

An active fish tank and a flock of roast ducks hanging near the kitchen window should be your cue to sample Eat First's fresh shrimp, fried whole flounder and crisp-skinned duck.

Eat First's epic menu is bigger still for the numerous specials printed in Chinese (but with English subtitles) on colored strips of paper that hang from the mirrored walls. The seasonal suggestions might highlight sauteed lotus roots, baby bok choy with Chinese sausage or a verdant heap of stir-fried sweet potato leaves. A bland duck soup here and a greasy eggplant dish there are disappointments, but infrequent ones. More likely, baked chicken dusted with salt and green chilies and pearly shrimp with caramelized walnuts will have you sending clean plates back to the kitchen.

Lunch: M-F 11-3 *Entrees:* $3.95-$5.25
Dinner: SUN-TH 3 PM-2 AM, F-SAT 3 PM-3 AM *Entrees:* $7.95-$24.95
Credit Cards: AE, V *Reservations:* RECOMMENDED
Dress: CASUAL *Cross Street:* SIXTH
Parking: STREET *Metro:* GALLERY PLACE-CHINATOWN

★ ★

EL CHALAN

1924 I ST. NW, WASHINGTON, DC (DOWNTOWN) 202-293-2765
www.elchalanrestaurant.com

PATRONS LEAVE WASHINGTON at the door when they enter the small English basement that for nearly three decades has housed this Peruvian restaurant. Listen: Most of the conversations around you unfold in Spanish. Look around: The low ceilings, carved chairs, tile floors and religious paintings suggest a faraway sanctuary in Lima.

Now taste: The fish seviche, colorful with corn and sweet potatoes, pulses with lemon, chilies and red onion. Bony but tender chunks of goat dominate a main-course stew that's tangy with vinegar and beer and balanced with soft-cooked white beans. Peruvians love their potatoes, and you will, too, after a taste of them mashed with fish, then chilled, sliced and served with a cilantro-laced salad of red onions. And regulars know that the little white dish of salsa picante, a wicked condiment here, is meant to be slathered on the bread that precedes your meal. (Ouch! More!)

Look around: The low ceilings, carved chairs, tile floors and religious paintings suggest a faraway sanctuary in Lima.

Shredded chicken in a light blanket of peanut sauce is merely decent, and the seating is so tight, you get to hear all the juicy details about your neighbor's new job or last date whether you care to or not. Service is indifferent; the beef hearts, spunky from their marinade of lemon, vinegar and paprika, are anything but.

Lunch: M-F 11:30-3 *Entrees:* $11.95-$24.25
Dinner: M-F 5:30-10, SAT 1-10, SUN 1-8 *Entrees:* $12.75-$24.25
Credit Cards: ALL MAJOR *Reservations:* RECOMMENDED FOR PARTIES OF 5 OR MORE
Dress: CASUAL *Cross Street:* 20TH
Parking: STREET *Metro:* FARRAGUT WEST

★

ELI'S

1253 20TH ST. NW, WASHINGTON, DC (DUPONT CIRCLE) 202-785-4314
www.elisdc.com

WHEN IT CAME TIME to name his kosher restaurant in Washington, Sina Soumerkian suggested his entire family—wife Ellen and children Ilana, Noah and Eli—vote on the matter. The majority ruled it should be named for the youngest member of the family, so Eli's it is.

"A good deli name," says the proud patriarch, who also owns Siena's pizzeria in Rockville.

Painted in a shade between pink and purple, the 65-seat restaurant sports wood floors, glass-topped tables, old-fashioned light fixtures and a basin in the rear, at which some patrons wash their hands and say a blessing before they eat.

The lunch menu of salads and sandwiches is intentionally simple: "People have an hour for lunch," explains Soumerkian. Dinner finds more options, including roast chicken, meat loaf, and fish and chips. What to eat? Chicken soup is thick with noodles, celery, carrots and slivers of the featured ingredient; one of the best sandwiches partners chopped liver and pastrami between thick slices of delicious rye bread.

One of the best sandwiches partners chopped liver and pastrami between thick slices of delicious rye bread.

Eli's—which takes the place of Kozy Korner in the city's West End and closes on Saturdays—sits on a corner surrounded by office workers, hotel guests and more than a few students from nearby George Washington University. "I hit the jackpot," concedes the man who now feeds many of them.

Lunch: SUN-TH 11-4, F 11-3 ***Entrees:*** $5.99-$12.99
Dinner: SUN-TH 4-9 ***Entrees:*** $6.99-$24.99
Closed: F AFTER 3, SAT ***Credit Cards:*** AE, MC, V ***Reservations:*** NO
Dress: CASUAL ***Cross Street:*** N STREET NW
Parking: STREET ***Metro:*** DUPONT CIRCLE

★ ★

EQUINOX

818 CONNECTICUT AVENUE NW, WASHINGTON, DC (DOWNTOWN) 202-331-8118
www.equinoxrestaurant.com

JUST LIKE PEOPLE, restaurants have their good seasons and their lesser ones. The thought occurred to me most recently after dining at Equinox, which in years past has been among my favorite places to tuck into lunch or dinner in downtown Washington. Todd Gray—its co-owner, chef and increasingly busy entrepreneur— typically is a careful shopper and a fine cook, but those talents haven't been as evident of late.

Consider a meal in late autumn: Butternut squash soup radiates orange and bobs with bits of lamb sausage, yet the liquid falls flat on the palate. Chicken shows up dry, sliced over a wet bed of nutty black rice and a vague foie gras sauce. "Herb-roasted" striped bass tastes blank despite the promise of seasoning, a flaw highlighted by a base of bland lentils.

Some dishes show better than others—cassoulet is respectable, as is cannelloni stuffed with shredded pork and draped with a delicate bechamel—but too much of the cooking these days resembles its appearance: beige (as in pleasant but neutral). Even the desserts are upstaged by the gratis sweets—a plate of tiny cookies, truffles and orange-flavored tuiles—that follow them.

Some dishes show better than others—cassoulet is respectable, as is cannelloni stuffed with shredded pork.

Roast scallops accented with Virginia ham, and polished service, are reminders of the good old days at Equinox. They also give me hope that the current state of affairs is just a blip, not a trend.

Lunch: M-F 11:30-2 *Entrees:* $18-$27
Dinner: M-F 5:30-10, SAT 5:30-10:30, SUN 5-9
Tasting Menus: 3-COURSE $55, 4-COURSE $70, 6-COURSE $85
Credit Cards: ALL MAJOR *Reservations:* RECOMMENDED
Dress: BUSINESS CASUAL *Cross Street:* I STREET NW
Parking: $5 VALET AT DINNER *Metro:* FARRAGUT WEST

Critic's Pick
★ ★

ETETE

1942 NINTH ST. NW, WASHINGTON, DC (SHAW) 202-232-7600
www.eteterestaurant.com

SAVE FOR A FEW BASKET-TABLES near the front window, Etete could pass for a stylish American bistro. Its long red banquette, sleek black chairs and peach-colored walls all suggest this is so. But the hubcap-sized platters exiting the kitchen give away the restaurant's identity: There's no mistaking the floppy folds of tangy bread—injera—or the earth-toned dollops of stews and salads that decorate that base as anything other than Ethiopian cooking.

Named for its owner and chef, Tiwaltenigus "Etete" Shenegelgn, known in the Ethiopian community for catering dozens of weddings each year, this narrow retreat serves food (sometimes sloooowly) that pulses with personality.

Derek tibs translates as crusty bites of sauteed beef sweetened with caramelized onion strings, chopped tomato and slivers of green pepper; accompanying the entree are zesty, brick-colored lentils and a dab of what looks like ketchup but turns out to be (watch out!) berbere, Ethiopia's famously fiery ground hot pepper seasoning. More elaborate is the "special" kitfo, which lives up to the descriptor when the raw minced beef is arranged on its platter with several kinds of seasoned cottage cheeses and collard greens, then ceremoniously dressed with melted butter. A feast—and a little trip to Ethiopia—for $12!

Derek tibs translates as crusty bites of sauteed beef sweetened with caramelized onion strings, chopped tomato and slivers of green pepper.

Open: DAILY 11:30-MIDNIGHT ***Entrees:*** $10-$12
Credit Cards: ALL MAJOR ***Reservations:*** RECOMMENDED
Dress: CASUAL ***Cross Street:*** U STREET NW
Parking: STREET ***Metro:*** SHAW-HOWARD U

★ ½

FAMOUS LUIGI'S

1132 19TH ST. NW, WASHINGTON, DC (DOWNTOWN) 202-331-7574
www.famousluigis.com

IN THE SAME SPACE SINCE 1943, this is the kind of spaghetti house that's become increasingly hard to find, with red-and-white-check table covers and not a whiff of truffle oil to be sniffed. Think lasagna and pizza as opposed to beef carpaccio and braised baby octopus.

"Inside or out?" a waiter might ask, nodding first to the glass-enclosed front room, then to the darker interior that houses Luigi's bar. Beneath whirling overhead fans, both spaces are crammed with tables set with shakers of red pepper flakes and grated Parmesan. Sometimes friendly, other times curt, the service invariably leans to the quick and efficient—a good thing, too, since the restaurant is particularly popular with groups, who show up in streams at lunchtime.

Head for whatever looks homey on the menu. Vegetable soup yields a Mom-like bowl of golden broth brimming with peas, celery, tomatoes, big soft chunks of carrot and more. Just the ticket on a cold winter's day. A brick-size slab of lasagna soothes its takers with layers of noodles, cheese, cubed beef and pleasantly sweet tomato sauce. And fans of carbonara will find happiness in the version here, a steaming turban of spaghetti showered with crisp bacon bits and enough cream sauce to moisten but not overwhelm the pasta. Nothing too fussy, everything doled out as if a friend were feeding you—Famous Luigi's hits the spot.

A brick-size slab of lasagna soothes its takers with layers of noodles, cheese, cubed beef and pleasantly sweet tomato sauce.

Lunch: M-SAT 11-3, SUN NOON-3 *Entrees:* $7.75-$15.25
Dinner: DAILY 3-MIDNIGHT *Entrees:* $10.75-$17.95
Credit Cards: ALL MAJOR *Reservations:* RECOMMENDED FOR PARTIES OF 7 OR MORE
Dress: CASUAL *Cross Street:* M STREET NW
Parking: STREET *Metro:* DUPONT CIRCLE

Critic's Pick

★ ★ 1/2

FIREFLY

1310 NEW HAMPSHIRE AVE. NW, WASHINGTON, DC (DUPONT CIRCLE) 202-861-1310
www.firefly-dc.com

ARE WE INSIDE OR OUT? It's hard to tell at Firefly, where birch branches line the wall, stone frames the kitchen window, and the host stand sits beneath a faux tree dangling tiny lanterns from its branches. No matter what kind of day you've had, walking into this small, golden-lighted room will make you feel better.

Often, the cooking follows suit. Chef John Wabeck comes up with plates that tend to comfort diners rather than challenge their palates, though he likes to slip in something unexpected, like buckwheat noodles in a big bowl of chicken soup "our way." Familiar food gets a twist or two: Roast chicken comes with a casserole of tortillas, salsa and cheese, while spaghetti and meatballs are updated here to include housemade pasta, lashings of pecorino cheese and meatballs made from venison. And good as the skin-on red snapper is, the fish is nearly upstaged by its creamy moat of caramelized, spice-redolent onions and fingerling potatoes. Roast squash soup is dull. Hand-chopped lamb tartare served with celery root remoulade is anything but.

No matter what kind of day you've had, walking into this small, golden-lighted room will make you feel better.

Desserts sound better than they really are (where's the punch in the espresso poundcake?) but the wine program is a winner. Wabeck, a grape nut, seems to spend as much time chatting up customers at the bar as he does in the kitchen, and regulars know that whatever he enjoys sipping is probably going to find its way to his intelligent list.

Breakfast: M-SUN 7-10 ***Entrees:*** $13
Lunch: M-F 11:30-2:30 ***Entrees:*** $11.50-$18
Dinner: M-TH 5:30-10:30, F-SAT 5:30-11, SUN 5:30-10:15 ***Entrees:*** $18.50-$26
Brunch: SUN 11-2:30 ***Entrees:*** $14-$19
Credit Cards: ALL MAJOR ***Reservations:*** RECOMMENDED
Dress: CASUAL ***Cross Street:*** N STREET NW
Parking: $8 VALET AT DINNER TH, SAT ***Metro:*** DUPONT CIRCLE

★ ★

FORTUNE

6249 SEVEN CORNERS CENTER, FALLS CHURCH, VA
703-538-3333

IF YOU THINK TRAFFIC JAMS occur only on paved surfaces, you haven't seen Fortune during rush hour—otherwise known as dim sum service on the weekend.

That's when a fleet of metal carts wends its way through a sea of tables, stopping here to unload a dish of sticky rice or there to offer a steamer basket of shumai (steamed dumplings). The food in this Falls Church dining hall comes out with lightning speed, and the staff is quick to explain the options, making this a good place to know about if you have children or impatient appetites in tow.

Better yet, much of the cooking is very good. Among the hits: bite-size, sesame-seed-flecked pastries filled with sweet barbecued pork; shrimp paste wrapped around sugar cane and fried to a golden crisp; translucent scallop dumplings; and pork-and-chive dumplings. Clams get drenched in a too-thick brown sauce, and Chinese watercress is oily, but there are dozens of other plates to make you glad to be here, including roast chicken served with peppery salt, and wrinkly green beans in garlic sauce.

Among the hits: bite-size, sesame-seed-flecked pastries filled with sweet barbecued pork; shrimp paste wrapped around sugar cane and fried to a golden crisp; translucent scallop dumplings; and pork-and-chive dumplings.

The catch? The decor, or what amounts to it. Purple drapes, and walls that should be any other color than they are, cry out for a visit from the crew of "Trading Spaces."

Lunch: DAILY 11-3 ***Entrees:*** $5.50-$8 (DIM SUM: $1.95-$5.50)
Dinner: DAILY 3-10:30 ***Credit Cards:*** D, MC, V
Reservations: RECOMMENDED FOR PARTIES OF 10 OR MORE
Dress: CASUAL ***Cross Street:*** ARLINGTON BOULEVARD
Parking: LOT ***Metro:*** EAST FALLS CHURCH
Second Location: FORTUNE OF RESTON, 1428 N. POINT VILLAGE CENTER, RESTON, VA, 703-318-8898

Critic's Pick
★ ★ ★

FOTI'S

219 E. DAVIS ST., CULPEPER, VA
540-829-8400

FOTI'S IS A TEXTBOOK EXAMPLE of what a good education will do for you. The principals behind this fresh face in Culpeper spent a combined total of 14 years at the esteemed Inn at Little Washington. In their new environment, the trio demonstrates, meal after meal, how much they absorbed from some of the best teachers in the business.

Remember this name: Frank Maragos. He's the quietly captivating, thirty-something chef whose Greek nickname explains the restaurant's title and whose appearances in the dining room to say hello and share a story make any dinner more delicious. While at the Inn, he served as executive sous-chef.

The sunny presence at the door, the woman who watches over the dining room like a nanny with a fine sense of humor? That's the chef's English-born fiancée, Sue Wilson, who was a server at the Inn and who continues to pamper customers as if she were still there. The jolly fellow helping you select something to drink, meanwhile, is Tyler Packwood, the Inn's former cellar master.

While the menu changes frequently, you'll want to zero in on seafood, and anything with a Mediterranean flavor.

Don't expect a baby version of the Inn at Little Washington. Plan instead on a comfortable few hours and generally excellent food in a dining room that practically glitters with sparkling glassware and flickering candles but, with its brick walls and wood floors, stops short of making you wonder "How am I ever going to pay for this?"

While the menu changes frequently, you'll want to zero in on seafood, and anything with a Mediterranean flavor. Maragos's paella is a tour de force: Rice enriched with saffron, toasted garlic, wine and bay leaf serves as a luscious canvas for seafood — beautifully cooked lobster and shrimp — that have been assembled on the plate to look like a whole lobster. The paella's equal in the meat department: lamb served three different ways. A pesto-edged piece of loin is joined on its plate with a tender shank that collapses at the touch of a tine and lamb sausage that pulses with cumin and garlic. Desserts show the same thought as the savory dishes.

And the name Foti's? Maragos says it's derived from Foteos, the first name of the man who introduced the chef's grandparents to each other. In Greek, according to Maragos, it means "to enlighten" or "bring new." How very fitting.

Dinner: TU-SAT 5-9:30 ***Entrees:*** $14.95-$33.95
Closed: SUN-M ***Credit Cards:*** AE, MC, V ***Reservations:*** RECOMMENDED
Dress: CASUAL ***Cross Street:*** MAIN ***Parking:*** STREET ***Metro:*** NO

★ ★ 1/2

GALILEO

1110 21ST STREET NW, WASHINGTON, DC (DOWNTOWN) 202-293-7191
www.robertodonna.com

FIRST, LET'S COUNT THE WAYS chef-owner Roberto Donna makes so many diners happy: When the weather cooperates, he sometimes grills lunch outside, and his informal Osteria next to the bar offers lusty home-style Italian cooking for not much more than you'd pay for dinner at a chain. And no Italian in town puts on quite the fashion show that Donna does in his intimate, glass-fronted Laboratorio, a 12-course, hours-long tour of Italy that doesn't involve jet lag, only lots of grand eating.

The problem? The main dining room, which is where most people aim when making a reservation at Galileo. Aside from the cozy alcoves along one wall, the space is unglamorous, and there's often a slightly chaotic feel to the service. While some of the food is very good—ravioli stuffed with sea bass and soft shell crabs scattered with morels made for nice spring memories, and the cheese cart is unrivaled downtown—other dishes don't live up to the chef's considerable reputation or the cost of dining here. A less than great hunk of beef partnered with artichokes and a dollop of potatoes yields mighty ordinary eating. Unfortunately, it has company elsewhere on the bill of fare.

Famous faces are fawned over; mortals are sometimes treated as if they were lucky to get in the door.

Who you are seriously matters. Famous faces are fawned over; mortals are sometimes treated as if they were lucky to get in the door. Few restaurants are as simultaneously adored and despised as this one. Frustratingly, there's no way of predicting what kind of experience you'll have. Which is why I prefer doing Galileo on the cheap (way up front, in the Osteria) or on Daddy Warbuck's expense account (in the Laboratorio).

Lunch: M-F 11:30-2 *Entrees:* $15-$20
Dinner: M-SUN 5:30-10 *Entrees:* $26-$37
Tasting Menu: 5-COURSE PRIX FIXE $145
Chef's Table: DAILY 5:30-10 4-COURSE $69, 5-COURSE $85, 7-COURSE $95
Pre-Theater: DAILY 5:30-6:30, 3-COURSE PRIX FIXE $33
Credit Cards: AE, D, MC, V *Reservations:* RECOMMENDED
Dress: BUSINESS CASUAL *Cross Street:* L STREET NW
Parking: $6 VALET M-SAT AFTER 6 *Metro:* FARRAGUT NORTH

★ ★ ½

GERARD'S PLACE

915 15TH STREET NW, WASHINGTON, DC (DOWNTOWN)
202-737-4445

THE WOMAN AT THE NEXT TABLE lets out a little gasp, and having eaten the same appetizer as she is savoring, I understand: Chef Gerard Pangaud's scallops have the ability to transport diners from here to heaven. The plate is elegant in its simplicity—four sweet coins of crisp-edged scallops on a shimmering green pool of parsley sauce, enhanced with a garlic flan that's as soft as a whisper—and a star-filled introduction to dinner.

There's more where that came from. An extraordinary mushroom tart brims with "the first cepes of the season," the chic hostess announces as the earthy dish is brought out. Sauteed foie gras, paired with caramelized mango, cuts like soft butter at the mere touch of a knife. Baby lamb is staged on a large plate and divided into quarters, each of which displays a different exquisite treatment (my favorite: roasted tenderloin with chanterelles). And a crisp square of cod stars in a "bouillabaisse" whose near-melting ribbons of sweet peppers and subtly tangy broth won't let you stop eating them. Too bad the wine list is priced for moguls.

Sauteed foie gras, paired with caramelized mango, cuts like soft butter at the mere touch of a knife.

Desserts are made to order and take time; your patience is rewarded with every bite of a souffle of tropical fruit and a fragile tart arranged with wine-soaked pears and walnut cream. Pangaud's work in his native France resulted in two Michelin stars; more than a decade after opening Gerard's Place in Washington, he's still on track.

Food is not all, however. People paying for first-class should also expect service that is more polished ("Where did my waiter disappear to?") and a dining room with more panache. Cozy as it is with its red walls and tentlike ceiling, Gerard's Place looks as if Pottery Barn had a hand in dressing it. And the plain white plates are right out of a college cafeteria. Pangaud's subtle art deserves a finer frame.

Lunch: M-F 11:30-2:30 *Entrees:* $24-$45
Dinner: M-SAT 5:30-9:30 *Entrees:* $28-$52
Tasting Menu: 5-COURSE $85
Closed: SUN *Credit Cards:* AE, DC, MC, V
Reservations: RECOMMENDED
Dress: BUSINESS CASUAL *Cross Street:* K STREET NW
Parking: STREET *Metro:* MCPHERSON SQUARE

☆ ☆

GOM BA WOO

7133-C COLUMBIA PIKE, ANNANDALE, VA
703-642-1577

BY THE TIME I RETIRE, I hope to be able to declare a "best" among the dozens of Korean restaurants that blanket the Northern Virginian landscape. Until then, I'm happy to take my steamed dumplings and barbecued meat at this homey shoebox, sandwiched between a Vietnamese noodle shop and a Japanese seafood buffet in a modest shopping center.

English is clearly a foreign language for the hard-working servers, so it helps to show up knowing what to order. I gravitate to the enormous bowls of soup: baby clams and crumbled tofu in a brick-red stock that brings tears to the eyes; kimchi with fatty bites of pork; or a milk-colored broth of marrow with shaved beef that is ordinary on its own but becomes enormously satisfying with a dash of salt, a sprinkle of chopped scallions and a dollop of chili paste (fear not, a waitress will mime instructions for proper seasoning).

English is clearly a foreign language for the hard-working servers, so it helps to show up knowing what to order.

The little snacks, or panchan, that accompany every meal negate the need for appetizers, and they are replenished if you deplete them. On the other hand, don't expect a lot of finesse. Drinks can be forgotten, empty tables find new diners even before the previous occupant's dishes are cleared and your lunch might be interrupted by the sight of a grocery cart, piled high with raw beef and produce, being pushed from parking lot to kitchen by a worker.

Still, surrounded by Korean business types, seniors and even families, I take comfort that this is the right place to be exploring.

Open: DAILY 7:30-11 *Entrees:* $6.95-$16.95
Credit Cards: AE, MC, V *Reservations:* RECOMMENDED
Dress: CASUAL *Cross Street:* ANNANDALE CENTER DRIVE
Parking: LOT *Metro:* NO

☆ ☆

GOOD FORTUNE

2646 UNIVERSITY BLVD. W., WHEATON, MD
301-929-8818

TAKE A TOUR OF AREA DIM SUM RESTAURANTS, and it becomes clear: There's a sameness to most of the scripts. Everyone serves shrimp dumplings, beef-filled rice noodles and baked barbecued pork buns, and everyone follows them with egg custard tarts. The menu at Good Fortune in Wheaton reads like a lot of the competition, but execution is what nudges this long-running restaurant, which employs three dim sum chefs, ahead of the pack. (Note: Carts are used only on weekends and holidays.)

For the most part, this is cooking with finesse. Spring rolls show up hot and crisp. Dumpling wrappers are sheer and light, pretty as porcelain, their ground shrimp centers subtly sweet. And 8-Treasure Sweet Rice in Lotus Leaves is not just poetry on paper; buried within the mound of sticky rice are goodies such as mushrooms, Chinese sausage and chicken, and the grains take on the fine, slightly nutty fragrance of the lotus leaves they're bound in. Here's the place to try ribbony tripe, garnished with scallions, as well as shrimp paste wrapped in a spindly web of fried taro root. Green beans retain a welcome crispness, while barbecued pork finds a nice home in big, soft, yeast-redolent buns.

Dumpling wrappers are sheer and light, pretty as porcelain, their ground shrimp centers subtly sweet.

All this good eating takes place in two large rooms that look like fast-food outlets, save for a few token Chinese knickknacks, but whose servers go about their work with slightly more gentility, and more civilized pacing, than the competition.

Open: M-TH 11:30 AM-1 AM, F 11:30 AM-2 AM, SAT 11 AM-2 AM, SUN 11 AM-1 AM
Entrees: $9.95-$24.95 ***Credit Cards:*** MC, V
Reservations: RECOMMENDED ***Dress:*** CASUAL
Cross Street: VIERS MILL ROAD ***Parking:*** STREET ***Metro:*** WHEATON

☆ ☆

GREEN PAPAYA

4922 ELM ST., BETHESDA, MD 301-654-8986
www.greenpapayabethesda.com

EVERYWHERE YOU LOOK in this Vietnamese restaurant there's something to catch the eye: handsome wall hangings, a tall banana tree fashioned from wood, mammoth vases, even a wall of water running over turquoise tiles in the bar. Softly lighted and backed by an eclectic soundtrack, the room would be an impressive place to seal a deal or woo a partner, though the prices are gentle enough to make Green Papaya a habit.

The kitchen can encourage return engagements, too. Settle in with squid salad tossed with green papaya and red onion and sparked with fresh herbs, maybe, or grilled quail, better after a dip in the accompanying sauce, which prickles with black pepper. And from the list of specials might come a light roll of Vietnamese sausage, chestnuts and dried shrimp bound in rice paper and served with black plum sauce. It would be easy to compose a little feast from just the appetizers, yet that would mean forgoing such pleasures as bo luc lac, a rib sticker of stir-fried beef, onions and potato.

It would be easy to compose a little feast from just the appetizers, yet that would mean forgoing such pleasures as bo luc lac, a rib sticker of stir-fried beef, onions and potato.

The waiters in their smart orange jackets are unfailingly pleasant but can also be inattentive—Some water, please? The bill?—and the flavors in the food tend to be less bright, the cooking techniques less polished than at such Vietnamese pace-setters as Minh's in Arlington and Huong Que in Falls Church. But the occasional overcooked rack of lamb with limp snow peas is balanced by thin cigars of ground beef wrapped in vine leaves and dusted with fried onions and crushed peanuts. The odds are in your favor.

Lunch: M-F 11:30-2:30 ***Entrees:*** $7.50-$21.95
Dinner: M-F 5-10, SAT 12:30-10, SUN 5-9:30 ***Entrees:*** $7.95-$21.95
Credit Cards: ALL MAJOR ***Reservations:*** RECOMMENDED
Dress: CASUAL ***Cross Street:*** WOODMONT AVENUE
Parking: STREET ***Metro:*** BETHESDA

Critic's Pick

★★

GUAJILLO

1727 WILSON BLVD., ARLINGTON, VA 703-807-0840
www.guajillogrill.com

WHILE THE MEXICAN RESTAURANT of my dreams continues to elude me in the Washington area, a few get points for trying harder than others. One of the handful of places that routinely rises above the routine is Guajillo, which takes its name from a chili pepper and is handsomely dressed with burnt-orange walls, "cloudy" blue skies on the ceiling and scooped cowhide chairs.

Details count here. Light chips come with a dusky salsa and a side of pale orange habanero sauce, "if you like it hotter," a server explains. Fried cheese with peppers and onions—queso fundido—is not any better than the competition, but the chicken tamales are, thanks to their dark red sauce.

Still, the best memories tend to be made from the list of specials. "Three flavor" mole reminds us that there's more than the famous chocolate-and-nut sauce in the Mexican repertoire; equally haunting are the green mole, made with tomatillo and pumpkin seeds, and the red mole, with three different chilies. In the pork carnitas, tender chunks of meat are arranged with bright guacamole, black beans and a quesadilla fat with cheese and the corn fungus known as huitlacoche; the whole assembly amounts to a strapping feast, prettily served on a banana leaf.

Light chips come with a dusky salsa and a side of pale orange habanero sauce, "if you like it hotter," a server explains.

Lunch: M-F 11:30-2:30 ***Entrees:*** $6.50-$10
Dinner: M-TH 5-10, FRI-SAT 5-11, SUN 5-10 ***Entrees:*** $9-$15
Brunch: SUN NOON-3 ***Entrees:*** $8-$12
Credit Cards: AE, D, MC, V ***Reservations:*** RECOMMENDED
Dress: CASUAL ***Cross Street:*** RHODES
Parking: LOT ***Metro:*** COURT HOUSE

Critic's Pick

★ ★ 1/2

HANK'S OYSTER BAR

1624 Q ST. NW, WASHINGTON, DC (DUPONT CIRCLE) 202-462-4265
www.hanksdc.com

A TESTAMENT TO THE HEAPIN' HELPIN' of medicore restaurants populating 17th Street in Dupont Circle: the line that frequently spills out the door at Hank's Oyster Bar.

The tidy seafood restaurant replaces the scruffy Trio Pizza & Subs and is headed by Jamie Leeds, the chef who made Logan Circle a better place to eat with 15 ria in the Washington Terrace Hotel. Hank's, the chef says, is a nod to her late father, an avid fisherman. It's also "reminiscent of the places I love to go," she says, including the counter-only Swan Oyster Depot in San Francisco and the pint-size Pearl Oyster Bar in New York, restaurants revered for their clean looks and sublime ingredients.

The menu is concise and (surprise, surprise) heavily populated by ingredients from the ocean. Following the current fashion, it is also divided into "Small Plates" and "Large Plates"—those would be appetizers and entrees—and it throws a bone to carnivores with "Meat & Two." Carryovers from 15 ria, these entrees change with the day and include a choice of two side dishes.

> ***The unfussy food tends to highlight ingredients rather than the chef's ego.***

But first, there are appetizers to think about. One that should be at the top of your to-do list is the popcorn shrimp and calamari. Lightly battered, the bite-size shrimp burst with juices, while the calamari are simultaneously tender and crisp. Take a cue from the restaurant's name and try the oysters. They come raw on the half shell, bedded on ice; dipped in buttermilk, then floured and deftly fried; or as the star in a shot glass. The last version is clever and refreshing, a briny Kumomoto oyster topped off with Bloody Mary-like juice and a splash of sake.

The unfussy food tends to highlight ingredients rather than the chef's ego. Thus, at Hank's, a special of perfectly cooked halibut is simply dressed with a tomato-lemon relish, and soft-shell crabs come with nothing more than a brush stroke or two of citrus butter. Sweet chunks of lobster and celery are bound with just a suggestion of mayonnaise, then slipped inside a pillowy bun, crisped from a moment on the griddle. Dad would be proud.

Dinner: W-TH 5:30-11, F-SAT 5:30-11:30, SUN-M 5:30-10 ***Entrees:*** $13-$19
Brunch: SAT-SUN 11-3 ***Entrees:*** $5-$17
Closed: TU ***Credit Cards:*** AE, D, MC, V ***Reservations:*** NO
Dress: CASUAL ***Cross Street:*** 17TH
Parking: $10 VALET W-SAT AT 6 PM ***Metro:*** DUPONT CIRCLE

★ ★

HAN SUNG OAK

6341 COLUMBIA PIKE, FALLS CHURCH, VA
703-642-0808

THE AROMA OF GRILLED MEAT, garlic and chilies greets diners right at the door. But the welcome to this handsome restaurant continues with the blue-uniformed waitresses, as pleasant and engaging as you will meet in any local Korean restaurant.

The women are quick to smile, eager to steer you to dishes you might like and happy to demonstrate the tabletop grills almost everyone ends up using. Squid, tripe, pork, beef short ribs—the flames take on those and other marinated ingredients, which are then served with steamed rice and crisp lettuce leaves for bundling.

Squid, tripe, pork, beef short ribs—the flames take on those and other marinated ingredients, which are then served with steamed rice and crisp lettuce leaves for bundling.

To begin, though, there are fried dumplings, meat-stuffed green peppers and a savory "pancake" veined with red and green bell peppers, slivers of squid and oysters. As is customary in Korean restaurants, half a dozen or so little taste treats, or panchan, precede the main event, crowding the large table. Each snack dish is different and delicious, be it chewy marinated soybeans, cucumber salad, strings of lightly pickled radish or the chili-stoked cabbage known as kimchi, so prized a dish that it merits a museum back home in Seoul.

Open: DAILY 11-11 *Entrees:* $8.95-$40
Credit Cards: AE, MC, V *Reservations:* RECOMMENDED
Dress: CASUAL *Cross Street:* ASHWOOD PLACE
Parking: STREET *Metro:* VAN DORN STREET

★ ★

HARRIS CRAB HOUSE

433 KENT NARROWS WAY N., GRASONVILLE, MD 410-827-9500
www.harriscrabhouse.com

BIG, WELCOMING—and far from thoughts of the office. That's Harris Crab House, one of the worst-kept secrets on the Eastern Shore. No problem: The restaurant has 400 seats, including some on a dock outside.

For more than two decades now, people have been pulling up to Harris' brown-paper-covered tables for the chance to get down and dirty with some steamed hard-shell crabs, sold in four sizes and stinging with paprika, mustard and salt. You don't have to lift a mallet for a sweet taste of crab if you don't want to, though; the crab imperial and the crab cakes are made with choice lump crabmeat.

For more than two decades now, people have been pulling up to Harris' brown-paper-covered tables for the chance to get down and dirty with some steamed hard-shell crabs, sold in four sizes and stinging with paprika, mustard and salt.

Beyond crab, think steamed or fried oysters, shrimp, mussels and clams. The platters arrive with a choice of two sides, the best of which are the mustardy potato salad and creamy slaw. Of course you'll have a Bud with that. And for sure you've saved room for a Nutty Buddy. Covered in chocolate and nuts, that locally dipped ice cream novelty is practically a draw in itself.

Open: DAILY 11-9 ***Entrees:*** $4.75-$24.95
Credit Cards: AE, D, MC, V ***Reservations:*** NO
Dress: CASUAL ***Cross Street:*** ROUTE 50
Parking: LOT ***Metro:*** NO

Critic's Pick
★ ★ ★

HERITAGE INDIA

2400 WISCONSIN AVE. NW, WASHINGTON, DC (GLOVER PARK) 202-333-3120
www.heritageindiageorgetown.com

ONE DAY, HERITAGE INDIA might decide to train its staff to better interact with its clientele, so as not to give diners the impression of rushing them through their meals—or forgetting them altogether.

Despite that annoying habit, the two-story dining room in Glover Park (there's also a branch downtown) gets my nod for Indian cooking that is as sophisticated as it gets in Washington. There's much to compete for your attention, from delicate vegetable fritters to juicy chicken tikka, from zesty strips of grouper blended with tomatoes and peppers to velvety baby eggplant draped in a creamy sesame sauce. Herb-laced spinach, possibly the best palak makai in town, reminds me that the menu welcomes vegetarians with open arms, while the lamb vindaloo beckons (and satisfies) fire eaters.

There's much to compete for your attention, from delicate vegetable fritters to juicy chicken tikka.

The sauces are distinct, the tandoor-baked breads hot and tasty. And the setting is at once rich and comfortable. Heritage India's spacious dining areas are painted in soothing pumpkin colors, graced with handsome portraits and swathed in elegant fabrics.

Lunch: DAILY 11:30-2:30 ***Entrees:*** $7.95-$12.95
Dinner: DAILY 5:30-10:30 ***Entrees:*** $9.95-$23.95
Credit Cards: ALL MAJOR ***Reservations:*** RECOMMENDED
Dress: BUSINESS CASUAL ***Cross Street:*** CALVERT
Parking: $5 VALET AFTER 6 ***Metro:*** TENLEYTOWN-AU
Second Location: 1337 CONNECTICUT AVE. NW, WASHINGTON, DC, 202-331-1414

★ ★

HOLLYWOOD EAST CAFE ON THE BOULEVARD

2621 UNIVERSITY BLVD. W., WHEATON, MD 240-290-9988
www.hollywoodeastcafe.com

"GOOD IN FOOD, good in service, good in decor" is how owner Janet Yu describes her longtime aspirations for Hollywood East Cafe in Wheaton. The place generally delivered on the cooking and attentiveness fronts but, dark and cramped, fell short in the looks department. Even Yu says, "We always lacked in decor."

Her solution was to open a second restaurant, dress it up and, for the convenience of her regulars, do it all in Wheaton, just three blocks away from the original. The result—Hollywood East Cafe on the Boulevard—is a prettier place to eat Chinese food. Yu went on a shopping trip to Guangzhou and Hong Kong to collect the banquet chairs, teapots and other appointments that, along with walls painted a cool pink and handsome gold dragons, help make it inviting.

The differences between the first and the second restaurant are more than cosmetic, though. The newer establishment boasts a larger menu, which is hard to imagine given the printed list of hundreds of dishes—and the numerous specials highlighted on strips of colored paper decorating the walls—at the original Hollywood East. The newcomer's menu combines the standing menu and those specials; better, at lunch the new kitchen also prepares the small plates of dumplings and other Chinese snacks poetically known as dim sum, or "heart's delight." Don't miss the finger-long hot green peppers filled with minced shrimp and garlicky crumbs, or the steamed turnip cake sweetened with bits of Chinese sausage and splashed with soy sauce.

Don't miss the finger-long hot green peppers filled with minced shrimp and garlicky crumbs.

Also elevating this kitchen above so much of the competition: Fried baby clams (No. 74 on the menu), arranged on their plate like petals on a flower and enhanced by a scattering of bread crumbs mixed with minced red and green bell peppers for color; sugar snap peas tossed with velvety mushrooms and chunks of sweet pineapple (No. 212); and a white mound of "salt & pepper" anchovies (No. 24), lightly crunchy and ignited with jalapenos. The last is the kind of tease that, like peanuts at a bar, keeps a diner moving from a nibble to a sip of beer and back—and eager to eat more.

Breakfast: SAT-SUN 10:30-3 ***Dim Sum:*** $2.50-$5.95 ***Lunch:*** M-F 11-3 ***Entrees:*** $6-$8
Dinner: SUN-TH 3-1 AM, F-SAT 3-2 AM ***Entrees:*** $10-$35
Credit Cards: ALL MAJOR ***Reservations:*** RECOMMENDED
Dress: CASUAL ***Cross Street:*** GEORGIA AVENUE ***Parking:*** LOT ***Metro:*** WHEATON
Second Location: HOLLYWOOD EAST CAFE, 2312 PRICE AVE., WHEATON, MD, 301-942-8282

★ ★ ½

HUONG QUE (FOUR SISTERS)

6769 WILSON BLVD., FALLS CHURCH, VA
703-538-6717

THE BUZZ ON THE GRAPEVINE ABOUT THIS, my longtime favorite spot for Vietnamese food, made me curious to pay it a visit. Was the restaurant affectionately known as Four Sisters, for the young women who work there, resting on its abundant laurels?

A bite of one of the house specialties, sauteed shrimp with walnuts, revealed less than sparklingly fresh seafood. And the giant yellow rice crepe stuffed with "shrimp, pork and steamed bean sprouts" was skimpy on the protein and overwhelmed with sprouts. My heart sank. Then I sampled a plate of tender squid tossed with pleasantly sour cabbage. Delicious! Shrimp toast showed delicacy, and sweetly spiced morsels of meat from skewers of beef found a fine home inside sheer rice wraps, bundled with rice noodles and bright herbs. Asparagus punched up with slivers of garlic glistened.

At least a couple of the four sisters were in evidence at that meal, pampering their many guests and showing newcomers how to eat this or dip that. "Do you work 24 hours a day?" a regular customer asked one of the siblings. "No, just 23," she shot back with a smile. Not every dish is wonderful at Huong Que, but the service always is.

Was the restaurant affectionately known as Four Sisters, for the young women who work there, resting on its abundant laurels?

Open: SUN-TH 10:30-10, F-SAT 10:30 AM-11 PM ***Entrees:*** $5.95-$25.95
Credit Cards: AE, MC, V ***Reservations:*** RECOMMENDED ON WEEKENDS
Dress: CASUAL ***Cross Street:*** ARLINGTON BOULEVARD / ROUTE 7
Parking: LOT ***Metro:*** EAST FALLS CHURCH

Critic's Pick
★ ★ ★

INN AT EASTON

28 S. HARRISON ST., EASTON, MD 410-822-4910
www.theinnateaston.com

THE WORLD HAS INFLUENCED chef Andrew Evans. As a child, he visited France, Spain, Lebanon and Israel with his "hippie mom"; as an adult, he spent seven years in Australia, where he learned what a "bay bug" is, received accolades for his work in a Vietnamese restaurant and met his wife, Liz, with whom he now runs a boutique inn in the heart of Easton, Md.

The chef's menu, which changes every three weeks or so, is exciting testament to his travels. "Everything is good," a server tells me, in one of the few instances where such praise rings true. Among those enticements are those bay bugs (slipper lobsters) in fragrant green Thai curry; sliced pork over Asian noodles; a juicy steak with top-notch french fries for conservative palates; and dishes like braised baby octopus layered with thin sheets of caramelized eggplant, everything sealed with Asiago cheese—a terrine of note for adventurers. And if you forgo the signature dessert, sticky fig pudding, you'll miss out on one of Australia's great exports.

The chef's menu, which changes every three weeks or so, is exciting testament to his travels.

The 45-seat dining room is civilized but never stuffy, its soft green walls graced with Russian impressionist paintings and its tables set with glass bowls of lively fish instead of flowers. Psst: If you're seeking a little privacy, there's no cozier nook than the alcove table for two, aptly known as Table No. 1.

Dinner: W-SUN 5:30-9 ***Entrees:*** $24-$38; 4-COURSE PRIX FIXE MENU $65; 6-COURSE CHEF'S TASTING MENU $85 ***Closed:*** M-TU ***Credit Cards:*** AE, MC, V
Reservations: RECOMMENDED ***Dress:*** BUSINESS CASUAL
Cross Street: SOUTH ***Parking:*** STREET ***Metro:*** NO

Critic's Pick
☆ ☆ ☆ ☆

INN AT LITTLE WASHINGTON

MIDDLE AND MAIN STREETS, WASHINGTON, VA 540-675-3800
www.theinnatlittlewashington.com

"TAKE AS MANY AS YOU WISH," a server whispers as he proffers a tray of Lilliputian savories moments after my friends and I have been ushered into a cocoon of comfort and luxury. Everywhere we look there are beautiful paintings, plush seats, flattering light and men and women who look very pleased to be dining in one of the dreamiest restaurants, anywhere.

Chef Patrick O'Connell's background in theater is evident on every whimsically staged plate, be it risotto served in the hollow of a big tomato, vegetable "sushi" that manages to make red peppers and hearts of palm look like raw fish, or a chocolate-robed birthday cake that is sliced to reveal a checkerboard of pistachio and white chocolate ice creams.

Those are but a few of the many fine dishes that make up this very American and seasonally-tuned script, whose charms also include crab cakes sandwiched between fried green tomato; minced squab, local peanuts and mushrooms scooped into cool lettuce wrappers; and beef "two ways" (as a perfect little filet mignon banded in Swiss chard and as tender short ribs, barbecued and crunchy with pecans).

Chef Patrick O'Connell's background in theater is evident on every whimsically staged plate.

Under the direction of co-owner Reinhardt Lynch, service is hushed and haute, but also full of humor; someone in your party has to order cheese just to hear the faux cow it's served on "moo," and kitchen tours are preceded by a robed young man waving incense at the door.

In-the-know romantics ask for Table 66 in the intimate terrace room looking onto the garden, a destination so popular, jokes O'Connell, that these days, "All the tables there are number 66. We have 66A, 66B, 66C . . ."

Dinner: M-TH 6-9:30, F 5:30-9:30, SAT 5:15-9:30, SUN 4-8:15
Entrees: 7-COURSE PRIX FIXE SUN-TH $138, F $148, SAT $168
Chef's Table: NIGHTLY 7-COURSE TASTING MENUS $178-$208
Closed: TU (JULY TO MID-SEPTEMBER, MID-NOVEMBER TO MID-APRIL)
Credit Cards: AE, MC, V ***Reservations:*** RECOMMENDED
Dress: BUSINESS CASUAL ***Parking:*** COMPLIMENTARY VALET ***Metro:*** NO

★ ★

ISLANDER CARIBBEAN

1201 U ST. NW, WASHINGTON, DC (U STREET CORRIDOR)
202-234-4955

A GLASS OF GENTLY SWEET and delicately floral Christmas-red sorrel juice gets a meal off to a tropical start at this modest corner storefront along the U Street corridor. Accras—piping-hot cod fritters partnered with a creamy pink dip—enhance the mood.

Just about everything that comes out of the kitchen of chef Addie Green, a native of Trinidad, makes the islands appear very close to where you're eating. I'm partial to the tender (if bony) goat curry and the "calypso chicken," braised and cloaked in a tantalizing sauce of onions, pimentos and basil—two of a dozen or so dishes that diners can pick from to create their own sampler. But just as appealing are Green's peppery mango chicken wings—move over, Buffalo—and moist whole red snapper served beneath a tangle of soft-cooked bell peppers and cabbage. The Islander is also a rare city source for roti, the unleavened bread tucked around generous and mild curried fillings of fish, vegetables, beef or shrimp; wrapped in waxed paper, these hefty pockets average $8 and amount to a meal on their own. In all, this is confident, comforting and spirited cooking (if you think all ginger ale tastes the same, you haven't tried the drink here, which packs a refreshing wallop).

Just about everything that comes out of the kitchen makes the islands appear very close to where you're eating.

Alas, the pace can be a little too authentically tropical (it's sloooow), but a greeting from the raspy-voiced Green, who has a habit of checking in on her charges in the dining room, smoothes over any bumps. "I might sit down and eat with you," she is known to tease her guests.

Open: TU-SAT 5:30-11, SUN 5:30-10:30 ***Entrees:*** $10.95-$27.95
Closed: M ***Credit Cards:*** D, MC, V ***Reservations:*** RECOMMENDED
Dress: CASUAL ***Cross Street:*** 12TH
Parking: STREET ***Metro:*** U ST / AFRICAN AMER CIVIL WAR MEMORIAL / CARDOZO

Critic's Pick

★★½

JACKIE'S

8081 GEORGIA AVE., SILVER SPRING, MD 301-565-9700
www.jackiesrestaurant.com

A GREEN SHAG RUG lights up the floor of the lounge and the vinyl booths in the brick-walled dining room run hot pink. What used to be an auto-parts garage has been winningly transformed into a space where the 1960s converge with industrial chic. It's a groovy scene that niftily suits co-owner Jackie Greenbaum's Day-Glo personality.

So it's hard not to smile right when you walk in. And it's tough to decide what to eat when the choices embrace such tempters as "mini Elvis burgers" and daily-changing "nostalgia" platters that reflect what some of us grew up on: Tuesday means beef brisket, Wednesday finds fried chicken hot from the skillet and Sunday is honored with catfish, coleslaw and hush puppies. Yum. That said, the open kitchen demonstrates its range with a starter of mussels, bound in shredded phyllo and enhanced with garlicky mayonnaise, and a main course of organic pork chop teamed with crisp yuca slices and snappy red-pepper ketchup.

It's tough to decide what to eat when the choices embrace such tempters as "mini Elvis burgers."

Even on a weekday, Jackie's—friendly and festive—feels like the weekend.

Dinner: SUN, TU-TH 5:30-10, F-SAT 5:30-10:30 ***Entrees:*** $12-$29
Brunch: SUN 11:30-2:30 ***Entrees:*** $7-$12
Closed: M ***Credit Cards:*** AE, D, MC, V ***Reservations:*** RECOMMENDED
Dress: CASUAL ***Cross Street:*** SLIGO AVENUE
Parking: STREET ***Metro:*** SILVER SPRING

Critic's Pick
★ ★ ★

JALEO

480 SEVENTH ST. NW, WASHINGTON (PENN QUARTER) 202-628-7949
www.jaleo.com

THE MORE I EAT TAPAS EVERYWHERE ELSE, the more I appreciate the little plates of Spanish flavors created by chef Jose Andres. The 70-plus choices are available hot or cold, with or without meat, mild or wild in flavor, light or hearty. Potato omelet, garlic shrimp, figs with ham—there's something for every mood.

If you get bored with this menu, you're not looking closely enough; Andres and his crew are constantly tweaking and upgrading it. A visit to the copper-topped bar might find quail filled with pork, raisins and foie gras; squid tossed with soft, sweet onions; near-melting codfish with parsley oil and a red, fish-infused sauce; and, in a nod to the chef's experimental food at minibar, skewers of watermelon and tomatoes drizzled with mint sauce and sea salt. Wow! (Less thrilling: ordinary pork in orange sauce.)

If you get bored with this menu, you're not looking closely enough; Andres and his crew are constantly tweaking and upgrading it.

Spanish dancers are depicted on a mural in the original Washington location—and show up in the flesh on Wednesday nights. But you don't need to be in the District to take in the fun, thanks to Jaleo's expansion to Bethesda and Arlington.

Lunch: M-SAT 11:30-2:30 ***Entrees:*** $6.95-$16.95 ***Tapas:*** $3.95-$9.99
Dinner: SUN-M 5-10, TU-TH 5-11:30, F-SAT 5-MIDNIGHT ***Entrees:*** $14.95-$16.95
Tapas: $3.95-$9.95 ***Brunch:*** SUN 11:30-3 ***Tapas:*** $4.25-$6.25
Credit Cards: ALL MAJOR ***Reservations:*** RECOMMENDED FOR LUNCH
PRE-THEATER (5-6:30) ONLY FOR DINNER ***Dress:*** CASUAL ***Cross Street:*** E STREET NW
Parking: $8 VALET AT DINNER M-SAT ***Metro:*** GALLERY PLACE-CHINATOWN
Second Locations: 7271 WOODMONT AVE., BETHESDA, MD, 301-913-0003
2250-A CRYSTAL DR., ARLINGTON, VA, 703-413-8181

Critic's Pick
★ ★

JERRY'S SEAFOOD

9364 LANHAM-SEVERN RD., SEABROOK, MD 301-577-0333
www.jerrys-seafood.com

IF YOU DROP BY AT PRIME TIME, expect to wait: Jerry's doesn't take reservations and the family-run destination has a long history of serving top-notch seafood.

Sweet crab finds its way into cream of crab soup, crab bisque and (my favorite) Maryland crab soup, chockablock with corn, tomato and lima beans in the mix. Then there are the famous crab "bombs" to consider; six to 10 ounces of hand-picked crab, seasoned with Old Bay, bound with a bit of mayonnaise, and baked to a light golden tan. Heaven!

Feel free to venture beyond that comfort zone, however: Skewered fried shrimp and daily specials like rockfish splashed with garlic butter elicit smiles of satisfaction, too. Meals come with a choice of two sides; coleslaw is fresh and creamy, stewed tomatoes are sweet enough to qualify as fruit soup.

Skewered fried shrimp and daily specials like rockfish splashed with garlic butter elicit smiles of satisfaction.

Aside from some stuffed fish swimming on its walls, the boxy dining room isn't much to look at. But the details are rich: red napkins tied with boat rope, an iced mug for your beer and first-rate hospitality. "Is this your first time?" I heard a young waiter ask a guest. "Let me bring you tastes of our soups." Which he then did (and which they enthusiastically finished).

Lunch: M-F 11-2:30 ***Entrees:*** $9.95-$25.95
Dinner: TU-TH 5-8, F 5-9:30, SAT 11:30-9:30, SUN 1-5 ***Entrees:*** $19.95-$33.95
Credit Cards: AE, MC, V ***Reservations:*** NO
Dress: CASUAL ***Cross Street:*** CARTER AVENUE
Parking: LOT ***Metro:*** NEW CARROLLTON
Second Location: 108 SECOND ST., LEWES, DE, 302-645-6611

★ ★

JOE'S NOODLE HOUSE

1488-C ROCKVILLE PIKE, ROCKVILLE, MD 301-881-5518
www.joesnoodlehouse.com

THERE'S NO LONGER A JOE, but there are plenty of noodles at this spare storefront Chinese restaurant. Some are thick and white, like the "drunken" rice noodles topped with crumbled beef and crisp slivers of green bell pepper; others are thin and glassy, like the ones in a big bowl of soup, blazing with red chilies and teeming with soft pieces of fish. These and hundreds of other dishes are yours by ordering from a counter in the rear, taking a number sign to your table and waiting for the goods to be delivered whenever they happen to be ready. (Translation: Entrees might arrive before appetizers.)

Regulars pick up a paper menu at the front door and make their decisions before getting to the cashier-hostess; they know they can't miss with fried baby smelt tossed with peanuts, pleasantly chewy baby conch laced with basil, squid paired with tangy cabbage and pungent garlic or delectable, head-on "salty and crispy" shrimp. Ah, but then there are all the specials posted behind the counter, too! Of course those who know Joe's want to add a plate of hot-and-sour fish to their order. On the other hand, vegetable lo mein is a bit oily, the Chinese beer is served too warm, and gingery pork dumplings are weighed down with too-thick wrappers.

A sign that you've come to the right place: lots of Asian faces in the small mirrored dining room.

A sign that you've come to the right place: lots of Asian faces in the small, mirrored dining room. Even more promising were the words of the Taiwanese native who generously shared his table with a friend and me during a weekend lunch rush. "This food reminds me of home."

Lunch: M-F 11:30-3, SAT-SUN 11-3 *Entrees:* $4.95-$5.95
Dinner: M-F 11:30-10, SAT-SUN 11-10 *Entrees:* $6.95-$10.95
Credit Cards: D, MC, V *Reservations:* RECOMMENDED FOR PARTIES OF 6 OR MORE
Dress: CASUAL *Cross Street:* TEMPLETON PLACE
Parking: LOT *Metro:* TWINBROOK

Critic's Pick
★ ★ ★

JOHNNY'S HALF SHELL

2002 P ST. NW, WASHINGTON, DC (DUPONT CIRCLE) 202-296-2021
www.johnnyshalfshell.net

TREATS ON THE HALF SHELL—glistening oysters and clams—are mere warm-up acts on a bill of fare that is so enticing, a seafood fancier will fantasize about ordering "one of everything, please."

Squid is grilled to retain tenderness, and tossed with crunchy shallots and wisps of wild arugula for a seafood salad of distinction. Oyster stew finds the lead ingredient in a bath of warm cream dusted with cayenne for kicks. Lunch means po' boys stuffed with crunchy-juicy fried shrimp inside toasted buns and dinner yields simple but serious entrees, like crab imperial and wood-grilled steak teased with green-chile butter.

While Johnny's is best known for fresh seafood, the trim restaurant also pours nice wines by the glass.

Indeed, while Johnny's is best known for fresh seafood, the trim restaurant also pours nice wines by the glass and churns out lovely endings (bracing lime sorbet, burnt sugar ice cream). I adore the marble bar, backed with an aquarium, and the green booths, their backs tall enough to prevent eavesdropping. But so do a lot of people: Be prepared for some clamor with your lobster.

Lunch: M-SAT 11:30-5 ***Entrees:*** $6.95-$25.95
Dinner: M-TH 5-10:30, F-SAT 5-11 ***Entrees:*** $19.95-$25.95
Closed: SUN ***Credit Cards:*** AE, MC, V ***Reservations:*** RECOMMENDED
Dress: CASUAL ***Cross Street:*** 20TH ***Parking:*** STREET ***Metro:*** DUPONT CIRCLE

★ ★

KANLAYA THAI CUISINE

740 SIXTH ST. NW, WASHINGTON, DC (CHINATOWN) 202-393-0088
www.kanlayathaicuisine.com

THANKS TO THE RICH INFUSION of restaurants near MCI Center over the years, that slice of Washington could probably make most of a United Nations delegation feel at home. Within a short walk of one another are kitchens that specialize in Spanish tapas, Chinese noodles, American barbecue and pizza, Indian curries, Mexican seviche, Irish corned beef and cabbage, and Japanese sushi. With the arrival of Kanlaya Thai Cuisine, the menu is broader still: Thailand gets recognized with green papaya salad and deep-fried bananas.

If you're a worker bee with not much time for lunch, or if you need to be in your seat for a game or concert in less than an hour, Kanlaya is a good place to find a meal. The food comes out very fast; indeed, sometimes everything you've ordered arrives at once. But you're bound to enjoy it anyway if you asked for larb gai, that zesty salad of crumbled chicken tossed with a dressing of lime and fresh mint, or a coconut milk soup packed with chicken and mushrooms, every spoonful of broth seesawing between sweet and tangy. The chicken satays, yellow with curry powder and plenty moist, are also a hit. Vegetables leave the kitchen bright and crisp; stir-fried Chinese broccoli, bold with oyster sauce, ranks as one of my favorites.

If you're a worker bee with not much time for lunch, or if you need to be in your seat for a game or concert in less than an hour, Kanlaya is a good place to find a meal.

The weak links in the chain include stolid and dense steamed Siam dumplings and Kanlaya grilled pork, which looks more like a thin hamburger and rests on a "bun" of gummy rice.

Some like it hot, and diners who do had better make that point clear to the staff. This is a kitchen that pulls its punches if you aren't insistent. Several dishes leave a nice tingling sensation on the lips, though, including stir-fried rice with chilies, garlic, fresh herbs and a choice of meat.

Kanlaya's dining room starts out big and pale yellow, but becomes more intimate in the back, where the space narrows, the walls turn burgundy and handsome banquettes foster a cozier atmosphere. Up front, facing the window, is a good spot for reading a newspaper; the back room is perfect cheap-date territory. Anywhere, it is fast food with a point of view.

Lunch: M-F 11:30-4 ***Entrees:*** $7.95-$10.95
Dinner: M-TH 4-10, F 4-10:30, SAT-SUN 11-10 ***Entrees:*** $8.95-$15.95
Credit Cards: D, MC, V ***Reservations:*** RECOMMENDED ***Dress:*** CASUAL ***Cross Street:*** H STREET NW
Parking: STREET ***Metro:*** GALLERY PLACE-CHINATOWN

Critic's Pick
☆ ☆ ☆

KAZ SUSHI BISTRO

1915 I ST. NW, WASHINGTON, DC (DOWNTOWN) 202-530-5500
www.kazsushibistro.com

IT WAS 95 DEGREES the last time I dropped by for lunch at Kaz Sushi Bistro, where I knew I could count on some sparkling sushi and chilled sake to revive me. What I hadn't anticipated was finding a colorful jumble of sashimi—scallops, salmon, tuna—in a deep white bowl of gazpacho, its orange liquid as cool as ice and teasing with rice wine vinegar. It was as elegant a soup as has ever crossed my lips. Then again, chef Kaz Okochi has long created Japanese food that goes beyond the familiar and frequently dips into the fabulous.

Originally trained to be an artist, he has a keen eye for picking ingredients—the finest rice, pristine fish—and making them sing. Tuna carpaccio has become a restaurant cliche, but it tastes new and different here, where Okochi swaps folds of tuna for ribbons of fish and presents it with jellylike cubes of carrot and feathery greens from his own garden. The best way to explore his range is to ask for a tasting menu or to focus on the daily specials; either might showcase flounder sashimi with plum sauce, cold sliced beef tongue anointed with a zippy miso sauce, or sweet baby clams floating in a shot glass of warm broth. Divine.

Chef Kaz Okochi has long created Japanese food that goes beyond the familiar and frequently dips into the fabulous.

Kaz Sushi Bistro is not the most beautiful Japanese dining room around, but to sweeten your stay, there's lovely service, fine sake and yuzu ice cream—a cool, fruity and elegant way to return to reality.

Lunch: M-F 11:30-2 ***Entrees:*** $10.50-$19.50
Dinner: M-SAT 6-10 ***Entrees:*** $13.75-$24
Tasting Menus: M-SAT 6-10, 4-COURSE $45, 8-COURSE $60-$75
Closed: SUN ***Credit Cards:*** ALL MAJOR ***Reservations:*** RECOMMENDED
Dress: CASUAL ***Cross Street:*** I STREET NW ***Parking:*** STREET ***Metro:*** FARRAGUT WEST

★ ★ ½

KINKEAD'S

2000 PENNSYLVANIA AVE. NW, WASHINGTON, DC (FOGGY BOTTOM) 202-296-7700
www.kinkead.com

ONE MEAL I'M SWOONING OVER a platter of glistening oysters, another visit I'm left scratching my head. Why is the kitchen trying to do Peking duck (and not pulling it off very well)?

At its best, this long-running seafood restaurant doles out a warm welcome with food so luscious you understand the wait for a table even early in the week. Fried Ipswich clams are still the best for 100 miles around and there's a reason wood-grilled squid on polenta never leaves the menu: It's fabulous. So is the wine list, crafted by ace sommelier Michael Flynn.

During lesser moments, you're looking at overmanipulated dishes that still appear to be auditioning for a spot on the program, and a staff that merely goes through the motions of serving you, treating you as if you're Customer No. 364. Anytime, Kinkead's proximity to the White House and other institutions means you're likely to spot a famous face in the crowd.

The second-floor main dining room is attractive enough (you'll know how you rate by how far you're led away from the action there). My preference is a stool at the convivial bar, which doesn't require reservations and serves the entire menu. If they're offered, zero in on crisp golden sea scallops lapped with a peanut-curry sauce and halibut paved in walnuts and lavished with a trembling cauliflower flan.

If they're offered, zero in on crisp golden sea scallops lapped with a peanut-curry sauce and halibut paved in walnuts and lavished with a trembling cauliflower flan.

Pleasures such as those help explain Kinkead's off-the-charts success—and keep critics coming back.

Lunch: M-F 11:30-2:30 *Entrees:* $16-$25
Dinner: SUN-TH 5:30-10, F-SAT 5:30-10:30 *Entrees:* $26-$36
Brunch: SUN 11:30-2:30 *Entrees:* $11-$25
Credit Cards: ALL MAJOR *Reservations:* RECOMMENDED
Dress: BUSINESS CASUAL *Cross Street:* 21ST
Parking: $5 VALET AT DINNER *Metro:* FOGGY BOTTOM-GWU

Critic's Pick
★ ★ ★

KOMI

1509 17TH ST. NW, WASHINGTON, DC (DUPONT CIRCLE)
202-332-9200

JOHNNY MONIS IS ONLY IN HIS TWENTIES but already cooks with the flair of someone who has spent a lifetime in the kitchen.

Seventeenth Street NW isn't known for quality places to eat, but Monis is helping turn the situation around, using a few tricks from the big boys. He bakes his own crackers and offers them in lieu of a bread basket. And there's always an amuse-bouche—most often a demitasse of soup—to savor before dinner. Where does he find his servers? They look like they stepped out of Teen Vogue and know the menu as if they have committed the recipes to memory.

Let them steer you to their favorites, maybe the very nice chicken-pistachio pâté or the poached lamb loin enhanced by black lentils and a tart cherry glaze. The narrow room is free of art on its soft green walls, the better to focus on what's on your plate. With the bill comes another fillip: lollipops in cold weather, or a cube of frozen watermelon with a drop of balsamic vinegar-spiked caramel in the heat of summer. Komi starts on a high and often stays there.

There's always an amuse-bouche—most often a demitasse of soup—to savor before dinner.

Dinner: TU-SAT 6-10 ***Entrees:*** $22-$27
Closed: SUN-M ***Credit Cards:*** ALL MAJOR ***Reservations:*** RECOMMENDED
Dress: BUSINESS CASUAL ***Cross Street:*** P STREET NW
Parking: STREET ***Metro:*** DUPONT CIRCLE

Critic's Pick

★ ★ 1/2

KOTOBUKI

4822 MACARTHUR BLVD. NW, 2ND FL., WASHINGTON, DC (PALISADES) 202-625-9080
www.kotobukiusa.com

YOU WON'T BELIEVE YOUR EYES when you see the prices on the menu. Can good sushi really be had for a buck a piece? Your taste buds confirm it's possible, and a rainbow of select raw fish awaits your call behind a glass display case.

Flounder is subtle, mackerel is divine, and sea urchin proves creamy as mousse and fresh as a sea breeze (and worth the extra 75 cents). If you're lucky, there's also toro, the sought-after underbelly of bluefin tuna. And to enhance the experience in this tiny, second-story oasis, which is simply decorated with painted Japanese characters and red banquettes, sake is poured into a small wood box and chef Hisao Abe sometimes prepares his own soy sauce.

Don't come expecting teriyaki, tempura or other mainstays of Japanese restaurants in the States.

Kotobuki's menu is small. Don't come expecting teriyaki, tempura or other mainstays of Japanese restaurants in the States. However, the kitchen does offer kamameshi, a rice casserole presented on a wooden stand and arranged with a choice of vegetables, chicken or eel (my pick).

Lunch: TU-SAT NOON-3 P.M. ***Entrees:*** $7.95-$12
Dinner: TU-TH 5-10, F-SAT 5-11, SUN 5-10 ***Entrees:*** $12-$15
Closed: M ***Credit Cards:*** MC, V ***Reservations:*** NO
Dress: CASUAL ***Cross Street:*** U STREET NW
Parking: STREET ***Metro:*** NO

★

KUMA

4441-B WISCONSIN AVE. NW, WASHINGTON, DC (TENLEYTOWN)
202-537-3717

THE EYES HAVE IT AT KUMA, whose pale wood floors, brown wood tables and assorted greenery make it an attractive place to hoist chopsticks. The ears pay a price for all those hard surfaces, however, as well as a musical loop that seems stuck on a thumping techno beat. And while I appreciate attention and efficiency in my servers, it would be nice to have a nanosecond to look over the menu before having to make any decisions. "Whatwouldyouliketodrink?" the otherwise congenial waiters tend to ask right away—once, before I even sat down.

Pretend you don't see the sushi bar in the rear, and feel free to skip over the first few pages of the menu, which leads off with a bunch of Japanese dishes, running from teriyaki to tempura. The sushi is pallid, and the tempura is leathery, a waste of decent vegetables.

To get to the best of Kuma—that's "bear" in Japanese—you have to concentrate on the page of Korean specials.

To get to the best of Kuma—that's "bear" in Japanese—you have to concentrate on the page of Korean specials. My favorite is the rice-based bibim bap, which diners hear before they see. Served in a deep clay bowl, the rice crackles against the heat of the vessel as noisily as fajitas do. The mound of grains is prettily arranged with crisp bean sprouts, threads of beef, batons of carrot and a sunny, runny egg, all of which are blended together at the table for a delectable and comforting one-dish meal. Kalbi is Korea's answer to barbecue, shavings of tender short ribs seasoned here with soy sauce, sesame oil, garlic, brown sugar and a bit of mashed pear, and served over a thin layer of cabbage. I'd like it more if it weren't so sweet. Of the soups, I'm partial to beef broth flavored with scallions and floating fat dumplings with soft beef-and-vegetable centers.

Kuma is easy to look at, easy on the budget and something of a rarity in the District. Within city limits, there aren't more than a few sources for Korean food. What in Annandale would be lost among a field of fierce competition is in Washington a modest find.

Lunch: M-SAT 11:30-2:30 ***Entrees:*** $8-$13
Dinner: DAILY 4:30-10 ***Entrees:*** $10-$24
Credit Cards: AE, D, MC, V ***Reservations:*** RECOMMENDED
Dress: CASUAL ***Cross Street:*** ALBEMARLE
Parking: STREET ***Metro:*** TENLEYTOWN-AU

Critic's Pick
★ ★ ★ ★

LABORATORIO DEL GALILEO

1110 21ST ST. NW, WASHINGTON, DC (DOWNTOWN) 202-331-0880
www.robertodonna.com

WHILE I DON'T GET TO ITALY nearly as often as I'd like, an evening spent in this restaurant-within-a-restaurant at Galileo always leaves me feeling as if I'd been in Milan or Rome for several hours. Unlike in the main dining room, it doesn't matter who you are or where you find yourself in this sunny-yellow space: Everyone is treated like a favored patron, and all 24 seats feel equal.

There's no predicting what you might find. Chef Roberto Donna—who amiably toils just feet in front of you in his gleaming open kitchen—changes his program constantly. But one thing is certain: You will dine very well, exquisitely even.

Chef Roberto Donna—who amiably toils just feet in front of you in his gleaming open kitchen—changes his program constantly.

Fond memories can be made from the likes of duck liver custard, served with warm peaches and thyme; house-made spaghetti decked out with rabbit sauce; risotto (one night with morel mushrooms, another with frog's legs and watercress foam); olive-stuffed lamb roulade and a world-class cheese trolley. Grape granita, tempura figs, hot doughnuts—the endings here are no less indulgent.

Twelve courses after you sat down, you're wondering how you will ever get up from the table—and when you can book a return trip.

Dinner: M-SAT 7:30 (ONE SITTING ONLY) ***Entrees:*** 10-12 COURSE PRIX FIXE MENU, $110 (M-TH), $125 (F-SAT) ***Closed:*** SUN
Credit Cards: AE, MC, V ***Reservations:*** REQUIRED
Dress: BUSINESS CASUAL ***Cross Street:*** L STREET NW
Parking: $6 VALET AT DINNER ***Metro:*** FARRAGUT NORTH

★ ★

LA FLOR DE LA CANELA

117 N. FREDERICK AVE., GAITHERSBURG, MD
301-519-9100

THE COCKTAIL OF CHOICE is a foam-capped pisco sour, the tables are crowded with potato dishes, and a wood carving on the wall depicts Lima as it used to be. Welcome to Peru!

Your tour should commence with either papa rellena or seviche. The first is mashed potatoes wrapped around ground beef, eggs and raisins, then deep-fried; the latter is citrus-splashed raw fish, and made to order. From there, feel free to fan out in the direction of beef (try the smoky lomo saltado), chicken (slow-roasted and herby) or something more adventurous (the tripe is irresistible—really). If you want to up the heat, add a bit of the wicked green chili sauce that accompanies the food as ketchup might in an American establishment.

If you want to up the heat, add a bit of the wicked green chili sauce that accompanies the food as ketchup might in an American establishment.

The name of the restaurant loosely translates as "cinnamon flower," which also happens to be the title of a folk song in Peru. It's a dreamy little name for a dreamy little outpost.

Open: M, W, TH 11:30-9:30, F 11:30-10:30, SAT NOON-10:30, SUN NOON-9 *Closed:* TU *Entrees:* $7-$16
Credit Cards: MC, V *Reservations:* RECOMMENDED FOR PARTIES OF 6 OR MORE
Dress: CASUAL *Cross Street:* CHESTNUT *Parking:* LOT *Metro:* SHADY GROVE

☆ ☆

L'AUBERGE CHEZ FRANCOIS

332 SPRINGVALE RD., GREAT FALLS, VA 703-759-3800
www.laubergechezfrancois.com

AT A TIME WHEN NOT MUCH in life is certain, it's comforting to know that some things around us never change. For nearly half a century—beginning in 1954 in Washington, then moving in 1976 to Great Falls—L'Auberge Chez Francois has been one of the region's most popular places to celebrate a graduation, toast an anniversary or bring together the family.

Inside, the four dining areas evoke a postcard-perfect Alsatian village. There are old beams overhead, stained glass in the windows and pressed white linens embroidered with tiny flowers.

It might be 90 degrees outside, but I still find myself drawn to the restaurant's four-course menu, and I can still muster interest in choucroute, a narrow bed of tangy sauerkraut piled with plump white and pink sausages, smoked pork loin and spiced apple. It's a strapping and immensely satisfying plate. Rack of lamb is patted with herbs and surrounded with a wreath of traditional turned carrots, zucchini, roast potatoes and even figs. As for innards, veal kidneys are particularly good; dense and tender, they show up beneath a mustardy cream sauce. There are lighter moments, too. Of the fish entrees, I'm partial to the fresh rainbow trout, scattered with slivered almonds and choice bites of crab.

Rack of lamb is patted with herbs and surrounded with a wreath of traditional turned carrots, zucchini, roast potatoes and even figs.

It would be easy to let nostalgia excuse the underachievers here. The truth is, some of the cooking is merely okay. Yet food is only part of the equation. The Old World service at L'Auberge is as impressive as anything on the menu. Take a cue from the dessert display and order a slice of the plum tart; heaped with what appears to be a small orchard of soft, ripe fruit, it's a long-time signature. A meal isn't finished, though, until the golden tuiles and dark chocolates arrive on a small tray. Just as they always have.

Dinner: TU-SAT 5:30-9:30, SUN 1:30-8 *Entrees:* 6-COURSE PRIX FIXE $58-$66
Closed: M *Credit Cards:* ALL MAJOR *Reservations:* REQUIRED
Dress: JACKET PREFERRED *Cross Street:* BEACH MILL ROAD
Parking: LOT *Metro:* NO

Critic's Pick

★ ★

LAYALINA

5216 WILSON BLVD., ARLINGTON, VA 703-525-1170
www.layalinarestaurant.com

RIMA KODSI IS ONE OF THE BEST MATCHMAKERS I've ever encountered. Few restaurateurs are so eager to connect you with their cooking. One moment she's at your table telling you what she made special that day, later in her introduction she's detailing what's typically Syrian.

She's also quick to translate for anyone unfamiliar with her highly personal Middle Eastern menu. So a salad of chopped cabbage, herbs and lemon becomes "Middle Eastern coleslaw." And her recipe for baba ghanouj—roasted, pureed eggplant—"gets lightened with zucchini."

It's hard to order wrong, though some dishes are more equal than others. Kodsi's thick dip of red peppers and nuts is a fine way to launch, as are her kibbe filled with ground meat and onions or just green peppers. Chicken arranged with shards of pita, yogurt and chickpeas adds up to a lovely shawarma, and requesting the special might yield eggplant with slivers of lamb and rice, a huge and homey comfort.

Kodsi's thick dip of red peppers and nuts is a fine way to launch, as are her kibbe filled with ground meat and onions or just green peppers.

Every square inch of the cozy place is claimed by a rug, a musical instrument, a photo of a VIP. Mention a birthday and out comes a doll that belly dances on your table. Meanwhile, the soundtrack sounds strangely familiar to a boomer's ears: "That's 'I Will Survive,' in Arabic," a young server translates.

Open: TU-TH 11:30-10, F-SAT 11:30-10:30, SUN 2-9:30 ***Entrees:*** $7.95-$18.95
Closed: M ***Credit Cards:*** ALL MAJOR ***Reservations:*** RECOMMENDED
Dress: CASUAL ***Cross Street:*** GEORGE MASON DRIVE
Parking: STREET ***Metro:*** BALLSTON-MU

Critic's Pick

★★½

LE MANNEQUIN PIS

18064 GEORGIA AVE., OLNEY, MD 301-570-4800
www.mannequinpis.com

FOR ALL THE COOKING I EXPLORED on a recent trip to Brussels, the Belgian restaurant that I'm most smitten with turns out to be a 50-minute drive from downtown Washington.

Handsome with yellow walls and red velvet drapes, Le Mannequin Pis is a lot like many of the smart little dining rooms I observed abroad. Its list of beers runs long and serious. Jacques Brel entertains in the background.

Take advantage of the tightly packed tables to see what looks good at your neighbors'. It could be cheese croquettes served with mustardy pickled vegetables, a deep pot of plump mussels in a rich saffron cream sauce, or a hefty piece of peppery beef with a hillock of excellent fries (for a real treat, let them soak up the pan juices).

Specials tend to be just that; I'm still dreaming of one night's pasta gilded with sea urchin. And if you've got stoemp on the brain, here's where you want to order that soothing Belgian tradition of mashed potatoes and other vegetables. The stern warnings on the menu (sorry, no cell phones, and, sorry, this isn't a vegetarian restaurant) are balanced by an otherwise gracious staff.

Take advantage of the tightly packed tables to see what looks good at your neighbors'.

The name of the restaurant, Le Mannequin Pis, comes from the famous fountain near the Grand Place in Brussels.

Dinner: DAILY 5-10 *Entrees:* $15.50-$23
Credit Cards: MC, V *Reservations:* RECOMMENDED
Dress: CASUAL *Cross Street:* ROUTE 108 / OLNEY-BLADENSBURG ROAD
Parking: LOT *Metro:* NO

★ ★ 1/2

LE PARADOU

678 INDIANA AVE. NW, WASHINGTON, DC (PENN QUARTER) 202-347-6780
www.leparadou.net

LITTLE EXCLAMATION POINTS go off in my head as I taste the lobster "purse" fashioned by Yannick Cam at Le Paradou. It looks like dim sum as imagined by a contemporary French artist: Its folds of pasta are sheer and delicate, and they hide generous bites of seafood so pure and rich, they taste like lobster just minutes out of the water in Maine. A drizzle of dark orange sauce—sweet carrot and zesty ginger—brightens the subtle canvas. The first course would be right at home in a Parisian temple of haute cuisine.

Like only some of the food at Le Paradou these days, this dish reveals the hand of a great chef, which is what Cam—who memorably entertained Washington audiences at Le Pavillon in the 1980s—clearly can be.

A few dishes are nothing short of exquisite. Wild salmon tartare is served as two tiny towers of rich, glistening fish, set on buttons of fine pastry and crowned with caviar. Cam's creamy risotto, redolent of tomatoes and summer truffles when I tried it, is as grand as you might ever encounter. This food is served in a room of beauty, stylishly understated with hardwood floors and a muted color scheme. No matter the weather outside, "stars" twinkle above your head in the dining room, thanks to some fiber optics.

Caviar and foie gras are doled out with abandon, which means sumptuous dining but, with wine factored in, also breathtaking tabs.

And yet, dining here can be an oddly joyless event. The waiters can be stiff and the air hangs heavy with pretension. Dry bread and bland pigeon do not help, either.

Caviar and foie gras are doled out with abandon, which means sumptuous dining but, with wine factored in, also breathtaking tabs. So any dish that is less than exceptional can be hard to swallow. "The lamb is the best you have ever tasted," a server promises, but the meat, though tender, doesn't quite deliver. At another dinner, a first course featuring sea urchin roe contains an unexpected ingredient: grit. Yet dessert might deliver an exquisite fig tart paired with a refreshing fennel sorbet.

Le Paradou soars and dips, sometimes at the same meal.

Lunch: M-F 11:45-2:30 ***Entrees:*** $18-$34
Dinner: M-TH 5:30-10:30 F-SAT 5:15-11 ***Entrees:*** $22-$44
Pre-Theater: M-SAT 5:15-6:30 3-COURSE PRIX FIXE $45
Closed: SUN ***Credit Cards:*** ALL MAJOR ***Reservations:*** RECOMMENDED
Dress: JACKET REQUIRED ***Cross Street:*** SEVENTH
Parking: $5 VALET AT DINNER ***Metro:*** ARCHIVES-NAVY MEMORIAL

★ ★

LES HALLES

1201 PENNSYLVANIA AVE. NW, WASHINGTON, DC (DOWNTOWN) 202-347-6848
www.leshalles.net

THE WAITERS' FRENCH ACCENTS, the pressed-tin ceiling, the steaming choucroute that lands on the next table—everything about Les Halles suggests that you're sitting in a neighborhood dining room in Paris.

Some of the food is very good, particularly anything based on meat, such as the house-made pâté served with mustardy greens, and steak tartare, a cool mound of chopped raw beef seasoned just the way you ask for it and flanked by a pile of french fries. And I'm a fool for the warm salad of potatoes accented with goat cheese and black olives.

I'm a fool for the warm salad of potatoes accented with goat cheese and black olives.

Salmon lapped with red wine sauce is best for its accessories—a bed of soft leeks and chopped shallots atop the fish—and much as I like the nest of frisee tossed with fried potatoes and browned garlic that cushions an entree of duck confit, the bird itself is tough and dry.

From the pastry chef come desserts both traditional (profiteroles, souffles, crepes) and more fashion forward (passion-fruit-and-raspberry flan, pineapple-coconut tart); there are about two dozen endings to consider, and they are available throughout the day, from 11:30 a.m. to midnight.

Underpinned by well-worn floors and pretty with half curtains in its picture windows, Les Halles's prime location near the Mall and several theaters means you'll find tourists in sweatshirts and tennis shoes alongside patrons dressed for a big night out—and dishes as simple as steamed mussels and macaroni and cheese or as serious as steak au poivre and tripe braised in cider.

Lunch: DAILY 11:30-4 *Entrees:* $9.50-$26
Dinner: DAILY 4-MIDNIGHT *Entrees:* $11.50-$26
Pre-Theater: M-SAT 5:30-7 2-COURSE PRIX FIXE $17.89
Brunch: SAT-SUN 11:30-4 *Entrees:* 3-COURSE PRIX FIXE $17.89
Credit Cards: ALL MAJOR *Reservations:* RECOMMENDED
Dress: CASUAL *Cross Street:* 13TH
Parking: $5 VALET TU-SAT STARTING AT 5 *Metro:* METRO CENTER

Critic's Pick
★ ★ 1/2

LEWNES' STEAKHOUSE

401 FOURTH STREET, ANNAPOLIS, MD 410-263-1617
www.lewnessteakhouse.com

FOR YEARS, I've been driving past this two-story, family-run steakhouse on my way to fresh fish at the nearby O'Learys in Annapolis.

Here's what I recently discovered I had been missing: A warm welcome at the door. Delicious clams casino. Terrific meat. Lewnes' serves only U.S. prime beef, revered for its tenderness and marbling, and grills its steaks and chops under super-hot broilers, after which they're topped with butter.

The result? One of the most succulent porterhouse steaks you'll ever slice into, and one of the juiciest prime ribs, stoked with fresh horseradish, within 60 miles. The pleasure is interrupted by gloppy creamed spinach, but buoyed by crisp, bracelet-size onion rings and fine red wine. And the waiters in their white jackets couldn't be more accommodating. Want to split the signature Greek salad? No problem (and no extra charge, either). Can't decide between the Lyonnaise and french fried potatoes? Your server is happy to bring you a plate with both for the same price.

Lewnes' serves only U.S. prime beef, revered for its tenderness and marbling.

More than many restaurants, Lewnes' lets us have it *our* way.

Open: DAILY 5-MIDNIGHT ***Entrees:*** $16.95-$32.95
Credit Cards: AE, DC, MC, V ***Reservations:*** RECOMMENDED
Dress: CASUAL ***Cross Street:*** SEVERN AVENUE
Parking: STREET ***Metro:*** NO

Critic's Pick
★★★★

MAESTRO

RITZ-CARLTON HOTEL, 1700 TYSONS BLVD., MCLEAN, VA 703-821-1515
www.maestrorestaurant.com

WANT TO CATCH A GREAT SHOW? Some of the finest dinner theater around unfolds at this big stage set of an open kitchen, where a cast of cooks and waiters led by Fabio Trabocchi routinely dazzles those patrons who have the good fortune to be seated close to the action.

The kitchen is all gleaming pots, white toques and serious concentration; the dining room is all oohs and ahhs as Trabocchi and crew send out dish after dish of pleasure. Diners have the option of composing a multi-course dinner from a vast range of traditional and experimental Italian dishes, but experience has taught me to leave such difficult decisions to the chef and order his "creation" menu.

Little waves of surprises follow. Think you know carpaccio? Think again. At Maestro, it comes not as thin sheets of sliced raw meat but as ruddy beef wrapped around a nugget of tofu and alternating with silken bites of foie gras in a long, clear glass cylinder, the dimples of which support each treat, along with a splash of aged balsamic vinegar. Clever! (But also delicious.) A nest of wire-thin pasta picks up some bite from silvery anchovies and minced chilies, while the most extraordinary roast pigeon is accompanied by a vial of lavender-perfumed sauce and a dark dab of paste that ricochets from coriander to nutmeg to orange to cloves—and beyond.

The dining room is all oohs and ahhs as Trabocchi and crew send out dish after dish of pleasure.

Maestro's cheese course is first-rate and so are desserts. My current favorite is a tall and airy peppermint souffle flanked by a velvety scoop of lemon verbena ice cream. Sommelier Vincent Feraud wears a tux, but that doesn't stop him from joking with you as he watches after your liquid needs as ably as the kitchen feeds you.

Breakfast: M-F 6:30-11 ***Entrees:*** $8.50-$16.50
Dinner: TU-TH 6-9, F 6-9:30, SAT 5-10 PRIX FIXE MENUS, 3-COURSE $85, 4-COURSE $98, 5-COURSE $110, 7-COURSE $135
Brunch: SUN 10:30-2:30 ***Buffet:*** $61 PER ADULT, $25 PER CHILD
Credit Cards: ALL MAJOR ***Reservations:*** RECOMMENDED
Dress: BUSINESS CASUAL ***Cross Street:*** INTERNATIONAL DRIVE
Parking: COMPLIMENTARY VALET TU-SAT ***Metro:*** WEST FALLS CHURCH-VT / UVA

Critic's Pick

★ ★ 1/2

MAJESTIC CAFE

911 KING ST., ALEXANDRIA, VA 703-837-9117
www.majesticcafe.com

When Susan McCreight Lindeborg left Old Town Alexandria for her native Las Vegas, N.M., fans worried about what would become of the popular American restaurant she left behind. Any fears should be dismissed: The veteran chef left Majestic Cafe in the hands of her trusted sidekick, Joe Raffa, who knows her soulful style as well as anyone, having helped McCreight Lindeborg open the place in 2001. And he's keeping her memory fresh while expanding the script to include more Southern accents.

I'm talking black-eyed pea soup, its bourbon-laced broth swirled with matchsticks of Virginia ham, and deviled eggs treated to a carrot salad sweetened with raisins. Lightly grilled catfish arrives on a loose base of hominy, buttery spinach and pickled corn. Not every dish merits a high five—a refreshing Asian slaw of snow peas and water chestnuts is forced to share its plate with arid chicken-filled spring rolls—but plenty do. Be sure to add a side dish or two to any order: Stewed tomatoes, sweet potato with orange-hazelnut butter and hush puppies gussied up with remoulade are particularly good choices. Much like the sunny space, with its charming old black-and-white photos running across the walls, the cooking here is clean and light.

If there's any place in Alexandria where you shouldn't forgo dessert, it's here.

If there's any place in Alexandria where you shouldn't forgo dessert, it's here. Pastry chef Valerie Hill's high and lovely coffee walnut cake and dreamy sweet potato pie make but two compelling cases.

Lunch: TU-SAT 11:30-2:30 ***Entrees:*** $9.25-$14
Dinner: TU-TH, SUN 5:30-10, F-SAT 5:30-11 ***Entrees:*** $18-$25
Brunch: SUN 11-2:30 ***Entrees:*** $9.25-$13
Closed: M ***Credit Cards:*** ALL MAJOR ***Reservations:*** RECOMMENDED
Dress: CASUAL ***Cross Street:*** PATRICK
Parking: STREET ***Metro:*** KING STREET

Critic's Pick

★ ★ ★

MAKOTO

4822 MACARTHUR BLVD. NW, WASHINGTON, DC (PALISADES)
202-298-6866

WEAR CLEAN SOCKS. That's my advice to anyone interested in a meal at this most Japanese of Washington restaurants, whose patrons are asked to shed their shoes at the door before entering the spare, narrow, low-ceilinged dining room.

No one just drops by Makoto. With only 28 seats, including a small sushi bar, reservations are essential. Looking around, and eavesdropping, I often think half the diplomatic corps must come here to hoist chopsticks and drink sake (from a fragrant wood box instead of a glass).

I imagine such diners feel at home perched on the wood seats that double as coat holders, feasting on pristine sushi, flounder bound in cherry leaf, or soft-shell crab crunchy in a coat of rice-cracker crumbs and garnished with leek flower stems. Chef-owner Yoshiaki Itoh makes his own soy sauce and serves only fresh wasabi, details that further elevate a meal here. This is all beautiful food, right down to the sparkling grape ice that signals the end of the $49 tasting menu.

With only 28 seats, including a small sushi bar, reservations are essential.

A seat at the counter, overlooking the kitchen and three chefs, provides one of the most engaging cooking shows you're likely to tune in to. For a few hushed hours, you'll also feel far, far removed from the bustle of the city.

Lunch: TU-SAT NOON-2 ***Entrees:*** $8.95-$19.50
Dinner: TU-SUN 6-10 ***Tasting Menu:*** $49
Closed: M ***Credit Cards:*** MC, V ***Reservations:*** REQUIRED
Dress: BUSINESS CASUAL ***Cross Street:*** RESERVOIR ROAD NW
Parking: STREET ***Metro:*** NO

★ ★

MANDALAY

930 BONIFANT ST., SILVER SPRING, MD 301-585-0500
www.mandalayrestaurantcafe.com

ONE OF THE MOST EXOTIC VACATIONS from workaday Washington is a meal at Mandalay, home to pork stew bulked up with pickled mango and sauteed shrimp made sassy with cilantro, onions and sour mustard leaves. Both Burmese dishes are irresistible. Both also face stiff competition for a diner's attention on a long menu that underscores Burma's connections to China, India and Southeast Asia with noodles, spices including cumin and curry leaves and fermented fish and shrimp pastes.

Prime detours include any of the refreshing salads (make mine pickled tea leaves).

Prime detours include any of the refreshing salads (make mine pickled tea leaves); beef in a gravy of tomato and onion and a sprinkling of (yeow!) red chili flakes; and mohingar, Burma's famous fish-and-rice noodle soup.

The dining room is only slightly dressy with dark wood tables and booths covered in orange-gold fabric, and the service runs hot or cold. Food—fragrant, nuanced and somewhat mysterious—offered at gentle prices is what really keeps you coming back.

Lunch: M-SAT 11:30-3 P.M., SUN NOON-3 *Entrees:* $8-$11
Dinner: SUN-TH 5-10, F-SAT 5-10:30 *Entrees:* $8-$11
Credit Cards: MC, V *Reservations:* NO
Dress: CASUAL *Cross Street:* GEORGIA AVENUE
Parking: STREET *Metro:* SILVER SPRING

★ ★ ½

MARCEL'S

2401 PENNSYLVANIA AVE. NW, WASHINGTON, DC (FOGGY BOTTOM) 202-296-1166
www.marcelsdc.com

THIS ELEGANT RESTAURANT looks better than ever, thanks to a little redo—notice the regal new carpet and plush chairs?—and it feels a little less stodgy now that the servers are in suits rather than tuxes. As always, the golden lighting makes even tired faces appear as if they just returned from a long holiday.

Working from a raised open kitchen that allows him to peek at his audience, Robert Wiedmaier prepares a menu that's mostly rich and primarily French. Boudin blanc is a signature, and you'll know why the chef can't remove it from his list after you taste the plump and mousselike appetizer, poised on celery root puree and lapped with a truffled wine sauce. That said, the show-stopper among first courses is the ultrarich lobster bisque hidden beneath a warm balloon of hot pastry; diners break the cover as if it were a souffle to get to the luxurious soup. Fun!

Less glorious is what follows: halibut overcooked by a precious minute, maybe, or rack of lamb whose muted flavor doesn't warrant a $42 price tag. Saving the day are the accompaniments to those entrees. The fish comes to the table atop a fine spinach risotto, while the meat gets an escort of silken pureed potatoes and a hot marble of spiced lamb sausage. And I'd be tempted to order the "farm house chicken" for its sidekick alone, a fat cake of shredded potatoes made decadent with Gruyere. Desserts are less inspiring these days, too. The bland chocolate souffle is not worth the wait, though I ate every lick of its mandarin orange ice cream.

The show-stopper among first courses is the ultrarich lobster bisque hidden beneath a warm balloon of hot pastry.

I always love sitting here. I sometimes feel the price of admission is worth it.

Dinner: M-TH 5-10, F-SAT 5-11, SUN 5-9:30 ***Entrees:*** $33-$39
Tasting Menus: 3-COURSE $58, 4-COURSE $78, 5-COURSE $98
Pre-Theater: DAILY 5-7 3-COURSE PRIX FIXE $48
Credit Cards: ALL MAJOR ***Reservations:*** RECOMMENDED
Dress: BUSINESS CASUAL ***Cross Street:*** 24TH ***Parking:*** DAILY $5 VALET AFTER 5:30
Metro: FOGGY BOTTOM-GWU

★ ★

MARK AND ORLANDO'S

2020 P ST. NW, WASHINGTON, DC (DUPONT CIRCLE) 202-223-8463
www.markandorlandos.com

THEY MET OVER A DOZEN YEARS AGO at Vidalia, became fast friends and talked for a long time about opening a restaurant of their own. In the summer of 2005, Mark Medley, a former waiter at the nearby Pesce, and his pal Orlando Hitzig, an alumnus of the kitchens at Blue Point Grill in Alexandria and 701 in Washington's Penn Quarter, finally made good on their daydreaming. Mark and Orlando's, two ideas in one, is the result of their Dupont Circle collaboration.

The ground floor is known as Orlando's, "the serious" part of the restaurant, says Hitzig. The chef's meals start with a quartet of bread spreads (tomato butter, bean dip, peanut butter and regular butter) and conclude with house-churned ice cream in rare flavors such as basil and curry. In between, diners might encounter fetching salads (scallops and red bell peppers in a vanilla-scented vinaigrette); delicious soups (tomato enhanced with beer); and entrees running from light crab cakes to robust pork stuffed with apples, pancetta and blue cheese. Not all of the kitchen's ideas work, but enough of them do, and you can be assured of sipping well: Medley, the host and wine maven, has assembled a nicely edited collection of labels that underscores both quality and value.

The ground floor is known as Orlando's, the "serious" part of the restaurant, says Hitzig.

Upstairs awaits Mark's, which celebrates "the lighter side of the world," according to Hitzig. In contrast with the small dining room on the street level—paved with a marble floor and decorated with copper cooking equipment and French maps—Mark's displays a flat-screen TV, parquet floors and a cocktail list. Look for a respectably juicy hamburger, a cheese plate, chicken wings and a few items from downstairs, like a smoked fish plate and grilled (really) Caesar salad, in this evening-only venue.

Handsome stone steps lead up to the entrance. The work of local artists and copper pots brighten the interior. From bottom to top, Mark and Orlando's is a pleaser.

Lunch: M-F 11:30-2:30 *Entrees:* $9-$14
Dinner: M-F 5:30-10, F-SAT 5:30-10:30, SUN 5:30-9:30 *Entrees:* $18-$22
Credit Cards: AE, D, MC, V *Reservations:* RECOMMENDED
Dress: CASUAL *Cross Street:* 20TH
Parking: STREET *Metro:* DUPONT CIRCLE

★ ★

MATCHBOX

743 H ST. NW, WASHINGTON, DC (CHINATOWN) 202-289-4441
www.matchboxdc.com

THE WOOD-BURNING BRICK OVEN in the rear of Matchbox is your clue for what to order at this three-story Chinatown magnet: pizza, natch. The restaurant's owners looked to some of New York's venerable pizza makers for inspiration, and it shows here, on blistered and smoke-perfumed crusts scattered with tasty toppings (I'll take spicy meatball or prosciutto with olives and ricotta cheese, please). The indecisive are in luck: Just ask, and the kitchen will decorate a pie half and half, with two different covers.

But Matchbox—which starts as a narrow bar with tall tables hugging a brick wall and climbs to a booth-lined dining room upstairs—is more than just a pizza joint. Salads are better than you expect them to be; I'm partial to the hillock of greens and roasted peppers tossed with rings of fried squid and balsamic vinegar, the aptly billed "sweet and tangy" calamari salad. And if some of the fare is a bit heavy handed, like the baseball-size crab cake bound in ribbons of phyllo and doused with remoulade, it's also more satisfying. Other dishes evoke American home cooking. Chicken pebbled with chopped pecans and set on a mound of whipped sweet potatoes, everything ringed in a gravy colored with finely diced carrot, adds up to a delicious rib-sticker. And the pizza gets heavy competition from another signature, a plate of baby hamburgers crowned with lacy onion rings offered on toasted brioche. (Bet you can't stop at just one.)

The pizza gets heavy competition from another signature, a plate of baby hamburgers crowned with lacy onion rings offered on toasted brioche.

All that good food at reasonable prices can mean a wait for one of the 75 seats at prime time. Matchbox hopes to remedy that situation: The restaurant is doubling its capacity by expanding next door, a project its owners hope to complete by the end of January 2006.

Open: M-TH 11-10, F 11-11, SAT NOON-11 ***Entrees:*** $11-$25
Closed: SUN ***Credit Cards:*** AE, MC, V ***Reservations:*** NO
Dress: CASUAL ***Cross Street:*** SEVENTH
Parking: STREET ***Metro:*** GALLERY PLACE-CHINATOWN

★ 1/2

MATSUTAKE

RONALD REAGAN WASHINGTON NATIONAL AIRPORT, ARLINGTON, VA
703-417-0521

I ONCE TURNED A DELAYED FLIGHT into a delicious advantage when I discovered a fine place to eat at Ronald Reagan Washington National Airport: Matsutake, a small Japanese eatery in the B terminal near gate No. 23.

An offshoot of a restaurant of the same name in Herndon, the venue offers a welcome alternative to fast food. A blond wood sushi bar and walls the color of wasabi create a soothing pit stop, and a diner can count on helpful recommendations from the chefs: "Giant clams just came in today," one of them said, steering me to a firm, pleasantly chewy and sea-scented sushi option; just as satisfying were buttery toro (fatty tuna) and subtle raw sweet shrimp. Prices average about $4 for two pieces, all of good quality (though the rice might not be as vinegared as you'd prefer).

There's more than just raw fish to consider: Japanese dumplings, noodle soups, spider rolls crunchy with soft-shell crab, and deep-fried vanilla ice cream round out the menu.

There's more than just raw fish to consider: Japanese dumplings, noodle soups, spider rolls crunchy with soft-shell crab, and deep-fried vanilla ice cream round out the menu. As an unexpected bonus, my waiter even volunteered to check the airline schedule posted out front so I wouldn't miss my flight.

All in all, it sure beats a bag of pretzels at 30,000 feet.

Open: DAILY 11-9 ***Entrees*** $6.95-$34.95
Credit Cards: ALL MAJOR ***Reservations:*** NO (RECOMMENDED AT OTHER LOCATIONS)
Dress: CASUAL ***Parking:*** GARAGE ***Metro:*** RONALD REAGAN WASHINGTON NATIONAL AIRPORT
Other Locations: 320 23RD ST., ARLINGTON, VA, 703-412-5301
4121 WILSON BLVD., ARLINGTON, VA, 703-351-8787
13049 WORLDGATE DR., HERNDON, VA, 703-787-3700

☆ ☆

MERKADO KITCHEN

1443 P ST. NW, WASHINGTON, DC (LOGAN CIRCLE) 202-299-0018
www.merkadodc.com

FIRST, SOME ADMISSIONS: One, I'm not a big fan of fusion cooking. And two, I can't recall a meal at Grillfish or Logan Tavern that made me eager to return to either one. I mention their names because both Washington restaurants are owned by David Winer, who recently opened Merkado Kitchen, which seasons Latin fare with Asian accents, on the same popular block as Logan Tavern.

Does everything sing? Everything does not. But plenty surpassed my expectations. Winer seems to be taking Merkado Kitchen more seriously than his earlier ventures, hiring a chef with a respectable résumé and creating an environment that is easy on the eyes, if not the ears. The owner also has outfitted the interior of the new restaurant with soothing colors, a kitchen visible behind glass and outsized paintings of faces that resemble the clientele that tends to flock here.

You're in luck if you like seafood, which makes up much of the menu. A trio of shrimp sports light tempura jackets and pink stripes of Thai chili paste mixed with mayonnaise, a presentation rounded out with a little nest of sesame-oil-splashed seaweed. More restrained are raw scallops, sliced into thick ivory coins, sprinkled with sea salt and anointed with a citrus-laced vinaigrette for a simple, clean effect.

You're in luck if you like seafood, which makes up much of the menu.

You can't fault Merkado's food for being boring. Salmon glides to the table with a sweet miso-based reduction and a bed of "risotto" made with sushi rice and shrimp; it won't please risotto purists—one bite of the rice is creamy, another is dry and chewy—but the overall flavor is fine. Succulent skirt steak "Nuevo Latino" is fanned out on its plate, scattered with diced peppers and offered with fried plantains and a cool and refreshing salad of julienned jicama, apple, carrot and chayote.

Merkado Kitchen is not where you want to take an aging parent or a soft speaker. When the place is busy, as it has been every night I've dropped by, the noise approaches that of a rock club. But keep in mind that this is Logan Circle, vibrant and forward-thinking. Even with its lapses, the new kid on the block fits right in.

Dinner: DAILY 5-10 ***Entrees:*** $14-$22.75
Pre-Theater: DAILY 5-7 3-COURSE PRIX FIXE $25
Brunch: SAT-SUN 11-3 ***Entrees:*** $7.95-$17.50
Credit Cards: AE, MC, V ***Reservations:*** RECOMMENDED
Dress: CASUAL ***Cross Street:*** 14TH
Parking: STREET ***Metro:*** DUPONT CIRCLE

Critic's Pick
☆☆☆☆

MICHEL RICHARD CITRONELLE

3000 M ST., NW, WASHINGTON, DC (GEORGETOWN) 202-625-2150
www.citronelledc.com

FEELING JADED? Have Michel Richard make dinner for you. No other chef in town claims quite the eye, or the skill set, of this imaginative French native, whose cooking could be displayed in a contemporary museum if only it wouldn't spoil.

His show might begin with a miniature salad nicoise, tucked in an egg shell and containing a surprise: What looks like egg white and egg yolk is actually fresh mozzarella and yellow tomato. Is that a hamburger in front of me? No, it's a light-as-air bun sandwiching a fine blend of pig's feet, pig's ear, chicken mousse, mushrooms and shallots. Its flavor is at once earthy and luxurious. A tin of glistening beluga caviar is set down, and by now you know to expect a delicious joke; the "caviar" is pasta cooked in lobster consomme, enriched with butter and stained black with squid ink.

No other chef in town claims quite the eye, or the skill set, of this imaginative French native.

These brilliant sleights of hand are punctuated by dishes that are more straightforward—lamb edged in a brilliant herb crust, turbot paired with the sweetest peas imaginable—but just as divine. If the underground dining room is looking a bit dated these days, chances are you'll be too busy contemplating the art on your plate to dwell on the matter. Richard is in a league all his own.

Breakfast: M-F 6:30-10:30, SAT-SUN 6:30-11 ***Entrees:*** $6-$18
Dinner: M-TH 6-10, F-SAT 6-10:15, SUN 6-9:30
Entrees: PRIX FIXE MENU $85; TASTING MENU $150
Chef's Table: DAILY 6-7:30, 12-COURSE $275 (6-8 PEOPLE REQUIRED)
Credit Cards: ALL MAJOR ***Reservations:*** RECOMMENDED
Dress: JACKET REQUIRED ***Cross Street:*** 30TH
Parking: $10 VALET ***Metro:*** FOGGY BOTTOM-GWU

★ 1/2

MIMI'S AMERICAN BISTRO

2120 P ST. NW, WASHINGTON, DC (DUPONT CIRCLE) 202-464-6464
www.mimisdc.com

WANT A SIDE OF OPERA with your ravioli? It's possible at Mimi's American Bistro, whose likeable servers punctuate their order-taking and dish-delivering with arias—or ballads, torch songs or show tunes, depending upon the individual talent. Cross "American Idol" with (loud) dinner theater and you have an idea of what to expect from an evening here.

Given the theme, the food can seem like an afterthought, as can the service. Mushroom-filled ravioli are stodgy, and the Caesar salad, while bountiful, gets showered with what tastes like cheese from an industrial bag. The best part of a thin rib-eye steak are its plate mates of sweet onion rings and custardlike potato souffle. And the swampy, soupy paella is nothing a Spaniard would recognize, though its mussels, clams and scallops are just fine. These and other dishes might get auctioned off instead of brought to the people who actually ordered them, but hey, it's your waiter's big moment at the mike!

Cross "American Idol" with (loud) dinner theater and you have an idea of what to expect from an evening here.

Mimi's grills a respectable hamburger, though, and rainbow trout with couscous, baby carrots and a bright lime sauce shows that the kitchen can handle fish with care, too. Summer might yield a lovely gazpacho, made with yellow tomatoes and enriched with a garnish of guacamole in its center. Think fruit for dessert. Both the apple pie, with practically a bushel of cinnamon-spiced apples, and the Key lime pie, which highlights tang over sugar, outperform the stodgy bread pudding and frosting-like chocolate mousse.

The restaurant's industrial shell is made warm with rich curtains here, modern art there, and sidewalk seating for when the weather cooperates—or when you'd really rather have a heart-to-heart than listen to your waiter pretend to be Billy Joel.

Lunch: M-F 11:30-4, SAT-SUN 11-3 *Entrees:* $7.50-$22
Dinner: DAILY 4-MIDNIGHT *Entrees:* $8-$24
Credit Cards: ALL MAJOR *Reservations:* RECOMMENDED
Dress: CASUAL *Cross Street:* 21ST
Parking: $5 VALET F-SAT DINNER *Metro:* DUPONT CIRCLE

Critic's Pick

★ ★ 1/2

MINH'S

2500 WILSON BLVD., ARLINGTON, VA
703-525-2828

VISITORS HERE COULD USE A GUIDE to sort through the more than 100 choices on the menu, including the daily specials on a chalkboard, and there always is one, be it a waiter or an owner, at this quietly stylish Vietnamese restaurant.

The hard-working staff has led me on some mouthwatering expeditions, one night introducing me to shrimp-and-potato cakes, bundled in crisp lettuce and dipped in tangy fish sauce; another time pointing out "sizzling" catfish, which does just that as it comes to the table, cubed and buried beneath a mound of fresh herbs, peanuts, slivered red onions and rice noodles. A meal gets off to a good start with stir-fried squid—crisp outside, pleasantly chewy inside—with onions and bell peppers. Season the mix with a pinch of the accompanying salt-and-pepper blend and a spritz of lime.

Like Vietnamese cuisine in general, the repertoire here borrows from Chinese, French and even Indian kitchens. Since a lot of these dishes are variations on a theme, it's less of a stimulus overload than you might anticipate when you first see the list.

Like Vietnamese cuisine in general, the repertoire here borrows from Chinese, French and even Indian kitchens.

Even on my own, though, I've plucked winners from the lot, including crisp, sweet folds of beef with lemon grass, and a special of fried scallops with mint, onions and jalapenos served with a peppery dipping sauce.

Minh's wouldn't be my first choice for pho or a Vietnamese crepe. Still, as with so much of the cooking, a lot of thought has gone into the interior. Pretty with fancy pillows on the banquettes, aged-looking sideboards and walls in shades of olive and burgundy, it doesn't look like the kind of place where entrees average $9.

Open: M-TH 11-10, F-SAT 11-11, SUN 11-10 ***Entrees:*** $6-$14
Credit Cards: ALL MAJOR ***Reservations:*** RECOMMENDED FOR 5 OR MORE
Dress: BUSINESS CASUAL ***Cross Street:*** CLEVELAND
Parking: LOT ***Metro:*** COURT HOUSE

Critic's Pick

☆ ☆ ☆

MINIBAR AT CAFE ATLANTICO

405 EIGHTH ST. NW, WASHINGTON, DC (PENN QUARTER) 202-393-0812
www.cafeatlantico.com

IF THE CIRQUE DU SOLEIL served food, this is what it would look and taste like.

On the second floor of Cafe Atlantico, minibar is just a few stools at a bar facing a small cast of cooks led by chef Jose Andres (also of Jaleo, Oyamel and Zaytinya), who take diners on a wild culinary ride through more than 30 bite-size courses. Nothing is what you think it will be—and much of it is more appealing than you'd imagine, knowing what you're popping in your mouth.

That sweet, salty and airy snack you get when you're first seated? That's caramelized pork rinds with maple syrup. What looks like green marbles might show up in front of you. "Japanese baby peaches with yogurt," a cook explains. I'm told to sip my demitasse of foie gras soup like a cappuccino; it is cool on the foamy top and hot (and rich) beneath the surface. A dish created expressly for wine guru Robert Parker, one of many famous foodies to check out this novel show, is simply brilliant: The "deconstructed glass of wine" finds a translucent layer of grape gelatin decorated on the surface with pinches of mint, orange peel, vanilla—a line of flavors commonly found in wine. At minibar, "ravioli" is created from mango and "air" (frothy foam) might be flavored with lime.

The "deconstructed glass of wine" finds a translucent layer of grape gelatin decorated on the surface with pinches of mint, orange peel, vanilla.

Andres's near-constant experimenting means there's always something fresh to look forward to, and anything you don't like is soon forgotten in the whirl.

Dinner: TU-SAT SEATINGS AT 6 AND 8:30 *Entrees:* TASTING MENU $85
Credit Cards: ALL MAJOR *Reservations:* REQUIRED
Dress: BUSINESS CASUAL *Cross Street:* D STREET NW
Parking: $10 VALET *Metro:* ARCHIVES-NAVY MEMORIAL

Critic's Pick
☆ ☆

MITSITAM NATIVE FOODS CAFE

NATIONAL MUSEUM OF THE AMERICAN INDIAN
FOURTH STREET AND INDEPENDENCE AVENUE SW, WASHINGTON, DC (NATIONAL MALL)
202-633-7038 www.nmai.si.edu

THERE ARE FEW reliable places to eat on the Mall. Mitsitam Cafe is a delightful exception. Located on the ground floor of the National Museum of the American Indian, this nod to the culinary traditions of Indians from around the Americas is both tasty and eye-catching. Different food stations serve up the likes of salmon cakes from the Pacific Northwest, chicken-stuffed tamales from South America, buffalo burgers from the Great Plains and shredded pork tacos and tomato rice from the Meso.

Most of the selections are very satisfying, with a few silly exceptions: The Indian tacos from the Plains heap iceberg lettuce, grated cheddar cheese and chili on saucer-size fry bread, the effect of which is more T.G.I. Friday than true to history books. And I seriously doubt any Indians from way back when finished their meals with fruit tarts or coconut macaroons, both of which are also available here. But the success stories prevail over the lapses, and the setting—airy, open and warmed up with orange and earth tones—gives "government cafeteria" a good name.

The success stories prevail over the lapses, and the setting—airy, open and warmed up with orange and earth tones—gives "government cafeteria" a good name.

The best seats overlook a curved glass wall that frames a nice nature scene—water splashing over rocks—and keeps kids of all ages mesmerized.

Open: DAILY 10-5 ***Entrees:*** $6.95-$13.95
Credit Cards: ALL MAJOR ***Reservations:*** NO
Dress: CASUAL ***Cross Street:*** FOURTH
Parking: STREET ***Metro:*** L'ENFANT PLAZA

★ ★ ½

MONTMARTRE

327 SEVENTH ST. SE, WASHINGTON, DC (CAPITOL HILL) 202-544-1244
www.montmartre.us

THE STAMP-SIZE RAVIOLI, brushed with a lovely arugula sauce, truly melt on the tongue. Braised rabbit—sharp with olives and arranged on creamy, truffle-perfumed pasta—proves deliciously moist. And brunch delivers a fluffy omelet and a pretty green salad.

Close your eyes at Montmartre and you could swear you were eating in one of Washington's starrier restaurants. Instead, you're sitting at a rough wooden table in a cozy 48-seat dining room on Capitol Hill, in view of Stephane Lezla, at work behind the counter of his open kitchen.

The chef's food reveals passion and experience; before Montmartre, Lezla worked at Bistrot Lepic, Lavandou and Provence under the watch of Yannick Cam. You can point just about anywhere on the menu and score a success. The dessert tray is as fetching as a jewelry case; the tortes look gorgeous and taste handcrafted.

The dessert tray is as fetching as a jewelry case; the tortes look gorgeous and taste handcrafted.

Not every meal is a dream come true. I've encountered tough veal kidneys and get an occasional gripe about snippy service. But more often than not, this is where I like to be when the mood calls for French but my budget demands restraint. Montmartre may not be perfect, but it's a perfect neighborhood restaurant.

Lunch: TU-F 11:30-2:30 ***Entrees:*** $12.95-$18.95
Dinner: TU-TH 5:30-10, F-SAT 5:30-10:30, SUN 5:30-9 ***Entrees:*** $16.95-$19.95
Brunch: SAT-SUN 11:30-2:30 ***Entrees:*** $7.95-$18.95
Closed: M ***Credit Cards:*** AE, DC, MC, V ***Reservations:*** RECOMMENDED
Dress: CASUAL ***Cross Street:*** PENNSYLVANIA AVENUE SE
Parking: STREET ***Metro:*** EASTERN MARKET

★ ★

MOURAYO

1732 CONNECTICUT AVE. NW, WASHINGTON, DC (DUPONT CIRCLE)
202-667-2100

SOFT GREEK MUSIC plays in the narrow restaurant, which is decorated to suggest a sleek yacht. Faux portholes dot the clean white walls, and servers in Greek sailors' caps and shirts navigate the tightly packed tables.

Mourayo is not the place to expect chicken-and-egg-yolk soup, moussaka or even baklava. Instead of sending out a fleet of the traditional dishes found in many Greek restaurants on this side of the Atlantic, this restaurant attempts to expand its customers' horizons. A meal can commence with squid ink soup, as dark as midnight and mysterious in flavor. Grilled octopus shows up as a single curled tentacle, thick as a garden hose, with a dab of fava bean puree and octopus ink vinaigrette. Daunting as that sounds, the seafood is tender and pleasantly smoky.

Alternatively, there are more familiar savory pastries, such as the pretty phyllo triangles, flaky as can be (psst, the dough is made right here) and filled with molten white cheese. Beggars' purses fashioned from phyllo contain both cheese and roasted peppers, and cheese is again the focus in a third appetizer, sesame-crusted ovals of goat cheese delivered with a grape-strewn lettuce salad. With several exceptions, the homier-sounding dishes are the ones to seek out. Soujoukakia—ground beef spiked with fennel, cumin and anise and shaped into fat bullets—is a special that deserves frequent play on the menu.

Mourayo is not the place to expect chicken-and-egg-yolk soup, moussaka or even baklava.

Now and then, the food here tastes as if no one's minding the kitchen. Some of the dips on the sampling platter are as dense as paste (fava bean puree) or lack proper seasoning (garlic and lemon are AWOL in the hummus). And lamb chops, nicely flavored and lapped with a wine and shallot sauce, tend to be overcooked.

Mourayo is not as ambitious as the first-class Zaytinya downtown, with its dozens of innovative mezze, nor is it as traditional as the Mykonos Grill in Rockville, which serves spinach pies and stuffed grape leaves in a room painted to look like a Greek village. What this newcomer does is offer enough enticements to lure you in and enough attractions to keep you coming back, even as you wish the sailing were sometimes just a bit smoother.

Lunch: M-F 11:30-3:30 ***Entrees:*** $10.25-$14.95
Dinner: M-TH 5:30-10:30, F-SAT 5:30-11, SUN 5:30-10 ***Entrees:*** $14.95-$23.95
Credit Cards: AE, D, MC, V ***Reservations:*** RECOMMENDED ***Dress:*** CASUAL ***Cross Street:*** 17TH
Parking: $6 VALET AFTER 5:30 F-SAT ***Metro:*** DUPONT CIRCLE

★ ½

MR. CHEN'S ORGANIC CHINESE CUISINE

2604 CONNECTICUT AVE. NW, WASHINGTON, DC (WOODLEY PARK) 202-797-0668
www.mrchens.com

ROAST DUCK AND HOISIN SAUCE wrapped in thin pancakes. Broccoli invigorated with a kicky sauce of ginger and garlic. Sichuan beef that lives up to the fiery promise of its name.

Those are a few of my favorite things at Mr. Chen's Organic Chinese Cuisine, a below-ground dining room and carryout just a few steps removed from the Metro stop in Woodley Park. Though a little frayed around the edges these days, the space is nevertheless clean and modestly attractive. Drawings of playful pandas and bucolic landscapes grace pale blue walls; tinkling Chinese music sets an appropriate backdrop to a menu that also includes satisfying versions of sweet-and-sour shrimp and General Tso's chicken.

Sichuan beef lives up to the fiery promise of its name.

Generally reliable cooking is just one draw; Mr. Chen's also makes deliveries, can steam most dishes on request and offers many of its entrees in two sizes, small and large. And the price is right—the two dozen or so lunch specials average $5.50, rice included.

Lunch: M-F 11-3 *Entrees:* $4.85-$6.85
Dinner: M-TH 3-10:30, F 3-11, SAT 11-11, SUN NOON-10 *Entrees:* $6.75-$10.95
Credit Cards: AE, D, MC, V *Reservations:* NO
Dress: CASUAL *Cross Street:* CALVERT
Parking: STREET *Metro:* WOODLEY PARK-ZOO / ADAMS MORGAN

★ ★

MYKONOS GRILL

121 CONGRESSIONAL LA., ROCKVILLE, MD 301-770-5999
www.mykonosgrill.com

GREECE SPRINGS TO LIFE in this convivial suburban idyll. One cozy room suggests a faraway village courtyard in blue paint and white plaster; another looks onto an Aegean seascape (even if only by way of a mural). And in good weather, tables and pots of hanging flowers adorn an outdoor patio.

The menu plays along. Begin with stuffed grape leaves, whipped fish roe or eggplant split and filled with a blend of tomato, onion, white raisins and pine nuts. Venture further into the meal with tender pan-fried squid with garlicky potato dip, trout stuffed with spinach, or a trio of lamb chops accompanied by homey roast potatoes, carrots and soft-cooked green beans tossed with tomatoes. If you like your food on the rare side, pipe up: The kitchen tends to overcook things by a minute or so.

There's nothing on the menu that you probably haven't encountered before, but even the standards are prepared with care. Rich green spinach and tangy feta cheese weave between sheets of crackling phyllo in an order of spanakopita, for instance, while moussaka translates into a surprisingly light sliced eggplant layered with meat and mashed potatoes so satiny that they resemble custard.

There's nothing on the menu that you probably haven't encountered before, but even the standards are prepared with care.

Periodically, a burst of flames interrupts conversation in the dining room, a spectacle that's a reminder to try the pan-fried kasseri cheese, sprinkled with lemon juice and brandy and ignited at the table. Sure, the fireworks are fun, but even better is what happens as your tongue absorbs the crisp golden crust, gently sparked with citrus and alcohol, followed by a molten rivulet of cheese.

Given the setting and the cooking, it's small wonder that Sunday night looks like a party, nearly every seat filled. Is the host a bit gruff? Are the waiters too serious? At least their suggestions are helpful. When I begged off ordering dessert on a hot summer night, my server couldn't resist sending me a gratis treat anyway: bites of watermelon with a few lovely cookies.

Lunch: TU-SUN 11:30-3:30 ***Entrees:*** $10.95-$19.95
Dinner: SUN, TU-TH 3:30-9:30, F-SAT 3:30-10:30 ***Entrees:*** $11.25-$21.95
Closed: M ***Credit Cards:*** ALL MAJOR ***Reservations:*** RECOMMENDED
Dress: BUSINESS CASUAL ***Cross Street:*** ROCKVILLE PIKE
Parking: LOT ***Metro:*** TWINBROOK

★ ½

NATTA THAI

153 GLYNDON ST. SE, VIENNA, VA
703-242-4323

DON'T EVERYBODY RUSH THE PLACE for a wicked plate of seafood stir-fried with chilies, garlic and basil. I've seen closets that are bigger than this fledgling Thai eatery, which probably accounts for its healthy carryout business.

Stick around to eat your food, though, and you'll experience sweet service in a pretty shoebox framed in peach-colored walls with pale blue trim. Ease in with bulbous chicken wings plumped with a mousselike filling of shrimp, crab and mushrooms or a slightly caramelized beef satay, juicy beneath its subtle curry seasoning. Then move on to pork and tender bamboo shoots draped in a creamy green curry, or whatever special your waitress encourages you to try. "The soft-shell crabs are fresh, not frozen," one of them shared on a midsummer visit.

Ease in with bulbous chicken wings plumped with a mousselike filling of shrimp, crab and mushrooms.

Not every dish makes my hit parade. The shrimp in a bowl of nicely tangy hot-and-sour soup could be fresher, and the steamed vegetable dumplings are pasty and less appealing for their cloying soy sauce (note to kitchen: Turn down the sugar dial). Natta Thai is good to know about if you find yourself nearby, hungry and in search of a bit of pampering with your garden roll or duck salad.

Lunch: M-SAT 11-3 *Entrees:* $4.95-$8.95
Dinner: DAILY 5-10 *Entrees:* $6.95-$12.95
Credit Cards: ALL MAJOR *Reservations:* NO
Dress: CASUAL *Cross Street:* MAPLE AVENUE
Parking: LOT *Metro:* VIENNA / FAIRFAX-GMU

☆ ☆

NEW FORTUNE

16515 S. FREDERICK AVE., GAITHERSBURG, MD
301-926-8828

A WASH IN RED CARPET and illuminated with chandeliers, this Chinese feeding hall is about as intimate as Tiananmen Square. With 450 seats and a stage for banquets, it's built on the scale of a country with more than a billion citizens.

A diner could visit every day for half a year and still not sample every dish on the epic menu. Seafood dishes, including "salt and pepper" squid and scallops, tend to be the kitchen's strong suit. At lunch, when dim sum is served, New Fortune feels like a trip to Canton. A flotilla of food carts crisscrosses the expanse, their bow-tied attendants hawking everything from appetizer-size plates of roast duck to rice gruel, from spidery deep-fried taro cakes to spareribs draped in black bean sauce.

A diner could visit every day for half a year and still not sample every dish on the epic menu.

Kids love the show, and parents appreciate the speedy service. Late dinner hours (until 1 a.m. weekdays, 2 a.m. weekends) and modest tabs make up for the occasional clinker from the kitchen.

Open: SUN-TH 11 AM-1 AM F-SAT 11 AM-2 AM ***Entrees:*** $7.95-$14.95
Credit Cards: ALL MAJOR ***Reservations:*** RECOMMENDED
Dress: CASUAL ***Cross Street:*** S. WESTLAND DRIVE
Parking: LOT ***Metro:*** SHADY GROVE

★ ★

NIRVANA

1810 K ST. NW, WASHINGTON, DC (DOWNTOWN) 202-223-5043
www.dcnirvana.com

IF YOUR IDEA OF INDIAN FOOD is limited to samosas and a curry or two, the family-run Nirvana will open your eyes to a richer world. Slender banana peppers stuffed with a paste of coconut, coriander, mint and nuts, all cushioned in a chickpea batter, practically tap-dance in your mouth. The zippy khasta kachori looks like a toy top but is actually an edible flower shell inside which cloves, red pepper and cumin wait to tease your tongue.

Nirvana also sets out a lunch buffet, and it changes daily to reflect a different region of India.

More familiar but no less satisfying are the crepelike dosas filled with vegetables and beds of fragrant Basmati rice, the best of which is flavored with tamarind, nuts and raisins. Nirvana also sets out a lunch buffet, and it changes daily to reflect a different region of India; for less than $10 a person, it adds up to a lusty little tour.

Watching over the pretty—and sometimes chaotic—dining room is the regal Doler Shah, elegant in a sari and eager to introduce you to her personal take on meatless cooking.

Lunch: M-F 11:30-3 ***Entrees:*** $7.95-$10.95
Dinner: M-TH 5-9, F-SAT 5-10 ***Entrees:*** $8.95-$10.95
Lunch Buffet: M-F $9.95 ***Brunch:*** SAT NOON-3 ***Price:*** $12.95
Closed: SUN ***Credit Cards:*** AE, D, MC, V ***Reservations:*** RECOMMENDED
Dress: BUSINESS CASUAL ***Cross Street:*** 18TH
Parking: STREET ***Metro:*** FARRAGUT WEST

★ 1/2

NORA

2132 FLORIDA AVE. NW, WASHINGTON, DC (DUPONT CIRCLE) 202-462-5143
www.noras.com

BACK WHEN THIS RESTAURANT opened in 1979, and many American chefs were just beginning to take their inspiration from gardens rather than cans, Nora Pouillon was enlightening diners with additive-free beef raised on a diet of alfalfa and seaweed. Zoom ahead to today. Free-range chicken and organic mixed greens are as much a part of the dining scene as cell phones and online restaurant reservations.

Now recognized as "America's First Certified Organic Restaurant," Nora can pride itself on many things, from its loyal clientele of famous names to its interesting, albeit pricey, wine list, featuring an all-star cast of pinot noirs from Burgundy and the United States. This is an expense-account dining room that dresses as if every day were Casual Friday: Quilts adorn the whitewashed brick walls, and a wooden model airplane drops from the center of the beamed ceiling.

For all the history and all the accolades, though, Nora requires some digging to find a meal to remember. Oh, a dewy cake of chopped raw yellowfin tuna with wiggly yellow cubes of tomato water is pretty and light. And house-made pâté with pumpkin chutney and poppy-seed crackers makes a nice nosh. But main courses in particular are more penance than pleasure. Rabbit "3 Ways"—as loin, leg and rack—with spaetzle is as dull as its beige palette. Pork roast with bacon and turnips is a bit better, but not much. When dinner costs more than $100 a head, I'd like something more clever than apple crisp for dessert and servers who extend more than the minimum effort in seeing to my needs.

This is an expense-account dining room that dresses as if every day were Casual Friday.

Consistency might not be a hallmark of Nora, but commitment is: Try to name another restaurant that bothers to triple-filter the water in your glass. Still, when the check comes, I'm left shaking my head and thinking of all the hauter restaurants around that would have made me happier—and for a lot less.

Dinner: M-TH 6-10 FRI-SAT 5:30-10:30 ***Entrees:*** $26-$31
Tasting Menus: $59-$69 ***Closed:*** SUN
Credit Cards: AE, D, MC, V ***Reservations:*** RECOMMENDED
Dress: CASUAL ***Cross Street:*** R STREET NW
Parking: $6 VALET ***Metro:*** DUPONT CIRCLE

Critic's Pick

★ ★ ★

NOTTI BIANCHE

824 NEW HAMPSHIRE AVE. NW, WASHINGTON, DC (FOGGY BOTTOM) 202-298-8085
www.nottibianche.com

AN ALUMNUS OF Equinox downtown, Anthony Chittum is serving some of the most appealing food around these days, and without resorting to any bells and whistles. If you're looking for a place to sup before an engagement at the Kennedy Center, which is within strolling distance, here's your ticket.

First, a caveat. Notti Bianche—"White Nights" in Italian—inherits some of the problems of its predecessors, the much-missed Nectar and Zuki Moon. The tables, particularly those facing the banquette, are placed so close together, you get to hear exactly what your neighbor got in her divorce settlement. The ceilings are low and industrial-looking, which detracts from the aesthetics. Do I sound whiney? Well, looks matter when you're dressed for a show and paying $20 for roast chicken.

It's a *really* good roast chicken, however, juicy as you could hope for and sporting a delightfully crisp skin. The entree is kept company by plate mates of kale, punched up with bits of pancetta, and a Parmesan-enriched puck of risotto. Had this dish been a play, it would have garnered a standing ovation. The same could be said of wild salmon, cooked so that the pink-orange fish fell away from my knife like hot butter, and delicately paved with a shimmering green coat of basil, spinach and Japanese bread crumbs. The young chef's fritto misto has few peers and his pastas are sublime.

The young chef's fritto misto has few peers and his pastas are sublime.

Like the menu, the concise wine list concentrates on things Italian. It also shows thought. The selection of 20 or so whites and reds embraces some unusual grape varieties (cortese, fiano di avellino) and a surprise or two. Never tried a Greek rose? Here's your chance.

Lunch: M-F 11:30-2:30 ***Entrees:*** $7-$25
Dinner: SUN-TH 5-10, FRI-SAT 5-11 ***Entrees:*** $7-$29
Pre-Theater: DAILY, 5-7 3-COURSE PRIX FIXE $35
Credit Cards: ALL MAJOR ***Reservations:*** RECOMMENDED
Dress: BUSINESS CASUAL ***Cross Street:*** I STREET NW
Parking: $6 VALET DAILY OFFERED THROUGH GWU INN ***Metro:*** FOGGY BOTTOM-GWU

Critic's Pick
☆ ☆ ☆

OBELISK

2029 P ST. NW, WASHINGTON, DC (DUPONT CIRCLE)
202-872-1180

THE PRICE HAS GONE UP—but so has the amount of food on the fixed-price menu—at Obelisk, which is again one of Washington's top performers after a season or so of merely good showings. Under the eye of owner Peter Pastan, the veteran Italian retreat tastes better than ever, and its muse has expanded the format so that dinner now begins with a flurry of mouthwatering antipasti—picture a thin slice of cured pork sausage (lardo) and tomato confit on bruschetta, shaved smoked duck breast, a pillow of soft white cheese (burrata) laced with extraordinary Tuscan olive oil—before moving on to four other courses.

Currently, there's not a more exciting place within the city limits to tuck into an Italian repast. Should anyone need proof, I can simply point to hand-cut noodles tossed with chanterelles and pancetta; the most extraordinary bluefun tuna served on a cushion of velvety roasted peppers; and a blissful pudding laced with dessert wine—among other heady memories from my most recent outing here. Italian cooking is all about finding the best ingredients and then not playing too much with them. Obelisk excels at that. Pappa al pommodoro is just a fancy way to spell out tomato and bread soup, yet that humble dish soars to new heights in this kitchen, where chef Jerry Corso has been hitting one home run after another since returning to the restaurant in April 2005.

Currently, there's not a more exciting place within the city limits to tuck into an Italian repast.

The narrow room is spare, decorated with not much more than a band of mirrors at eye level and a few prints. But the space allows diners to stretch out a bit more than before, thanks to the removal of a half-dozen seats. No more knocking over your neighbor's wand-size bread sticks when you sit or stand.

My biggest regret is a menu that changes between visits, meaning everything I long to eat again might not be around on my return. Of course, that's the thrill of a meal here, too: Just imagine what new dishes Pastan and Corso will have dreamed up by the time you get back!

Dinner: TU-SAT 6-10 ***Entrees:*** 5-COURSE MENU, TU-TH $60, F-SAT $65
Closed: SUN-M ***Credit Cards:*** DC, MC, V ***Reservations:*** RECOMMENDED
Dress: CASUAL ***Cross Street:*** 21ST
Parking: STREET ***Metro:*** DUPONT CIRCLE

★ ★ 1/2

OCCIDENTAL

1475 PENNSYLVANIA AVE. NW WASHINGTON, DC (DOWNTOWN) 202-783-1475
www.occidentaldc.com

ONE OF THE HISTORY LESSONS a lot of tourists miss in Washington is a meal at the Occidental, whose soaring walls are covered with hundreds of framed pictures of notables past and present. Look, it's Teddy Roosevelt! Also watching you eat are J. Edgar Hoover, baseball legend Walter Johnson and Sen. Hillary Rodham Clinton.

The room—which dates to 1906 and includes a gleaming wood bar—is steeped in yesteryear, yet the cooking is very much of the moment. Spring rolls, crunchy and fat with jerk chicken, include a mango-chili dip that is spicy but not searing. The ubiquitous tuna tartare gets personalized with wasabi vinaigrette and slender house-baked saltines. Oysters served warm in their shells with creamed spinach need to lose their manchego cheese covers, but the lobster roll, bound with celery and presented on toasted brioche, is a real catch. And lamb chops slathered with pesto and rounded out with barley risotto deliver plenty of savor, too.

The room—which dates to 1906 and includes a gleaming wood bar—is steeped in yesteryear, yet the cooking is very much of the moment.

This often-hearty food is accompanied by equally generous service—at the host stand, at the bar and especially in the dining room, where my last waiter was so adept at entertaining me with bits of trivia about this historic address that I wasn't surprised to hear he was planning to be a social studies teacher.

Lunch: DAILY 11:30-3 *Entrees:* $11-$23
Dinner: SUN 4:30-9:30, M-TH 4:30-10, F-SAT 4:30-10:30 *Entrees:* $23-$37
Credit Cards: AE, DC, MC, V *Reservations:* RECOMMENDED
Dress: BUSINESS CASUAL *Cross Street:* 14TH
Parking: COMPLIMENTARY VALET AT THE WILLARD HOTEL AFTER 6 PM *Metro:* METRO CENTER

Critic's Pick
★★½

OCEANAIRE SEAFOOD ROOM

1201 F ST. NW, WASHINGTON, DC (DOWNTOWN) 202-347-2277
www.theoceanaire.com

DINERS STEP BACK IN TIME at this dashing ode to fish, where meals begin with a complimentary relish tray, big band music plays in the background, and the bathroom doors indicate "Gents" or "Powder Room." Sleek as an ocean liner—say, the Queen Mary—the vast dining room is a looker, decorated as it is with outsized red leather booths and more curves than at Hugh Hefner's manse.

Consider some oysters on the half shell to start: There are typically a dozen varieties from which to choose, and they come to the table nicely shucked and glistening. "Try not to use these," a waiter instructs, pointing to the cocktail sauce and mignonette that accompany the bivalves, which are so fresh and sweet they shouldn't be slurped with anything but a sip of white wine.

The menu is epic and changes daily, but there are a few constants: lovely crab cakes, fine grilled squid, and shrimp de jonge, an old-fashioned recipe featuring baked butterflied shrimp, lightly breaded and spiked with cayenne and paprika. Pay attention to anything your waiter recommends, like the Panamanian "bigeye" tuna, which looks like steak, cuts like silk and gets an Asian accent with pickled ginger and seaweed salad. Crisp-seared coho salmon might sit on a pool of mustard cream, while sturgeon can be had "dirty"—lightly blackened in the Cajun fashion—yet balanced with mango relish.

Pay attention to anything your waiter recommends, like the Panamanian "bigeye" tuna, which looks like steak.

A seafood restaurant with the sensibility (and prices) of a steakhouse, Oceanaire is not for the faint-hearted. A side dish of creamed corn brims with almost a bushel's worth of that sweet vegetable; the hash browns are the size of a hub cap; and a request for fruit crisp yields enough dessert for a quartet of eaters. Look elsewhere if you prefer to dine in peace. During the lunch and dinner rushes, Oceanaire rocks and roars.

Lunch: M-F 11:30-5 ***Entrees:*** $8.95-$31.95
Dinner: M-TH 5-10, F-SAT 5-11, SUN 5-9 ***Entrees:*** $16.95-$50
Credit Cards: ALL MAJOR ***Reservations:*** RECOMMENDED
Dress: BUSINESS CASUAL ***Cross Street:*** 12TH
Parking: $7 VALET AT DINNER ***Metro:*** METRO CENTER

★ ★

OLD EBBITT GRILL

675 15TH ST. NW, WASHINGTION, DC (DOWNTOWN) 202-347-4800
www.ebbitt.com

SECRET SERVICE AGENTS, tourists, business types—everyone seems to end up in downtown Washington's grand Victorian-style saloon, conveniently located near the White House and dressed in dark wood, gleaming brass, antique gas chandeliers and enough green velvet and potted plants to suggest a forest. Murals of Washington in the main dining room lend a sense of place; a sunny atrium in back of this behemoth catches the inevitable overflow of people who want to eat here.

A member of the Clyde's restaurant empire, Old Ebbitt Grill is a great convenience: usually open for at least two meals a day, big enough to accommodate any size group, and offering a menu that takes into account plain and fancy tastes. And the service is as friendly as it gets: The bow-tied bartender is likely to introduce herself—and ask for your name in return.

Oyster lovers can always count on lots of choices of pristine bivalves.

The cooking ("good American food" I overheard a server explain the concept to a group of diners) is as straightforward and satisfying as the decor. Look for a decent hamburger, better fish and chips and a lobster roll that is full of its namesake—and mighty fine. Chicken wings are appropriately tangy, clam chowder appropriately hearty. If there's one thing that keeps me coming back, though, it's a raw bar of distinction: Oyster lovers can always count on lots of choices of pristine bivalves and something crisp and refreshing to knock them back with.

Breakfast: M-F 7:30-11 ***Entrees:*** $8.95-$10.95
Lunch: M-F 11-5 ***Entrees:*** $9.95-$15.95
Dinner: M-F 5-1 AM, SAT-SUN 4-1 AM ***Entrees:*** $13.95-$23.95
Brunch: SAT-SUN 8:30-4 ***Entrees:*** $9.95-$23.95
Credit Cards: ALL MAJOR ***Reservations:*** RECOMMENDED
Dress: CASUAL ***Cross Street:*** G STREET NW
Parking: COMPLIMENTARY VALET AFTER 6, ALL DAY SUN ***Metro:*** METRO CENTER

★ 1/2

OLD EUROPE

2434 WISCONSIN AVE. NW, WASHINGTON, DC (GLOVER PARK) 202-333-7600
www.old-europe.com

OLD EUROPE ON A FRIDAY NIGHT feels like Oktoberfest even in springtime, what with the tables pushed together to seat groups of beer-drinking friends and a pianist pounding out cheerful tunes.

Even at a quiet weekday lunch, there's no mistaking this room for anything but Teutonic. The air smells sweetly of pork and sauerkraut, and the walls are crammed with enough wood crests, antique steins and idyllic landscapes to outfit a small castle. It borders on a Disney-esque stereotype, except that it's just what you might find abroad.

The kitchen is determined that you won't leave hungry. Most of the appetizers are the size of light entrees, while the main courses appear to be built for two. Sauerbraten is flanked with light potato dumplings sauced with a subtle brown gravy and a nest of soft, shredded cabbage whose flavor dances from sweet to sour. Sausages of snap and savor ride to the table with crisp herbed potato pancakes and lush, caraway-scented sauerkraut. Wiener schnitzel, however, was a disappointment on my last visit, damp and bland. Acting like bookends to these hearty meals are seasonal beers and fine desserts (splurge on the decadent Sacher torte, chocolate cake punctuated with apricot filling).

The air smells sweetly of pork and sauerkraut, and the walls are crammed with enough wood crests, antique steins and idyllic landscapes to outfit a small castle.

In a field that doesn't encourage longevity, Old Europe is a grand dame with more than half a century of gemütlichkeit to its credit.

Lunch: TU-SAT 11:30-2:30, SUN 1-3:30 *Entrees:* $8.75-$11.50
Dinner: TU-TH 4-8:30, F-SAT 5-9:30, SUN 4-7:30 *Closed:* M
Credit Cards: ALL MAJOR *Reservations:* RECOMMENDED
Dress: CASUAL *Cross Street:* CALVERT
Parking: STREET *Metro:* TENLEYTOWN-AU

☆ ☆

O'LEARYS

310 THIRD ST., ANNAPOLIS, MD 410-263-0884
www.olearysseafood.com

ELSEWHERE, WAITERS TELL YOU what they like on the menu and leave it at that. At O'Learys, diners experience the results of thorough training. "The crab cakes are 16 parts crab to one part filler," my friendly server said, painting a picture that turned out to be accurate. The crab cakes in this charming seafood restaurant, with its partial views of boat masts and sea grass, are models of their kind, rich with the lead ingredient and expertly seasoned (that is, not much at all).

"The crab cakes are 16 parts crab to one part filler," my friendly server said, painting a picture that turned out to be accurate.

There are other fine ways to begin a meal: small steamed mussels in a broth infused with orange zest, or fried oysters that get a kick from fiery remoulade and tangy pickled vegetables. Entrees incorporate worldly accents, such as Thai barbecue glaze on the mahi-mahi, and black beans and rice with the grouper. Lobster is removed from its shell, simmered in butter and presented on a bed of crab-enriched risotto. "We do all the work for you!" our server said as it arrived at our table. Alas, the lobster meat was a tad soft, the risotto bland. Better: halibut dusted with cornmeal and brightened with haricots verts, corn relish and a creamy shrimp salad (this is a kitchen that pays delicious attention to its accompaniments).

Dinner: M-TH 5-10, F-SAT 5-11, SUN 5-9 ***Entrees:*** $24-$35
Credit Cards: ALL MAJOR ***Reservations:*** RECOMMENDED
Dress: BUSINESS CASUAL ***Cross Street:*** SEVERN AVENUE
Parking: LOT ***Metro:*** NO

★ ★ ½

OSTERIA DEL GALILEO

1110 21ST ST. NW, WASHINGTON, DC (DOWNTOWN) 202-293-7191
www.robertodonna.com

WHEN PEOPLE INQUIRE ABOUT GALILEO, I have to ask which space they're talking about, because chef-owner Roberto Donna now maintains three separate menus under one roof.

One is for the main dining room with its regional Italian focus. Another is for the glamorous Laboratorio with its gleaming open kitchen and extravagant tasting menu. The third is for diners who sit in his eight-table osteria next to the bar.

The last is easy on the wallet and easy to like, for it brings together comforting plates and pleasant service in a simple space that doesn't require you to dress for the occasion. There are only a few choices per course on the small menu, but what enticing choices! Shaved veal with tuna sauce is sublime. So is the baby roast chicken. Pastas taste home-made because they are (ricotta dumplings are a favorite) and the meat dishes seem to be channeled from the kitchen of an Italian grandmother (pork sausage is as lusty as it comes).

Pastas taste home-made because they are (ricotta dumplings are a favorite).

Continue with what's casual for dessert: Tonight's cannoli is worth tomorrow's reprimand from your trainer.

Dinner: TU-SAT 5:30-10 ***Entrees:*** $8-$10
Closed: SUN-M ***Credit Cards:*** AE, D, MC, V ***Reservations:*** NO
Dress: CASUAL ***Cross Street:*** L STREET NW
Parking: $6 VALET TU-SAT ***Metro:*** FARRAGUT NORTH

★ ★ ½

OVAL ROOM

800 CONNECTICUT AVE. NW, WASHINGTON, DC (DOWNTOWN) 202-463-8700
www.ovalroom.com

ITS PROXIMITY TO THE WHITE HOUSE and media outlets means there's always something, or someone, to liven a meal at the Oval Room, where Condi Rice and Brit Hume are known to refuel between foreign trips and TV appearances.

The two dining rooms, set off with celery-colored walls and splashy modern art, are designed for comfort. Velvet-covered banquettes make it easy to sit through a business discussion and the prime tables along the front windows allow their occupants to see and be seen but not overheard.

Meat-eaters are acknowledged with a tasty veal chop scattered with fleshy mushrooms.

Wisely, chef Paul Luna offers a tapaslike menu of small plates to start and many entrees in half portions, and his food is interesting but never over-the-top. Thus bite-size spring rolls are filled with ribbons of steak and garlic-perfumed seafood soup takes on a Brazilian accent. Meat-eaters are acknowledged with a tasty veal chop scattered with fleshy mushrooms, while vegetarians can content themselves with hats of pasta stuffed with minced roasted vegetables, dusted with shaved Parmesan and lapped with a delicate curry sauce.

Feeling adventurous? Grouper swaddled in crisp ribbons of plantain is a delicious destination. Looking for something sweet? Luna's free-form tiramisu, potent with espresso and rum, delivers a lovely twist on tradition.

Lunch: M-F 11:30-3 P.M. ***Entrees:*** $13-$28
Dinner: M-SAT 5-10:30 ***Entrees:*** $14-$28
Closed: SUN ***Credit Cards:*** ALL MAJOR ***Reservations:*** RECOMMENDED
Dress: BUSINESS CASUAL ***Cross Street:*** H STREET NW
Parking: COMPLIMENTARY VALET AT DINNER ***Metro:*** FARRAGUT WEST

Critic's Pick
★ ★ ½

OYAMEL COCINA MEXICANA

2250-B CRYSTAL DR., ARLINGTON, VA 703-413-2288
www.oyamel.com

EVERYWHERE YOU LOOK there's something to catch the eye in this sprawling, orange-and-gold ode to Mexican cooking: cooks patting out tortillas in the open kitchen, smartly fronted with counter seats; a swirl of tin butterflies floating before a panel of light blue "sky"; fanciful animal masks on the wall and a long communal table flanked by scooped cowhide seats.

Similarly, everywhere you look on the menu—designed by star chef Jose Andres of Cafe Atlantico, Jaleo, minibar and Zaytinya acclaim—there's something you simply have to try. Tacos, stuffed with such luscious fillings as baby pig, halibut or shredded duck with pineapple. Soups, brimming with the likes of hominy and spicy pork. Seviches sparkle, and you'll be missing out on some fun if you don't knock back a sassy margarita with one or more of the kitchen's many Mexican snacks, or antojitos.

Seviches sparkle, and you'll be missing out on some fun if you don't knock back a sassy margarita.

On the other hand, chicken with mole poblano is best for its mysterious sauce; the chicken is dull and dry. Come brunch, be sure to save room for some churros, donutlike twists sprinkled with cinnamon and served piping hot with a cup of rich hot chocolate. Dessert doesn't get any better.

Lunch: TU-F 11:30-4 ***Entrees:*** $5.50-$14.95
Dinner: SUN, TU-W 4-10, TH-SAT 4-11 ***Entrees:*** $4.95-$18.95
Brunch: SAT-SUN 11:30-4 ***Entrees:*** $4.95-$10
Closed: M ***Credit Cards:*** ALL MAJOR ***Reservations:*** RECOMMENDED
Dress: CASUAL ***Cross Street:*** 23RD
Parking: FREE PARKING AFTER 4 IN GARAGE NEXT TO RESTAURANT ***Metro:*** CRYSTAL CITY

Critic's Pick

★ ★ ★

PALENA

3529 CONNECTICUT AVE. NW, WASHINGTON, DC (CLEVELAND PARK) 202-537-9250
www.palenarestaurant.com

ORDER A "SUMMER SALAD" and that's precisely what you get. Yet, like everything that's served here, the dish bears the distinctive stamp of chef Frank Ruta: exquisite ingredients (in this example, lime-tickled fresh beans, shaved truffles, a slice of house-smoked ham, genuine mozzarella di buffalo) arranged as a lush still-life.

Unlike a lot of other star chefs, Ruta delights his audiences with subtlety, letting the ingredients get all the credit for his understated yet masterly performances. His gnocchi, fashioned from Yukon Gold potatoes, are tender as can be, and scattered with tiny, slightly nutty-tasting Japanese mushrooms and crumbled (and rarely seen) Castelmagno cheese for enhancement. An entree of veal arrives as a choice chop and luscious loin, handsomely sauced and accessorized with glazed baby fennel, carrots and onions.

The room, with its flickering votives and soothing colors, is much like the cooking—at once relaxed and delightful—and the staff sees to your needs as if you were the only person that mattered. From the bar come classic cocktails and from Ann Amernick come desserts that make you wish she still ran a bakery.

Ruta delights his audiences with subtlety, letting the ingredients get all the credit for his understated yet masterly performances.

During my most recent visit, Diana Krall was singing "Embraceable You" while I was eating. She could have been serenading the chef.

Dinner: CAFE M-SAT 5:30-10, DINING ROOM TU-SAT 5:30-10 ***Cafe Entrees:*** $10-$14
Dining Room: 3-COURSE PRIX FIXE $57; 4-COURSE $64; 5-COURSE $71
Closed: SUN ***Credit Cards:*** AE, D MC, V ***Reservations:*** DINING ROOM ONLY
Dress: CASUAL ***Cross Street:*** PORTER
Parking: STREET ***Metro:*** CLEVELAND PARK

★ ★

THE PALM

1225 19TH ST. NW, WASHINGTON, DC (DUPONT CIRCLE) 202-293-9091
www.thepalm.com

WHEN IT COMES TO FRESH GOSSIP and newsworthy names, no steakhouse in town can compete with the Palm. Day and night, the place swells with movers and shakers, some of whose likenesses are caricatured on the walls. Women are welcome, but the Palm is really a guy's place, back-slappingly boisterous and watched over by hosts who look as if they've seen it all and servers who play the roles of confidants.

After a chopped salad perked up with anchovies or a bowl of lobster bisque with enough cream to sink a ship, meat is the way to go, naturally: The rib-eye is thick and succulent, lamb chops come three plump models per order, and the New York strip tastes prime and aged because it is. Further, all the meat is cooked just the way you want it (not so the cottage fries, which might show up with an unfortunate bronze rather than a golden tan). Shrimp cocktail is standard issue, creamed spinach actually tastes of its vegetable, and the Key lime pie is too big and too sweet to finish.

The rib-eye is thick and succulent, lamb chops come three plump models per order, and the New York strip tastes prime and aged because it is.

The Palm isn't a wise choice for a romantic rendezvous: Its hardwood floors and pressed-tin ceiling trap the noise and make conversation difficult, particularly at prime time. But you'll feel like an insider when you look up from a great piece of meat to catch James Carville or Wolf Blitzer strolling in.

Lunch: M-F 11:45-3 ***Entrees:*** $10-$20
Dinner: M-F 3-10, SAT 6-10, SUN 5:30-9 ***Entrees:*** $17.50-$39
Credit Cards: ALL MAJOR ***Reservations:*** RECOMMENDED
Dress: CASUAL ***Cross Street:*** N STREET NW
Parking: COMPLIMENTARY VALET AT DINNER ***Metro:*** DUPONT CIRCLE
Second Location: 1750 TYSONS BLVD., MCLEAN, VA, 703-917-0200

★ ★

PATOWMACK FARM

42461 LOVETTSVILLE RD., LOVETTSVILLE, VA 540-822-9017
www.patowmackfarm.com

Beverly Morton Billand bought this 40-acre farm in northern Loudon County 20 years ago, hoping to grow and sell herbs for a living, but she quickly learned she had to do more to survive. So she started offering farm tours, and making and selling jams, vinegars and other food products. In the early years, she served dinner to up to 20 guests in a barn on the property; between entree and dessert, customers were taken on hayrides. "But fine dining was always my goal," Morton Billand says. The business grew over the years to include a gazebo and a new kitchen. Most recently, she opened a glass conservatory.

No two visits to Patowmack Farm are alike, since the food changes every week.

"The concept is farm-to-table," Morton Billand tells her visitors. Thus the multicourse menus incorporate lettuces from her garden and eggs from the 100 or so chickens that roost nearby. Wherever possible, the farm is used as a pantry.

No two visits to Patowmack Farm are alike, since the food changes every week. Thursdays and Fridays diners get to choose from a five- or seven-course tasting menu; Saturday nights the game plan is five courses, only one of which involves making a decision (there are three entree options). On Sunday, brunch is served.

Chances are, you'll start off on a high note. One cool spring night commenced with a "soup and sandwich," translated here as a creamy elixir of duck broth and onions with an island of crisp, goat-cheese-slathered toast floating in its center. Highlights from meals past have included grilled hanger steak flanked with vegetable-stuffed brown rice crepes and lapped with a truffle-fragrant butter sauce; salmon coated in sesame seeds and partnered with Asian-style summer rolls; and herby and moist roast Cornish game hen positioned on luscious creamy leeks.

The scenery is so enchanting, the sounds are so lulling—Hear the geese in the background? The train?—that it's tempting to overlook Patowmack Farm's flaws, like oversweetened sauces and oversalted entrees. But the thoughtful details add up: Menus bear the names of reservation holders and special requests ("One of the guests is a vegetarian") made in advance are honored without hesitation.

Dinner: TH-F SEATINGS 6:30-8, SAT SEATINGS AT 7
Tasting Menus: TH-F 5-COURSE $35, 7-COURSE $49 SAT 5-COURSE $70
Brunch: SUN 11-3 ***Price:*** $35
Closed: M-W ***Credit Cards:*** MC, V ***Reservations:*** REQUIRED
Dress: BUSINESS CASUAL ***Cross Street:*** ROUTE 15
Parking: LOT ***Metro:*** NO

Critic's Pick

★ ★ ★

PAZO

1425 ALICEANNA ST., BALTIMORE, MD 410-534-7296
www.pazorestaurant.com

OUTSIDE THE RESTAURANT on a Saturday night, there hangs a velvet rope and a couple of big guys with earphones.

Inside, you begin to understand why those props at the door might be necessary. Flocks of people are eating and drinking on multiple levels, some on the ground floor in tented nooks, others at balcony tables that overlook the happy congestion below. The center of the sprawling room contains enough sofas to stock a Pottery Barn; in the distance, an exhibition kitchen seems to stretch an entire block.

Riding a trend that is destined to be with us for a while, Pazo ("grand house" in the Catalan language) emphasizes Mediterranean-style tapas meant to be shared. Do not start yawning. Three or four of these small plates per person mean a crowded table, a delectable feast—and lots of contenders for seats.

Empanadas stuffed with ground pork and veal vanish within moments of landing on the table.

Meals are culled from categories including "sea," "land" and the vegetable-driven "field"—surf, turf and more turf—and choosing isn't easy, since there are well over 50 selections. Fritto misto is a collection of lightly fried calamari and shrimp, served piping hot but cooled down after a dip in the accompanying aioli. A thin slice of swordfish gets a saline lift from olives, a breezy lilt from fresh basil and some sweet, juicy punctuation from orange.

There are plenty of delicious discoveries on "land," too. Empanadas stuffed with ground pork and veal vanish within moments of landing on the table, as do braised veal cheeks, scattered with crisp pumpkin seeds and resting on pumpkin puree zipped up with sherry and garlic. Vegetarians will be pleased to see more than a dozen dishes celebrating ingredients from the "field," though even carnivores may find themselves ordering the glossy, garlicky sauteed spinach or the powerfully smoky eggplant dip. And one of the best dishes on the whole menu is goat cheese pasta with fresh-tasting arugula pesto.

Dinner: SUN-W 5-10, TH-SAT 5-1 AM ***Entrees:*** $12-$36 ***Tapas:*** $4-$12
Credit Cards: AE, D, MC, V ***Reservations:*** RECOMMENDED
Dress: BUSINESS CASUAL ***Cross Street:*** S. CAROLINE
Parking: COMPLIMENTARY VALET ***Metro:*** NO

Critic's Pick
☆☆ ½

PESCE

2016 P ST. NW, WASHINGTON, DC (DUPONT CIRCLE) 202-466-3474
www.pescebistro.com

CHEFS COME AND GO HERE, yet no matter who's in the kitchen, the mission is always the same: sparkling seafood, as befits the restaurant's straightforward Italian name.

Owner Regine Palladin, a frequent and graceful presence in the small dining room, wouldn't have it any other way. Pesce's menu, which changes daily, is written on a chalkboard and always poses some difficult choices. Will it be smoked trout and fusilli tossed with sweet peas and a light goat cheese sauce, or whole branzino, its sweet flesh countered by diced zucchini and juicy little tomatoes? Both are simple and both delicious.

Look for things that aren't exactly mainstream; your reward might be the likes of tilefish, utterly moist beneath a crumb coat and teamed with buttery pureed potatoes, thin green beans and a glossy red wine sauce. And count on finding here such seasonal treats as shad and soft-shell crabs, nice wines by the glass with which to savor them and service that is casual yet informed.

Pesce's menu, which changes daily, is written on a chalkboard and always poses some difficult choices.

Desserts sometimes taste like an afterthought, and the room, walled in bricks and glass windows, can be noisy. But those drawbacks are small in light of all the good catches.

Lunch: M-F 11:30-2:30 ***Entrees:*** $12.95-$17.95
Dinner: M-TH 5:30-10, F-SAT 5:30-10:30, SUN 5-9:30 ***Entrees:*** $19.95-$24.95
Credit Cards: ALL MAJOR ***Reservations:*** RECOMMENDED
Dress: CASUAL ***Cross Street:*** 21ST ***Parking:*** $5 VALET AT DINNER ***Metro:*** DUPONT CIRCLE

☆ ☆

PIZZERIA PARADISO

3282 M ST. NW, WASHINGTON, DC (GEORGETOWN) 202-337-1245
www.eatyourpizza.com

JUST WALKING INTO THE BIG GEORGETOWN BRANCH of the small Dupont Circle original puts a smile on my face. Brick walls, wood floors, a warm greeting at the door and a sunburst painted on the restaurant's pizza oven will do that.

Start with a glass of Italian wine, continue with a flossy salad and take a cue from the wood-fired oven in the rear when ordering your main course: The pies here are flavorsome from slow rising, and their crusts come scattered with fine ingredients. Potatoes, pesto and Parmesan decorate the "Genovese," while tomato, salami, olives and hot pepper flakes lend some oomph to the "Atomica." The panini are less successful. Roast pork hiding in a dull roll is a snooze of a sandwich, though I like the pickled carrots that accompany it.

Start with a glass of Italian wine, continue with a flossy salad and take a cue from the wood-fired oven in the rear when ordering your main course.

The staff runs young and cheerful; desserts embrace marsala-splashed baked pears and good gelato in such flavors as banana and pineapple-coconut. Hosting a party? Paradiso's low-ceilinged private dining room beckons downstairs. Looking for a deal on dinner? "Two for Tuesday" includes an appetizer, large pizza, a bottle of wine and a dessert sampler for $50 per couple.

Open: M-TH 11:30-11, F-SAT 11:30-MIDNIGHT, SUN NOON-10 ***Entrees:*** $8.95-$16.95
Credit Cards: D, DC, MC, V ***Reservations:*** NO
Dress: CASUAL ***Cross Street:*** POTOMAC
Parking: STREET ***Metro:*** FOGGY BOTTOM-GWU
Second Location: 2029 P ST. NW, WASHINGTON, DC, 202-223-1245

★ ★ ½

POSTE

555 EIGHTH ST. NW, WASHINGTON, DC (PENN QUARTER) 202-783-6060
www.postebrasserie.com

A FINE WARM-UP ACT to a concert at the nearby MCI Center or a play at the Shakespeare Theatre is dinner at Poste.

Housed in the Hotel Monaco, the high-ceilinged dining room always has a nice glow, a happy buzz, and from the exhibition kitchen come dishes that dare to be a little different. Garlicky snails don little caps of pastry and an arugula salad appears as a perfect hedge, breezy with mint and sweetened with figs.

Housed in the Hotel Monaco, the high-ceilinged dining room always has a nice glow, a happy buzz.

In winter, there might be roseate venison paired with Brussels sprouts, while spring can find herb-paved cod served with a tiny skillet of boulanger potatoes. Like strong performances, desserts like apple and quince tarte Tatin or a trio of tiny custards keep you in your seats.

Breakfast: M-F 7-10 ***Entrees:*** $7-$13
Lunch: M-F 11:30-2:30 ***Entrees:*** $10-$18
Dinner: M-TH 5-10, F-SAT 5-10:30, SUN 5-9 ***Entrees:*** $16-$28 ***Tasting Menu:*** $55
Pre-Theater: DAILY 5-7 3-COURSE PRIX FIXE $30.05
Brunch: SAT-SUN 9-2 ***Entrees:*** $10-$22
Credit Cards: ALL MAJOR ***Reservations:*** RECOMMENDED
Dress: CASUAL ***Cross Street:*** F STREET NW
Parking: STREET ***Metro:*** GALLERY PLACE-CHINATOWN

★ ★

PRIME RIB

2020 K STREET NW, WASHINGTON, DC (DOWNTOWN) 202-466-8811
www.theprimerib.com

ITS LOYAL CLIENTELE knows the Prime Rib as more than just a restaurant. Set off with Louis Icart lithographs of scantily clad women on gilt-edged black walls, the Prime Rib is a ritual, an event, a celebration of a time when real men didn't know what quiche was, let alone eat it. There are no female servers in evidence, but there is a dress code: "Jackets and ties are requested for gentlemen," callers are informed when they make reservations.

Take the place at its word and indulge in its signature attraction. The prime rib is as thick as the White Pages and as rosy as you request. Bursting with juices, the meat is served with a heap of horseradish for a bit of electricity. No other protein on the menu—not the veal chop, not the rack of lamb or the New York strip steak—can match the prime rib for savor. Of the fish dishes, rockfish is simply broiled and served with lemon.

No other protein on the menu—not the veal chop, not the rack of lamb or the New York strip steak—can match the prime rib for savor.

The appetizers embrace the usual steakhouse staples. Fat shrimp drape over the rim of a cocktail glass, poised to take a dip in a sinus-clearing cocktail sauce. Caesar salad comes out punching with a tangy dressing. The best of the beginnings are also the richest: creamy crab cakes and velvety lobster bisque. As for side dishes, the creamed spinach outshines steak fries that taste as if they originated in a factory rather than a field.

The Prime Rib refers to itself as "the civilized steak house," a promise it frequently delivers. But not always. Unless you are a known commodity, the greeting at the door can be gruff and the waiters tend to go through the motions of serving. And the china and wine glasses look as if they were rescued from a garage sale. For $100 a head, one expects more pampering and polish.

Even at its off moments, though, the Prime Rib has the competition beat as far as comfort is concerned, from the leather chairs to the live piano, even at lunch. There are more delicious places to go for a classic steak experience, but none are as steeped in tradition as this address.

Lunch: M-F 11:30-3 ***Entrees:*** $10-$26 ***Dinner:*** M-TH 5-11, F-SAT 5-11:30 ***Entrees:*** $19.95-$42.95
Closed: SUN ***Credit Cards:*** AE, DC, MC, V ***Reservations:*** RECOMMENDED
Dress: JACKET & TIE ***Cross Street:*** 20TH
Parking: COMPLIMENTARY VALET AT LUNCH (12:15-2:15) AND DINNER (7-10:30) ***Metro:*** FARRAGUT WEST
Second Location: 1101 N. CALVERT ST., BALTIMORE, MD, 410-539-1804

☆ ☆

RAKU

7240 WOODMONT AVE., BETHESDA, MD
301-718-8680

I'M OFTEN TEMPTED to ask for "one of everything, please" at this stylish pan-Asian retreat in the middle of one of Bethesda's jam-packed restaurant rows.

Oh, the plain sushi and dumplings are fine here, but the kitchen gives me some delicious reasons to walk on the wild side. Take the "Seoul Train Roll," its raw tuna center made crunchy with kimchi, or steamed pork and seafood dumplings whose wasabi-tinted wrappers scorch the tongue. Toro (fatty tuna) tartare bound in sliced cucumber, a special, is overwhelmed by too much sauce, but I like the idea of a tasting of three different kinds of yellowtail, another special, and the chance to experience it with fresh wasabi ($3 extra, and worth the splurge). Don't overlook the entrees, which include a lovely plate of sliced duck with tart cherries, crisp spaetzle and a little bacon-laced cabbage (a hit of ginger in its sauce is a reminder you're not eating in a German restaurant).

The setting—festive with colorful parasols overhead and bamboo on the walls—is as much fun as the food, and the staff couldn't be more accommodating.

The setting—festive with colorful parasols overhead and bamboo on the walls—is as much fun as the food, and the staff couldn't be more accommodating. When one of my pals jumps up from a booth to add money to a meter out front, the host stops him at the door: "Relax, you're eating dinner. I'll take care of it." Then he does.

Lunch: M-F 11:30-2:30, SAT-SUN NOON-3 *Entrees:* $7.25-$17.50
Dinner: SUN-TH 5-10, F-SAT 5-10:30 *Entrees:* $8.25-$24
Credit Cards: AE, MC, V *Reservations:* RECOMMENDED
Dress: CASUAL *Cross Street:* BETHESDA AVENUE
Parking: STREET *Metro:* BETHESDA
Second Location: 1900 Q ST. NW, WASHINGTON, DC, 202-265-7258

Critic's Pick

★ ★ 1/2

RAY'S THE STEAKS

1725 WILSON BLVD., ARLINGTON, VA
703-841-7297

WHAT THIS LOUD AND UNDERDRESSED Arlington steakhouse lacks in comfort and decor is more than made up for in beef of distinction. Owner Michael Landrum—he's the tall dude in the chef's whites watching over the host stand—competes with the big boys downtown with great cuts of meat that are judiciously seasoned and expertly grilled.

Take your pick from the New York strip steak lapped with brandy-laced mushroom sauce, prime rib spiked with Cajun seasonings or (my favorite) the very French onglet—ropy hanger steak oozing juices at every touch of a fork. Those and other slabs of protein are accompanied by little skillets of garlicky spinach and luscious, skin-on whipped potatoes; unlike at the competition, these sides are part of the cost of the entree rather than priced à la carte. And, unlike at other steakhouses, this one is low-key, which means you and your server can wear jeans.

Unlike at other steakhouses, this one is low-key, which means you and your server can wear jeans.

Dinner begins with spiced nuts and ends with peanut buttery fudge with the check. Sweet. The walls are bare and the tables are tightly packed, but guess what? There's a line out the door anyway.

Dinner: M-F 6-10:30, SAT 5-11, SUN 5-8:30 ***Entrees:*** $14.95-$31.95
Credit Cards: ALL MAJOR ***Reservations:*** REQUIRED
Dress: CASUAL ***Cross Street:*** RHODES ***Parking:*** LOT ***Metro:*** ROSSLYN

★ ★

REGENT THAI CUISINE

1910 18TH ST. NW, WASHINGTON, DC (DUPONT CIRCLE) 202-232-1781,1782
www.regentthai.com

THE LOUD SIZZLE preceding the arrival of my beef entree, neua krata, seems out of place in the context of the serene Regent Thai Cuisine, where the only other sounds on a slow weeknight have been gentle background music and the tinkle-tinkle of a nearby fountain. The dish sputters like beef fajitas but smells sweetly of Asian spices. A jumble of thin slices of marinated beef, snow peas and other vegetables strewn with sesame seeds, it is one of several signature dishes that set this Thai restaurant apart from the crowd. It's tasty, if a bit more expensive than what you tend to find at your typical issuer of papaya salad and drunken noodles.

The Regent is also prettier than much of its competition. There are two high-ceilinged rooms, and both give you a sense of being far away from Washington. A small forest of handsome wood carvings and moss green walls wrap visitors in style and comfort, and the blocky teak chairs and tables underscore the Thai theme.

Of the signature dishes, the standout is grilled whole trout. The fish is moist, meaty and—thanks to slices of lemon and lime as well as lemon grass tucked inside—also fragrant and flavorful. Presented on banana leaf, it's enhanced by a sharp dipping sauce fueled by garlic, lime juice and chilies.

Of the signature dishes, the standout is grilled whole trout.

Pork-and-seafood dumplings are too compact, and duck is limp and cloying with its honey sauce and dry watercress. Now and then, the kitchen also oversweetens things. But the winners outnumber the lesser choices. Ordering basil fried rice, for instance, brings a glistening mound of fragrant grains stir-fried with the namesake herb, strips of red pepper, a blazing chili sauce and a choice of meat or seafood. Drunken noodles here are thick, slippery and pleasantly smoky ribbons, punched up with a similar sauce and best ordered with tender scored squid. And everything brims with style: Your check is delivered in a sleek wood box rather than on the usual plastic tray.

Lunch: M-F 11:30-3, SAT NOON-3 ***Entrees:*** $7.95 TO $19.95
Dinner: M-TH 5-10, F-SAT 5-11, SUN 5-10 ***Entrees:*** $10.95 TO $19.95
Credit Cards: AE, MC, V ***Reservations:*** RECOMMENDED
Dress: CASUAL ***Cross Street:*** FLORIDA AVENUE NW
Parking: STREET ***Metro:*** DUPONT CIRCLE

Critic's Pick

★ ★ ★ ½

RESTAURANT EVE

110 S. PITT ST., ALEXANDRIA, VA 703-706-0450
www.restauranteve.com

EATING IN THE SERENE TASTING ROOM at Eve reminds me of dining in a garden. Pictures of fruits and vegetables on the walls set the scene, while the food that comes from the kitchen gives life to the al fresco fantasy.

If there are great tomatoes nearby, chef Cathal Armstrong finds them, and tucks them into a paper-thin pastry shell with biting Roquefort, infant basil and a vinaigrette of Sauternes. And if there's a humble ingredient that needs an ego boost, the Irish-born chef is just the guy for the job. Tripe is not something diners expect to find on the menu of a luxury restaurant, but tasting Armstrong's version—slowly braised in veal stock with citrus zest, arranged with housemade lamb sausage and scattered with chopped aromatics—makes a convincing case for the fit.

The chef's seasonally inspired tasting menus (take your pick from five or nine courses) are filled with pleasures great and small. Picture escolar, poached in olive oil, then sliced into bands and made haunting with a vinaigrette of smoked ham. Or lemon-kissed custard cake lavished with the sweetest blueberries ever.

The chef's seasonally inspired tasting menus (take your pick from five or nine courses) are filled with pleasures great and small.

This luscious food is delivered by gracious and intelligent servers and accompanied by fine wines and cocktails that raise the bar: Eve goes to the trouble of making its own tonic for its gin and tonic.

Lunch: M-F 11:30-2:30 ***Entrees:*** $14-$20
Dinner: M-SAT 5:30-10 ***Entrees:*** $25-$35, 5-COURSE PRIX FIXE MENU $75, 9-COURSE PRIX FIXE $98
Closed: SUN ***Credit Cards:*** ALL MAJOR ***Reservations:*** RECOMMENDED
Dress: BUSINESS CASUAL ***Cross Street:*** KING
Parking: STREET ***Metro:*** KING STREET

★ ★

ROCK CREEK

4917 ELM ST., BETHESDA, MD
301-907-7625

THE POTATO CHIPS that flank Fred Przyborowski's lean but tasty buffalo burger are not fried, they're sprayed with olive oil and baked. The chef's chocolate cake substitutes sour cream for butter. And once a week he meets with a nutritionist to make sure each entree has no more than 500 calories, preferably fewer.

"It's a totally different way of cooking," says the cutter of calories and the shaver of sugar.

It's also a totally different way of eating. Rock Creek opened in a former deli with the mission of serving food that is good for you, and tasty to boot.

The menu at Rock Creek opens like a regular list, with "small plates" (appetizers) followed by main courses. Flip the paper over, though, and you'll get a nutritional breakdown of each dish. Calorie counts, fat counts, sodium and fiber measures—it's plenty of information to help you make the decision that's right for you, and it reveals a few unexpected facts: At 530 calories, the vegetable sandwich weighs in heavier than that buffalo burger. (Pesto sauce is to blame, says the chef.)

The chef's lobster "bisque" tastes richly of the sea, with choice bites of lobster bobbing in a brick-colored liquid.

The biggest surprise, however, is how satisfying some of the food is, even if you're not trying to eat lighter or smarter. The chef's lobster "bisque" tastes richly of the sea, with choice bites of lobster bobbing in a brick-colored liquid; the trademark "creaminess" comes not from a dairy product but from pureed Yukon Gold potatoes and Basmati rice. Przyborowski's Mediterranean sampler would look very much at home at one of the area's mezze purveyors. Glossy stuffed grape leaves, garlicky hummus, some olives and a fluffy, herby tabbouleh make for delightful grazing.

Pasta heaped with broccoli rabe, mushrooms and tomato, though, is punishingly bland. Indeed, the presentation reminded me that what I was eating was supposed to be good for me. Who wants the visual lecture?

The brightest note in the last course is roasted pineapple served with a scoop of tangy yogurt sorbet and a sail of dried pineapple. This finale is refreshing, attractive and something you'd be inclined to come back for—whether or not you care that it's a mere 140 calories.

Lunch: M-F 11:30-2:30 *Entrees:* $7-$16 *Dinner:* M-TH 5-10, F-SAT 5-11, SUN 5-9 *Entrees:* $7-$27
Credit Cards: AE, MC, V *Reservations:* RECOMMENDED
Dress: BUSINESS CASUAL *Cross Street:* WOODMONT AVENUE
Parking: $5 VALET F-SAT AT DINNER *Metro:* BETHESDA

★ 1/2

ROSA MEXICANO

575 SEVENTH ST. NW, WASHINGTON, DC (PENN QUARTER) 202-783-5522
www.rosamexicano.com

THIS SPRAWLING MEXICAN RESTAURANT is all broad windows and soaring ceiling, a vast stage set pulsing in red, yellow and tangerine. On the rear wall, a thin curtain of water (sometimes) flows over about a million blue tiles, with a summer's worth of beautiful faux butterflies floating above the water's surface. Behind the bar, hundreds of rose petals are displayed within illuminated panels.

"Have a margarita!" the scene practically cries out. Just make sure it's a "clasica" shaken with Cointreau, lime juice and Herradura Silver tequila rather than the signature pomegranate version, which goes down like a vaguely alcoholic Slurpee. Waiters in handsome embroidered shirts brush by with lava-stone bowls full of bright guacamole or bubbling queso fundido, the warm white cheese scattered with poblano peppers and a crumble of chorizo.

Alas, your chance of eating well is 50-50. The same kitchen that welcomes its audience with a hearty soup of tender chicken and tortilla matchsticks—the familiar sopa de tortilla—and terrific beef short ribs with velvety peppers also serves muted seviche, too-tame lamb shanks and third-class desserts. At too many meals, Rosa Mexicano amounts to shiny packaging for middling food.

"Have a margarita!" the scene practically cries out. Just make sure it's a "clasica."

Lunch: M-F 11:30-3 ***Entrees:*** $9-$20
Dinner: M-TH 5-10:30, F-SAT 5-11:30, SUN 5-10 ***Entrees:*** $17-$26
Brunch: SAT-SUN NOON-3 ***Entrees:*** $9-$20
Credit Cards: ALL MAJOR ***Reservations:*** RECOMMENDED
Dress: CASUAL ***Cross Street:*** F STREET NW
Parking: $15 VALET AT DINNER ***Metro:*** GALLERY PLACE

★ ★ ★

SAKOONTRA

12300-C PRICE CLUB PLAZA, FAIRFAX, VA 703-818-8886
www.sakoontra.com

A LIFE-SIZE THAI TAXI in the foyer and walls splashed in blues and purples might pull you into one of Sakoontra's many seats, but it's the vivid cooking that will keep you transfixed.

Hot-and-sour lemon grass soup lives up to its description, and its many vegetables taste bright and fresh. Saucer-size shrimp cakes are nicely springy, their red curry seasoning balanced by a sweet sidekick of cucumbers and crushed peanuts. Slices of grilled beef, pink and crisp-edged, get tossed with red onions, herbs and brassy lime dressing for a steak salad to remember.

As the food shows up, always fast and graciously, the table takes on the appearance of a mouthwatering photo spread. There might be a pretty yellow mound of fried rice, veined with cashews, raisins, pineapple and diced ham, each spoonful redolent of curry. Or pearly stir-fried shrimp, shimmering in their coats of honey and balanced with pepper and garlic.

As the food shows up, always fast and graciously, the table takes on the appearance of a mouthwatering photo spread.

The person responsible for all this enticing food? Vilai Chivavibul. Most chefs of note in Thailand are women, and Sakoontra honors this tradition.

Lunch: DAILY 11:30-3 ***Entrees:*** $5.95-$14.95
Dinner: DAILY 3-9:30 ***Entrees:*** $6.95-$14.95
Credit Cards: AE, MC, DC, V ***Reservations:*** RECOMMENDED
Dress: CASUAL ***Cross Street:*** WEST OX ROAD
Parking: LOT ***Metro:*** NO

Critic's Pick

★ ★ ½

SAMANTHA'S

631 E. UNIVERSITY BLVD., SILVER SPRING, MD
301-445-7300

PARENTS WEARY OF ENCOUNTERING SIGHS when they walk into restaurants with kids in tow need to get acquainted with the family-run Samantha's: The staff actually smiles when this demographic shows up, quickly rearranging tables to accommodate whatever number of diners it is. (The restaurant's white napkins also make excellent diversions. One early evening, I spotted no fewer than three families playing peekaboo with their littlest diners.)

The menu, a mix of Mexican and Salvadoran flavors, proves long and enticing. Fried green plantains draped with mild white cheese, chicken-stuffed tamales and chicken soup with a small garden of vegetables all make great introductions. And take your server's advice when she steers you to her favorite beef dish or a daily fish special. The payoff might be one of the best skirt steaks (carne asada) you've ever cut into, or flounder stuffed with fresh spinach, both entrees made more memorable with lusty black beans and oiled white rice.

Fried green plantains draped with mild white cheese, chicken-stuffed tamales and chicken soup with a small garden of vegetables all make great introductions.

The portions are huge, but order dessert anyway. The flan is as soothing as a call from Mom, the tres leches cake ultramoist—and quick to disappear.

Open: SUN-TH 11-11, F-SAT 11-MIDNIGHT ***Entrees:*** $6.95-$23.95
Credit Cards: ALL MAJOR ***Reservations:*** NO
Dress: CASUAL ***Cross Street:*** PINEY BRANCH ROAD
Parking: LOT ***Metro:*** SILVER SPRING

☆ ☆

SETTE OSTERIA

1666 CONNECTICUT AVE. NW, WASHINGTON, DC (DUPONT CIRCLE) 202-483-3070
www.setteosteria.com

ON A MONDAY NIGHT, Sette Osteria jumps as if it were Saturday, with every table taken, and drinkers standing two and three deep at the bar. Sette's bare wood tables and hard tile floors, mixed with conversation and music, make for a lot of noise, but the restaurant feels like an event you want in on—not unlike Cafe Milano, the glamorous Georgetown restaurant from which this trattoria sprang. Sette (pronounced set-tay) means seven in Italian, and it's a number that creator and co-owner Franco Nuschese considers a lucky one.

The wood-fired pizza oven catches your eye right from the door, and its output is well worth investigating. The yeasty base of the pizza falls somewhere between thick and thin; the crust offers chew and character, thanks to skilled shaping, semolina on the bottom and a trace of soot that reminds you the pies are baked near an actual fire. The toppings (I'm partial to the four cheeses, and the more forceful combination of pork sausage, chili peppers and broccoli rabe) are doled out Italian style—that is, with a light hand—and underscore the kitchen's knack for finding good ingredients.

Sette (pronounced set-tay) means seven in Italian, and it's a number that creator and co-owner Franco Nuschese considers a lucky one.

Pasta is less consistent. At its best, Sette dishes out very good spaghetti scattered with shrimp, scallops and squid, and moistened with a light garlicky broth. But there can be flops, too, such as agnolotti stuffed with rabbit and served with a heavy quilt of pesto. Of the meat dishes, braciola is divine. Thin slices of beef are bundled with parsley and Parmesan, marinated in herbs and red wine, slowly cooked in tomato sauce, then presented with fingers of soft potato and verdant broccoli rabe.

Sette's street-corner location gives it a couple of advantages over the competition, including wide windows that allow you to people-watch from either side of the glass and a sidewalk patio to accommodate the crowd as the weather permits. Thoughtful little details abound, such as colorful pillows to soften the hard seats and wines poured by the half-glass as well as the standard six ounces.

Lunch: DAILY 11:30-4 *Entrees:* $9-$13
Dinner: SUN-TH 4-MIDNIGHT, F-SAT 4-1 *Entrees:* $10-$15
Brunch: SUN 11-3 *Entrees:* $10-$14
Credit Cards: ALL MAJOR *Reservations:* NO
Dress: CASUAL *Cross Street:* R STREET NW
Parking: STREET *Metro:* DUPONT CIRCLE

Critic's Pick

★ ★ ★

1789

1226 36TH ST. NW, WASHINGTON, DC (GEORGETOWN) 202-965-1789
www.1789restaurant.com

THE ONLY SURPRISE at this 1962-vintage Georgetown address is how delicious it remains after all these decades.

With her all-American crab cakes and rack of lamb, chef Ris Lacoste keeps long-time patrons happy with food that is familiar but never dull; the crab cakes get a nice assist from lemon-thyme aioli, while the lamb nods to modern tastes with feta-laced potatoes. And with her sublime grilled pork and Copper River King salmon, she makes food fashionistas feel at home; the former takes on a Southwestern accent with black beans and salsa, the latter (a late spring treat) sports a delicate crust of Parmesan and brioche crumbs.

Crab cakes get a nice assist from lemon-thyme aioli, while the lamb nods to modern tastes with feta-laced potatoes.

Waiters in white jackets and an enforced dress code—gentlemen, don't leave home without a suit coat—hark back to a more genteel era, as do the six intimate dining rooms spread over three stories. Early and late-comers can take advantage of another of the restaurant's assets: a three-course, pre- and post-theater menu for $35. Book now to savor Lacoste's creations since the chef is considering a new venture.

Dinner: M-TH 6-10, F 6-11, SAT 5:30-11, SUN 5:30-10 ***Entrees:*** $18-$36
Tasting Menu: 5-COURSE $60
Pre-Theater: DAILY UNTIL 6:45 3-COURSE PRIX FIXE $35
Credit Cards: ALL MAJOR ***Reservations:*** RECOMMENDED
Dress: JACKET REQUIRED ***Cross Street:*** PROSPECT
Parking: COMPLIMENTARY VALET ***Metro:*** FOGGY BOTTOM-GWU

Critic's Pick
★ ★ 1/2

SONOMA

223 PENNSYLVANIA AVE. SE, WASHINGTON, DC (CAPITOL HILL) 202-544-8088
www.sonomadc.com

SUDDENLY, A DINER CAN'T TURN AROUND in a new restaurant without bumping into charcuterie, plates of artisanal cheeses and more wines by the glass than Baskin-Robbins lists flavors.

Surely you've noticed, too. Every other Washington neighborhood now claims a spot where the vibe is easy and the food leans to the unpretentious (and, typically, Italian). The trend originated in spring 2005 when the owners of Mendocino Grille in Georgetown opened a second restaurant on tavern-heavy Capitol Hill and gave it a name that massages the California theme: Sonoma.

Even before a proper sign went up, residents flocked to the bar—which stocks 30 or so wines in a refrigerated case that also preserves the product once it's opened—and to the banquette, which runs along the side of the long and narrow dining room. Sonoma is like an Abercrombie & Fitch model: good-looking in a fresh sort of way. And the recently opened second-floor lounge, with its club chairs and fireplace, only expands Sonoma's appeal.

Order some sausage, and it arrives on a butcher block of wood that practically covers the table.

Order some sausage, and it arrives on a butcher block of wood that practically covers the table. There are six meats to consider: prosciutto, salami, speck (smoked prosciutto), mortadella (lightly smoked pork sausage), bresaola (air-dried beef) and a rich chicken liver pâté. Sharing the surface of the board are fat pieces of grilled bread and optional little pots of "accents"—herbed nuts, pickled red onions, wine-plumped figs—to spice up the eating.

Pastas make up the bulk of the "firsts," and they include some charmers, gnocchi and risotto included. "Seconds" yield a more varied collection of meat and seafood dishes, including a hamburger made with Wagyu beef that is sometimes bursting with flavor and other times, frankly, just a burger. I have no qualms about the plump roast chicken, whose flavor is enhanced by a long soak in lemon and in garlic oil.

At full throttle, Sonoma is uncomfortably loud. Yet, when I'm drinking a lovely glass of wine for less than the price of a matinee, and polishing off every last strand of pasta from my plate, I'm also pleased to know about an alternative to all the restaurants nearby that are merely cooking in place.

Lunch: M-F 11:30-2:30 ***Entrees:*** $8-$18
Dinner: SUN-TH 5:30-10, F-SAT 5:30-11 ***Entrees:*** $8-$18 ***Credit Cards:*** ALL MAJOR
Reservations: RECOMMENDED ***Dress:*** CASUAL ***Cross Street:*** SECOND
Parking: STREET ***Metro:*** CAPITOL SOUTH

Critic's Pick

★ ★ ½

SORAK GARDEN

4308 BACKLICK RD., ANNANDALE, VA
703-916-7600

PART OF THE FUN OF VISITING a Korean restaurant with friends who have never experienced the cuisine is to watch their faces when the customary panchan show up. Those are myriad little salads and nibbles that arrive after you've placed your order—and a measuring stick used by devotees of Korean restaurants.

On my most recent visit to Sorak Garden, my friend's eyes widened as our waitress appeared with a platter of tiny bowls moments after we'd been seated. "Dried squid," she said, introducing one snack. "Kimchi," she continued, placing a bowl of fermented cabbage on the table. "Eggplant." "Black beans." "Bean sprouts." "Mushrooms." She rattled off 10 different tastes, leaving us to graze on the mini-banquet and sip our beers.

The table got more crowded as our appetizers and entrees arrived in quick succession. A strapping bowl of porridge with bits of pleasantly chewy abalone grew tedious after a few spoonfuls, but we eagerly downed half-moon-shaped dumplings filled with crumbled beef. Shredded beef and thin strips of bell peppers and onions were heaped over glassy noodles. It was a filling and homey dish. My friend and I were also looking for some fire, and we found it, in an entree of spicy squid tossed with cucumbers and a wicked red sauce.

My friend and I were also looking for some fire, and we found it, in an entree of spicy squid tossed with cucumbers and a wicked red sauce.

Sorak Garden has a lot of competition among Korean restaurants in Northern Virginia, but with its rich wood, lush plants and handsome artifacts it remains the most stylish.

Open: M-SAT 11-11, SUN 11-10 ***Entrees:*** $10.95-$49.95
Credit Cards: AE, DC, MC, V ***Reservations:*** RECOMMENDED
Dress: CASUAL ***Cross Street:*** LITTLE RIVER TURNPIKE
Parking: LOT / COMPLIMENTARY VALET ***Metro:*** DUNN LORING-MERRIFIELD

★ ★ ½

SPICES

3333-A CONNECTICUT AVE. NW, WASHINGTON, DC (CLEVELAND PARK)
202-686-3833

SPICES GIVES US PLENTY OF REASONS to seek it out, one of them being its location across the street from the Uptown, one of the last great movie houses around.

Another is the restaurant's moderately priced menu of Japanese, Thai, Chinese and other Asian dishes. It's no problem if you want sashimi and your mate wants pad thai or Peking chicken, because the gang's all there, and delicious to boot—as are scallion pancakes invigorated with sweet-and-sour sauce, and curry puffs filled with gently spiced potatoes and ground chicken. The stir-fried pork is enlivened with basil and fiery with chilies, and I always make time for a refreshing house signature, the ginger salad.

It's no problem if you want sashimi and your mate wants pad thai or Peking chicken, because the gang's all there.

Did I mention how stylish the place looks? The long blond sushi bar is backed by soothing yellow-green walls, and a small alcove across from it assures privacy for anyone sitting there. The lilting music, the warm service, the fresh and appealing food served on lovely plates with twiglike chopsticks—all the senses are rewarded at Spices.

Lunch: M-F 11:30-3, SAT NOON-5 *Entrees:* $8-$19
Dinner: M-SAT NOON-11, SUN 5-10:30 *Entrees:* $8-$30
Credit Cards: ALL MAJOR *Reservations:* RECOMMENDED
Dress: CASUAL *Cross Street:* MACOMB *Parking:* STREET *Metro:* CLEVELAND PARK

★ ★

STONEY'S SEAFOOD HOUSE

3938 OYSTER HOUSE RD., BROOMES ISLAND, MD 410-586-1888
www.stoneysseafoodhouse.com

THERE ARE NO OBVIOUS MARKERS pointing the way to Stoney's Seafood House, 50 miles southeast of downtown Washington on Calvert County's Broomes Island, but in summer you know you're getting closer as the signs for fresh shrimp, crab, scallops, corn and peaches grow more plentiful along the roadside.

"Inside or out?" the hostess asks at the entrance. "Out," you should answer if you want the most vivid crab-eating experience. Beyond the mounted fish and hanging nets of the main dining room, the outdoor space unfolds on two levels, one of which is a solid deck, the other a wooden barge that creaks and moans as it bobs up and down in the water.

The star of the show is crab, which can be sampled almost a dozen different ways: It comes as a dip, as a salad, in bite-size "balls" or in excellent, crusty-edged half-pound cakes the size of muffins. All three of the kitchen's soups have crab in them, and if you order a Bloody Mary, a claw dangles on the rim of the glass. There's a sandwich plump with soft-shell crabs (in season) and then there's the primary reason for my visit: hard-shell crabs, gently steamed, accented with a peppery, brick-red seasoning and served on tables spread with brown paper. (Note: Hard-shells are not a meal for the Felix Ungers of the world.)

Plain is prime at Stoney's, where I prefer anything steamed to anything fried.

Plain is prime at Stoney's, where I prefer anything steamed to anything fried. Steamed shrimp (a half-pound makes a nice appetizer for two) with melted butter proves tender and sweet, a first-class introduction to lunch or dinner. Meaty cherrystone clams also taste recently plucked from the water. From the fryer, however, emerge virtually bulletproof hush puppies and stiff battered shrimp.

A customer doesn't have to eat seafood to appreciate Stoney's. The sleeper on the menu: barbecued pork, sweet and smoky shreds of which are tucked inside a soft bun and presented as a sandwich with coleslaw.

Open: DAILY 11:30-9 ***Entrees:*** $8-$51
Credit Cards: D, MC, V ***Reservations:*** NO
Dress: CASUAL ***Cross Street:*** ROUTE 4
Parking: LOT ***Metro:*** NO

★ ★

STRAITS OF MALAYA

1836 18TH ST. NW, WASHINGTON, DC (DUPONT CIRCLE) 202-483-1483
www.straitsofmalaya.com

NEW TO THE MALAYSIAN GAME? The servers here tend to ask if you are, and if you nod yes, you get a verbal pat on the back. "The food is served family-style and meant to be shared," your tour guide will inform you. "It comes out as it is done." Sure enough, one appetizer might precede another by several minutes, and entrees are staggered, too.

A cluster of snacks sparks conversation and gets fingers and forks flying (no knives, though, as is the custom in Malaysia). Owner Lawrence Tan offers a taste from home with his mother's recipe for five-spice roll. Ground beef is blended with cinnamon, nutmeg and other sweet spices, bound in sheer bean curd skins and fried so that the skins are crisp but the filling remains moist. Slices of the savory snack are served with a ginger- and chili-sharpened soy sauce that jousts nicely with the beef's seasoning. A dot of ground beef, this time scented with curry, fills the triangular and ultra-crisp curry puffs, which develop more personality after a dip in the accompanying sweet-hot sauce. An exotic riff on chicken noodle soup is laksa, a treasure of thin rice noodles, ribbons of chicken, cooked egg and coconut milk in a brown broth that tickles the throat with hot spices.

A cluster of appetizers sparks conversation and gets fingers and forks flying (no knives, though, as is the custom in Malaysia).

Straits sets out airy shrimp chips for munching as guests peruse the menu; the chips make a nice scoop for achar, an appetizer of pickled cucumbers, carrots and cabbage that amounts to Malaysia's version of chips and dip. The vivid red cocktail that brightens more than a few tables is that Singapore sling, sweet with fruit juice and potent with gin. The libation looks as innocent as a Shirley Temple but packs a seriously adult punch.

The seductions continue: Tamarind adds its mysterious sweet-tart accent to a chicken dish, stir-fried with tomatoes, onion and water chestnuts—nice. A standout among the seafood dishes is chili-spiked pearly shrimp with soft scallops, and flounder, fried to a delicate crunch and partnered with jasmine-scented steamed rice and vegetables in a light tomato sauce. Throw in a table on the rooftop and you've got a night to remember.

Dinner: SUN-TH 5:30-10:30, F-SAT 5:30-11 ***Entrees:*** $10.95-$21.95
Credit Cards: AE, D, MC, V ***Reservations:*** NO
Dress: CASUAL ***Cross Street:*** T STREET NW
Parking: STREET ***Metro:*** DUPONT CIRCLE

Critic's Pick

★★ 1/2

SUNFLOWER VEGETARIAN RESTAURANT

2531 CHAIN BRIDGE RD., VIENNA, VA 703-319-3888
www.crystalsunflower.com

AS CHEERFUL AS ITS NAME SUGGESTS, this trim vegetarian oasis is proof that a diner can eat healthfully and happily, even if he's a card-carrying carnivore.

Fashioned from white mushrooms and soy protein, morsels of fried "chicken" taste much like fowl—McNuggets with a conscience. And what looks just like sweet-and-sour pork, "Sweet & Sour Sensation" is actually crisp green bell peppers, pineapple, carrots and more swabbed with a lively red glaze of tomato, vinegar and pineapple juice. Wonton soup reveals a sumptuous treasure for only $2.50: Its flavorful mushroom stock floats threads of spinach and a trio of delicate dumplings.

Curry fried rice, abundant with crisp and colorful chopped vegetables, is both kicky and fragrant.

Not everything on the epic bill of fare tastes as poetic as it sounds. "Peace and Harmony" finds big pieces of eggplant and a sauce of sun-dried tomatoes and mushooms under a gooey cover of rice cheese. And pumpkin tofu pie reminds my pal (and me) of a wet protein bar. But the flavors are generally on target; curry fried rice, abundant with crisp and colorful chopped vegetables, is both kicky and fragrant.

As busy as it gets, the place feels serene. Sunflowers crop up everywhere: in pictures on the white stucco walls, in garlands hanging above the cashier's post, on the curtain separating foyer from dining room. And instead of the latest singing sensation, your ears are treated to what sounds like the backtrack to a day at the spa.

Lunch: DAILY 11:30-4 ***Entrees:*** $5.75-$6.50
Dinner: DAILY 4-10 ***Entrees:*** $5.50-$11
Credit Cards: ALL MAJOR ***Reservations:*** NO
Dress: CASUAL ***Cross Street:*** NUTLEY
Parking: LOT ***Metro:*** VIENNA / FAIRFAX-GMU

Critic's Pick

★ ★ ★

SUSHI-KO

2309 WISCONSIN AVE. NW, WASHINGTON, DC (GLOVER PARK) 202-333-4187
www.sushiko.us

WASHINGTON'S OLDEST SOURCE for raw fish and vinegared rice is also one of its best, thanks to a young chef with a clear idea of what's fresh and appealing and a deft way with a knife. Koji Terano isn't yet 30, but already he cooks like someone with decades of experience under his belt.

Koji Terano isn't yet 30, but already he cooks like someone with decades of experience under his belt.

The most engaging way to taste his work is to snare a coveted counter seat and request "omakase"—Japanese for "chef's choice"—after which a parade of lovely arrangements floats by. If you're fortunate, they might include crisped eel on slices of sheer cucumber; a seared fold of white tuna presented with avocado, Japanese mountain potato and chips of garlic; a mellow bowl of soup with a few choice morsels of lobster; maybe duck drizzled with a mustard-punched miso sauce and snowy, wine-flavored sorbets.

But you'll also find plenty to applaud on the standing menu and at a table on one of two spare floors, where informed servers deliver amazing rock shrimp tempura, a tasting flight of tunas and flounder sashimi, elegantly garnished with a halo of fried carrot threads and truffle vinaigrette.

Lunch: TU-F NOON-2:30 ***Entrees:*** $10-$20
Dinner: M-TH 6-10:30, F 6-11, SAT 5:30-11, SUN 5:30-10 ***Entrees:*** $10-$30
Credit Cards: AE, MC, V ***Reservations:*** RECOMMENDED
Dress: CASUAL ***Cross Street:*** CALVERT
Parking: $4 VALET AT DINNER ***Metro:*** TENLEYTOWN-AU

★ ★

SUSHI TARO

1503 17TH ST. NW, WASHINGTON, DC (DUPONT CIRCLE) 202-462-8999
www.sushitaro.com

I'VE NEVER BEEN TO TOKYO, but I imagine Sushi Taro would look right at home there. On any given night at this second-story restaurant, a throng of Japanese suits are pampered by waitresses in beautiful kimonos and by chefs in blue caps positioned behind a long stretch of a sushi counter. Handsome rice paper screens and a few low tables surrounded by shoeless diners complete the scene.

The sushi bar's prominence is my cue to go fish. Salmon, yellowtail, sweet shrimp—all the usual suspects show up on the sushi menu, and they taste as if they'd been caught that morning. But here's the place to venture beyond your comfort zone and try ingredients that you won't always find at your neighborhood sushi parlor. The display cases are lined with amberjack, three kinds of mackerel and even more varieties of clam, from arctic surf to orange. If you think all tuna tastes the same, conduct an experiment and request the three grades of tuna available here. You'll discover why the fattiest of the three (toro) costs almost twice as much as the regular (maguro, priced at $4.50 for two pieces) and a couple of dollars more than medium-fatty (chu-toro, $6.25). The toro is simply exquisite, like butter crossed with the sea. Sushi maestros will tell you that the little pillow of rice that supports the featured ingredient is just as important as the fish itself. At Sushi Taro, the grains are firm, plump and moist, their flavor a gentle balance of rice wine vinegar, salt, sugar and dried seaweed.

Salmon, yellowtail, sweet shrimp—all the usual suspects show up on the sushi menu, and they taste as if they'd been caught that morning.

There's more than just raw fish to be savored here. I'm particularly fond of the appetizers, including the delicate steamed dumplings (shumai), and it pays to ask if such seasonal treats as smelts or soft-shell crabs are available. The former, rich and meaty, are deep-fried and invigorated with a clear sauce that's at once subtly sweet and tangy; the latter are treated to a lightly crackling tempura batter that allows the clean, sweet flavor of the crab to rule. A parade of fried, broiled and simmered meats is also offered, but with fish as good as this, why stray beyond the raw deal?

Lunch: M-F 11:30-2 ***Entrees:*** $6.95-$18
Dinner: M-TH 5:30-10, F-SAT 5:30-10:30 ***Entrees:*** $13-$50
Closed: SUN ***Credit Cards:*** ALL MAJOR ***Reservations:*** RECOMMENDED
Dress: CASUAL ***Cross Street:*** P STREET NW
Parking: STREET ***Metro:*** DUPONT CIRCLE

★

SWEET MANGO CAFE

3701 NEW HAMPSHIRE AVE. NW (PETWORTH)
202-726-2646

A FEW YEARS BACK, a fire destroyed Sweet Mango Cafe. But hard work and money borrowed from family and friends helped its owner, Reginald James, rebuild his Jamaican retreat at the same location.

Conveniently parked across from the Georgia Avenue-Petworth Metro station, the reborn Sweet Mango Cafe unfolds on multiple levels and offers that rare restaurant asset: a rooftop patio. The ground floor is open and airy, with alternating mint-green and butter-yellow walls and a scattering of tables for those who opt to eat their food—oxtail, red snapper, cocoa bread—on the premises. (Sweet Mango does a brisk carryout business.)

Conveniently parked across from the Georgia Avenue-Petworth Metro station, the reborn Sweet Mango Cafe unfolds on multiple levels and offers that rare restaurant asset: a rooftop patio.

The signature dish remains jerk chicken, tingling with spices and utterly juicy. But I'm also a fan of the rustic curry goat, which is predictably bony but also tender and zippy. Like all the entrees, they are both rounded out with rice and peas and a warm cabbage salad. Only the savory beef- and chicken-filled patties are made elsewhere; the pocket-size snacks come from the respected Royal Caribbean Bakery in New York.

Stoking the charcoal fire in the open kitchen behind the counter is James's brother, George "Lenky" Beckford. What's the trick to his no-punches-pulled chicken? I asked, angling for his recipe. "You don't reveal the secret to your special!" says James politely but firmly declining to share his recipe.

Open: M-SAT 11-10, SUN 11-8 *Entrees:* $6.50-$10
Credit Cards: ALL MAJOR *Reservations:* NO
Dress: CASUAL *Cross Street:* GEORGIA AVENUE NW
Parking: STREET *Metro:* GEORGIA AVE-PETWORTH

☆ ☆

SWEETWATER TAVERN

14250 SWEETWATER LA., CENTREVILLE, VA 703-449-1100
www.greatamericanrestaurants.com

THIS BARN-SIZE RESTAURANT is part of a chain (the Fairfax-based Great American Restaurants), yet it goes out of its way to make you feel special. Curious about the beer made on site? A bartender is happy to provide a free taste in a frosted mini-mug. There is country music to tap your toes to, and there are cowboys and Indians depicted in a handsome mural. The room all but shouts "Howdy!"

So it seems appropriate to start with a Southwestern-style bean-cheese-avocado dip (eight layers, count 'em) and move on to a smoky pork chop, served with light brown gravy and brightened with corn salsa. Equally hearty is prime rib—thick and succulent—partnered with a big baked potato. Barbecued ribs? They're meaty if a tad too sweet, flanked by creamy coleslaw and fine, skin-on fries. Specials show the kitchen's range; halibut baked in banana leaf and presented with polenta is a dish I'd expect to find at an expense-account venue in the city.

It seems appropriate to start with a Southwestern-style bean-cheese-avocado dip (eight layers, count 'em) and move on to a smoky pork chop, served with light brown gravy and brightened with corn salsa.

Sweetwater's fresh-faced servers in striped shirts navigate the space with smiles and good cheer. Plus, they know the menu as well as the cooks do. More than once I've left here wondering, Why can't every restaurant be so hospitable?

Lunch: DAILY 11-4 *Entrees:* $8-$19
Dinner: SUN-M 4-10, TU-TH 4-11, F-SAT 4-MIDNIGHT *Entrees:* $8-$23
Credit Cards: ALL MAJOR *Reservations:* RECOMMENDED
Dress: CASUAL *Cross Street:* ROUTE 28
Parking: LOT *Metro:* VIENNA / FAIRFAX-GMU
Other Locations: 45980 WATERVIEW PLAZA, STERLING, VA, 571-434-6500
3066 GATEHOUSE PLAZA, FALLS CHURCH, VA, 703-645-8100

Critic's Pick
☆ ☆ 1/2

TABAQ BISTRO

1336 U ST. NW, WASHINGTON, DC (U STREET CORRIDOR) 202-265-0965
www.tabaqdc.com

FOR ANYONE WHO HAS TRIED to find a restaurant with a Washington backdrop and food that is equal to the scenery, the arrival of Tabaq is no small news flash. While the fourth-floor aerie of this multistory oasis requires a good heart and strong legs to reach, the reward for the cardio workout is a seductive, candle-lit dining room and bar beneath a high, tented glass ceiling—a ceiling that opens to let in the night air when it's balmy and closes at the first few drops of precipitation when it's not. "It will be beautiful up here when it snows," forecasts Omer Buyukbayrak, who owns Tabaq with his brother Melih.

The siblings hail from Meze in Adams Morgan and continue to do what they did at that Turkish-themed restaurant—small plates—only better and in tonier digs. The fun actually starts below ground, in an intimate lounge with low stools and continues on the narrow main floor with a long row of red seats before climbing to the roof.

There are more than 40 tapas to consider at Tabaq, and they span the realm of tastes, from liquid to solid, meatless to meaty, surf to turf.

By now, a regular restaurant-goer knows what to expect of a place where small plates rule: A server who explains the concept of tapas and the pleasure of sharing food. There are more than 40 tapas to consider at Tabaq, and they span the realm of tastes, from liquid to solid, meatless to meaty, surf to turf. Vegetarians will find a welcome mat in the form of grape leaves stuffed with rice, currants and pine nuts and stubby phyllo "cigars" fattened with warm feta cheese and spinach. Carnivores can gravitate to liver and onions tossed with bold herbs and crushed red pepper, and compact but juicy beef-and-lamb patties. Pine nuts in the blend make for a soft crunch, the grill imparts a nice char and dabs of tart yogurt lend cool contrast to the winning dish.

With its endearing service and sexy scene, Tabaq would be a fun place to hang out even if the food were half as good as it is. Throw in a postcard view, and you've got yourself a night to remember.

Dinner: SUN-TH 5-11, F 3-MIDNIGHT, SAT 5-MIDNIGHT *Entrees:* $13.95-$19.95
Brunch: SAT-SUN 11-4 *Entrees:* $6.75-$16.95
Credit Cards: ALL MAJOR *Reservations:* RECOMMENDED
Dress: BUSINESS CASUAL *Cross Street:* 14TH *Parking:* $10 VALET AFTER 6 DAILY
Metro: U ST / AFRICAN-AMER CIVIL WAR MEMORIAL / CARDOZO

Critic's Pick

★ ★ 1/2

TABARD INN

1739 N ST. NW WASHINGTON, DC (DUPONT CIRCLE) 202-833-2668
www.tabardinn.com

SOME OF US THINK of this tucked-away restaurant as a bit of a secret, at least until we go to the fire-lit lounge for drinks in winter and find every couch taken, or aim for the lovely garden patio in summer to see that others had the same idea. The Tabard Inn's low ceilings, dim lighting, snug seating and black-and-white tile floors provide just the right backdrop for dinner with an old friend or even a first date. Before "fresh" and "seasonal" were ubiquitous on American menus, this 30-year-old restaurant was developing relationships with growers and even claimed its own farm.

Its goal of serving simple good food is still true. Spring is trumpeted with a sublime puree of asparagus and watercress, winter might find flavorsome lamb with a flan of black trumpet mushrooms, and salads are anything but ordinary (keep an eye out for shaved pear and smoked trout). Tradition gets balanced with innovation, which means scallops come in a band of salmon and land on squid ink fettuccine moistened with a light butter sauce. Service is quietly efficient; the wine list is a gentle charmer. No wonder the word is out and the rooms are full.

Winter might find flavorsome lamb with a flan of black trumpet mushrooms, and salads are anything but ordinary.

Breakfast: M-F 7-10, SAT 8-10, SUN 8-9:30 *Entrees:* $6-$10
Lunch: M-F 11:30-2:30 *Entrees:* $10-$15
Dinner: DAILY 6-10 *Entrees:* $18-$29
Brunch: SAT 11-2:30, SUN 10:30-2:30 *Entrees:* $10-$15
Credit Cards: ALL MAJOR *Reservations:* RECOMMENDED
Dress: CASUAL *Cross Street:* 17TH
Parking: $5 VALET F-SAT DINNER, SUN BRUNCH *Metro:* DUPONT CIRCLE

☆ ☆

TABERNA DEL ALABARDERO

1776 I ST. NW, WASHINGTON, DC (DOWNTOWN) 202-429-2200
www.alabardero.com

A HOT COIN OF PASTRY-WRAPPED CHORIZO staves off hunger as you peruse the menu, and more people seem to be speaking Spanish than English. "Welcome to Madrid," this grandly formal restaurant, which includes a handsome tapas bar, seems to whisper.

Seducers know to request the plush red banquettes in the corners—cocoons of comfort strewn with handsome pillows and backed with frilly white lace—but even the broad chairs, covered in what looks like tapestry, are a treat to your seat. No matter where you find yourself in this pleasure palace, the lighting is gentle, the music is hushed and the servers, smartly attired in vests or tuxes, see to your well-being.

Seducers know to request the plush red banquettes in the corners.

The caveat? The cooking can be very good (fresh sardines tickled with tomato vinaigrette, artichoke stew jazzed up with garlic and pork cracklings, salt cod partnered with crimson roasted peppers) or truly underwhelming (lamb stew ringed with mashed potatoes suggests Dinty Moore had a hand in its creation). That said, you will always drink well from the epic wine list, and end on a little high with anything that jiggles: The kitchen's flans are all sublime.

Lunch: M-F 11:30-2:30 ***Entrees:*** $19-$28
Dinner: M-TH 5:30-10:30, F-SAT 5:30-11 ***Entrees:*** $27-$45
Closed: SUN ***Credit Cards:*** ALL MAJOR ***Reservations:*** RECOMMENDED
Dress: BUSINESS CASUAL ***Cross Street:*** 18TH
Parking: VALIDATED GARAGE AT DINNER ***Metro:*** FARRAGUT WEST

★ ★

TALLULA

2761 WASHINGTON BLVD., ARLINGTON, VA 703-778-5051
www.tallularestaurant.com

FRIENDLY AND FUN, Tallula is the discerning yupster's all-purpose place to refuel, with two lounges (one nonsmoking) and a dining room with a small fountain in its center and an open kitchen in the rear.

The menu encourages diners to start with some "appeteasers" from a long and varied list of two- and three-bite snacks. Steak tartare nestles in a little curl of Parmesan cheese, pulled pork and coleslaw pair up in what must be the smallest barbecue sandwich around and a $2 risotto fritter harks back, deliciously, to chef Nathan Anda's time at Equinox in Washington. There's even a mini-corn dog. As for main courses, wild salmon swims to the table on a creamy bed of diced parsnips ringed with a fine bordelaise sauce, but the protein that calls to me most here is braised short ribs; scattered with green tomato salsa and poised on a lake of cheesy grits, the dish is one of those rib-stickers you look forward to on a frigid day.

The menu encourages diners to start with some "appeteasers" from a long and varied list of two- and three-bite snacks.

Less pleasing: Dry roast chicken with oversalted greens and a dense pork chop garnished with a too-sweet onion confit. The kitchen isn't always consistent. However, desserts win diners over (ever had your banana cream pie in a martini glass?) and so does the wine list. Instead of playing it safe with obvious labels, Tallula's roster delves into the lesser-known treasures offered by small producers in Australia, Oregon and New Zealand. Better still, you can choose from 70 different wines in servings of 7 ounces or a little more than 3 ounces.

Dinner: SUN-TH 5:30-10, F-SAT 5:30-11 *Entrees:* $16-$28
Brunch: SAT-SUN 11-2:30 *Entrees:* $6-$15
Credit Cards: ALL MAJOR *Reservations:* RECOMMENDED
Dress: CASUAL *Cross Street:* PERSHING DRIVE
Parking: LOT *Metro:* CLARENDON

★ ★

TAQUERIA TRES REYES

5403 KENILWORTH AVENUE, RIVERDALE, MD
301-779-6060

DING-DONG! The bell rings every time someone walks through the door, which turns out to be a lot, even on a Sunday afternoon. If your weekend visit is anything like mine, expect to find a room full of Spanish speakers and a jukebox turned up to compete with their many voices.

The place is a confection of white walls, pink trim and too many fake flowers to count. Service? You line up at a counter in the rear to place your order from the small Mexican menu, take a number, then try to find a spare seat before the food is cooked (and delivered by a waitress who swims through the crowd as easily as a fish through water). Chances are, locating a free spot won't be easy.

If your weekend visit is anything like mine, expect to find a room full of Spanish speakers and a jukebox turned up to compete with their many voices.

But chances are, you're going to like whatever shows up on your table. Mucho. Tacos made with pork, tongue and even goat are all enormously satisfying, as is the shredded beef flauta beneath its cover of lettuce and cheese. Sliced radishes, scallions and lemon wedges dress up the plates; think of it all as fast food with slow-cooked appeal. Forget soda—a meal here begs for horchata, that milky and refreshing blend of rice, almonds, cinnamon and sugar.

Do your ears hurt? Are your taste buds happy? Si, on both counts.

Open: 10-10:30 ***Entrees:*** $2.25-$11
Credit Cards: NO ***Reservations:*** NO
Dress: CASUAL ***Cross Street:*** SPRINGBROOK TERRACE
Parking: LOT ***Metro:*** NO
Other Locations: 6056 GREENBELT ROAD, GREENBELT, MD, 301-441-8652
8562 MATHIS AVE., MANASSAS, VA 20110, 703-335-6663

TASTE OF MOROCCO

3211 N. WASHINGTON BLVD., ARLINGTON, VA 703-527-7468
www.tasteofmorocco.net

"WE LOOK FORWARD TO SEEING YOU," a host says after I reserve a table. Inside the restaurant, Moroccan music spirits guests far away as they sink deep into pillowed banquettes. Glistening olives and cubes of bread show up to ward off any hunger pangs as the menus are doled out. Instead of a pitch to order the most expensive items, a waiter volunteers that the multicourse "feasts," averaging $43 a couple at dinner, are the most economical way to enjoy the place.

The kitchen makes two kinds of bisteeya. One encases ground chicken, almonds and eggs—the classic filling—in onionskin-thin, flaky and buttery phyllo; as is customary, the surface is lightly dusted with sugar and cinnamon. Less common but even more delicious is bisteeya stuffed with squid, fish and fresh coriander along with glassy vermicelli that picks up the tint of the seasonings, including cumin and saffron.

Much of the rest of the menu is devoted to tagines, a word that refers both to Moroccan stews and to the glazed earthenware dishes, capped with conical lids, in which they're cooked.

If bisteeya sounds like too heavy a way to begin a meal, there are salads of cucumber and tomato, coriander-spiked carrot, and cumin-scented eggplant to mull over. They are all good and fresh tasting.

Much of the rest of the menu is devoted to tagines, a word that refers both to Moroccan stews and to the glazed earthenware dishes, capped with conical lids, in which they're cooked. My preference is for the lamb tagines, offered with soft-cooked vegetables in a saffron sauce, stewed with prunes and sprinkled with sesame seeds, or blended with almonds and raisins.

Belly dancing Thursday through Sunday turns dinner into dinner-and-a-show. If you've opted for one of the feasts, you're probably not going to have room for much more dessert than some minted tea, poured with dramatic flair into tiny glass cups.

Lunch: M-F 11-2:30 *Entrees:* $10.95-$12.95
Dinner: DAILY 5-11 *Entrees:* $12.95-$16.95
Credit Cards: AE, D, MC, V *Reservations:* RECOMMENDED
Dress: BUSINESS CASUAL *Cross Street:* WILSON BOULEVARD
Parking: LOT *Metro:* CLARENDON
Second Location: 8661 COLESVILLE RD., SILVER SPRING, MD, 301-588-4003

★ ★

TASTING ROOM

101 N. MARKET STREET, FREDERICK, MD
240-379-7772

WHEN HE LAUNCHED THIS CORNER RESTAURANT in downtown Frederick several years back, owner Michael Tauraso's mission was pretty straightforward: He hoped to offer "a place where people could come for a good plate of food and a good glass of wine."

He's done much to live up to that aim, and it's offered in a bustling, glass-wrapped bistro. Regulars drive from miles away for the Tasting Room's tender and juicy filet mignon, a fine piece of meat enhanced with bearnaise sauce and crisp-soft au gratin potatoes. The herby roast chicken is good, too, with its nice, garlic-laced gravy. Pan-roasted rockfish and loose, fat crab cakes reflect a kitchen that knows its way around seafood.

Pan-roasted rockfish and loose, fat crab cakes reflect a kitchen that knows its way around seafood.

Appetizers are less successful, though you'll find an exception in the sherry-laced lobster chowder, and if you order only one dessert, make sure it's the chocolate "fix"—and make sure you have strong elbows to fight off any competing forks.

Lunch: M-SAT 11-3 *Entrees:* $7.95-$15.95
Dinner: M-TH 5-10, F-SAT 5-11 *Entrees:* $17.95-$32.95
Closed: SUN *Credit Cards:* AE, DC, MC, V
Reservations: RECOMMENDED *Dress:* BUSINESS CASUAL
Cross Street: CHURCH *Parking:* STREET *Metro:* NO

★ ★

TAVIRA

8401 CONNECTICUT AVE., CHEVY CHASE, MD 301-652-8684
www.tavirarestaurant.com

FIRST, YOU HAVE TO GET PAST SOME HURDLES. Like the fact that the restaurant sits in a nondescript bank building—and it's underground.

Once you're seated, however, doubts fade to delight as your waiter introduces you to Tavira's Portuguese menu, starting with a recitation of specials that unwittingly pays homage to the Energizer Bunny (the list goes on and on and on).

If you've never been before, acquaint yourself with some of the regular dishes. Fried cod fritters and chicken massaged with a fiery pepper sauce are worth pursuing, more so than the casserole of tough pork, potatoes and clams. On the other hand, previous visitors to this cozy, low-ceilinged warren of four rooms should check out those specials. They might include baby squid in a light wash of garlic sauce or twice-roasted duck, its mahogany skin yielding to ample succulent meat, joined by a sublime risotto.

Fried cod fritters and chicken massaged with a fiery pepper sauce are worth pursuing, more so than the casserole of tough pork, potatoes and clams.

Lunch: M-F 11:30-2:30 ***Entrees:*** $6.95-$15.95
Dinner: M-SAT 5:30-10, SUN 5-9 ***Entrees:*** $17.95-$25.95
Credit Cards: ALL MAJOR ***Reservations:*** RECOMMENDED
Dress: CASUAL ***Cross Street:*** CHEVY CHASE LAKE DRIVE
Parking: LOT ***Metro:*** NO

Critic's Pick

★ ★ ½

TEMPTASIAN CAFE

6259 LITTLE RIVER TURNPIKE, ALEXANDRIA, VA
703-750-6801

DINERS CHOOSE BETWEEN TWO MENUS HERE. One is a holdover from the restaurant that preceded this one, also named TemptAsian. It lists standards such as orange beef and sweet-and-sour pork. The other menu starts with two pages of Chinese characters and goes on to include combinations that you aren't likely to see on a flyer from your neighborhood carry-out ("Spicy pig blood tofu in hot bowl," anyone?). It's been hundreds of restaurants ago that I last ate at the flame-throwing China Star in Fairfax, but I think I recognize its fiery food. The lone decoration on the wall confirms my hunch: It's a framed photograph of the restaurant's chef, Peter Chang, alongside a beaming Hu Jintao, the president of China. A native of Sichuan, Chang previously cooked at China Star.

That discovery makes it easier for me to order at TemptAsian. I simply seek out dishes I was fond of at the chef's former employer. The five-spice sliced beef appetizer, cool and fragrant, is every bit as luscious as I remember it, as is the spicy diced rabbit, ignited with chili oil (but still too bony to let you retrieve all the meat from the roughly chopped rabbit). A history with China Star isn't necessary, though; little drawings of chile peppers on the menu indicate which choices are spicy, and you can count on plenty of fire when you order them. Ordering "spicy dried bean curd," an excellent vegetarian starter, yields a cool mound of diced tofu splashed with a chili- and scallion-laced dressing. In "General Kwan spicy beef," a generous entree, soft slices of beef are all but concealed under a wicked cover of roasted red chilies.

You don't need to be a heat-seeker to eat well here.

You don't need to be a heat-seeker to eat well here. Steamed buns "with chicken flavor" translates as golf-ball-size dumplings containing chicken broth and a mild ground pork center, so that a warm rush of broth fills your mouth when you bite through the dough. A comforting casserole of glassy rice noodles, shredded pork and pickled cabbage is enough food for four to share, and a steal of a meal at only $8.50.

Lunch: M-F 11-3 *Entrees:* $5.25-$6.50
Dinner: M-TH 3-10, F-SAT 3-11 SUN 11-10 *Entrees:* $7.95-$12.95
Credit Cards: MC, V *Reservations:* NO
Dress: CASUAL *Cross Street:* BEAUREGARD
Parking: LOT *Metro:* VAN DORN STREET

★ 1/2

TENPENH

1001 PENNSYLVANIA AVE. NW, WASHINGTON, DC (DOWNTOWN) 202-393-4500
www.tenpenh.com

LIKE AN OPEN BOTTLE of bubbly left out overnight, TenPenh has lost much of its initial fizz. Oh, it's still a fun scene, crowded as ever with beautiful people and seductively dressed in silk and teak accents. The big marble bar is a swell spot for a cocktail and the seating expands to a sidewalk patio when the weather cooperates.

But have you eaten there lately? Charmingly served in the bowl of a coconut shell, chicken-coconut soup is all show, its super-sweetness begging for balance in the equation. Presented in a wicker basket, shrimp-stuffed dumplings are so tame as to put me to sleep. A noodle entree featuring honey- and soy-glazed duck is heavy and gloppy. The lone savory draw on my last visit: gently cooked halibut in a light coat of bread crumbs. Why can't there be more such dishes? The kitchen seems to be sleep-walking.

The lone savory draw on my last visit: gently cooked halibut in a light coat of bread crumbs.

A pal and I would have left hungry had it not been for dessert; fortunately, the kitchen still turns out some nice sweets, including a fine ginger poundcake. Meanwhile, the gratis shot of gazpacho and moist towel doled out upon arrival remind me that the restaurant—cleverly named for its address on the corner of 10th and Pennsylvania—is at least as thoughtful as ever.

Lunch: M-F 11:30-2:30 *Entrees:* $13-$18
Dinner: M-TH 5:30-10:30, F-SAT 5:30-11 *Entrees:* $13-$28
Closed: SUN *Credit Cards:* ALL MAJOR *Reservations:* RECOMMENDED
Dress: BUSINESS CASUAL *Cross Street:* 10TH
Parking: $6 VALET AT DINNER *Metro:* ARCHIVES-NAVY MEMORIAL

★ ★

THAI BASIL

14511-P LEE JACKSON MEMORIAL HWY., CHANTILLY, VA 703-631-8277
www.thaibasilchantilly.com

FOR PASSENGERS FLYING INTO or out of Dulles International Airport, or visitors to the National Air and Space Museum's outpost nearby, Thai Basil provides a convenient place to refuel.

The chef, Nongkran Daks, hails from Chumphon province in southern Thailand, where fish and seafood are abundant, coconuts are plentiful, and the food tends to be hot with chilies. This last detail is evident on her menu in dishes such as chicken (or pork or beef) in green curry; the tingling gravy, made with chilies, fish sauce and coconut milk, is sweet and complex. Crisp green beans and soft bamboo shoots fill out the entree.

Fish cakes are familiar finds on Thai menus, though the tongue-tingling patties served with cucumber relish at Thai Basil are zestier and lighter than much of the local competition. Even more enticing are shrimp cakes, an occasional special, seasoned with little more than soy sauce, and crunchy beneath their coats of Japanese bread crumbs. Whole shrimp bundled with scallions and julienned carrots, then fried to a gentle crisp, are wittily billed as "shrimp in a blanket." They're tasty.

Your server will ask how spicy you prefer your food, using a scale that starts with "American Hot," indicated by a single chili pepper.

Daks's soups pulse with flavor—and keep a diner reaching for his beer (or, better yet, his rice bowl; the starch is better than any liquid for taming the flames). Chicken and coconut milk are jump-started with lemon grass and lime in one heady bowl, while another choice finds tender shrimp bobbing in a brick-red broth that sears the tongue with blazing chilies. Your brain cries, "Stop!" but your taste buds say, "Bring it on, baby." Both soups are less than $3 at lunch, and both show off the layering of flavors that make Thai food so appealing.

Your server will ask how spicy you prefer your food, using a scale that starts with "American Hot," indicated by a single chili pepper, and tops out at "Laos Hot," signaled by four peppers—and plenty fiery, I should add. When ordered "Thai Hot" (three peppers), shaved beef in a creamy red curry is a blowtorch of a dish that still lets you taste ingredients other than its red chilies.

Lunch: DAILY 11-3 ***Entrees:*** $6.95-$10.95 ***Dinner:*** DAILY 5-10 ***Entrees:*** $8.95-$24.95
Credit Cards: AE, DC, MC, V ***Reservations:*** RECOMMENDED FOR GROUPS OF 5 OR MORE
Dress: CASUAL ***Cross Street:*** AVION PARKWAY
Parking: LOT ***Metro:*** NO

★ 1/2

THAI COAST

2514 L ST. NW, WASHINGTON, DC (FOGGY BOTTOM)
202-333-2460

GOOD-BYE, PASTA. HELLO, PAD THAI. Not a trace of the Italian restaurant Donatello's that once thrived here remains now that Thai Coast has settled into the airy, two-story space. It's pretty in soft blues, greens and exposed brick.

A spinoff of Taylay Thai on Capitol Hill, the restaurant does pretty well by the standards: crab-stuffed chicken wings are plump and juicy, fish cakes are pleasantly springy, and pork with green curry teases the tongue with gentle waves of heat.

Not a trace of the Italian restaurant Donatello's that once thrived in this space remains now that Thai Coast has settled into the airy, two-story space.

On the other hand, crispy whole flounder looks like the fish was on a diet when it was caught—it's scrawny—and the bland garden rolls aren't improved by a dipping sauce that is too sweet. If you don't demand too much from it, Thai Coast adds up to a satisfying lunch or dinner.

Feeling lazy? The restaurant delivers within a two-mile radius.

Open: M-TH 11:30-3 AND 4:30-10:30 F-SAT 11:30-11 SUN 11:30-10:30
Entrees: $6.95-$12.95
Credit Cards: AE, D, MC, V ***Reservations:*** RECOMMENDED
Dress: CASUAL ***Cross Street:*** PENNSYLVANIA AVENUE NW
Parking: STREET ***Metro:*** FOGGY BOTTOM-GWU

★ ★

THAIPHOON

2011 S ST. NW, WASHINGTON, DC (DUPONT CIRCLE) 202-667-3505
www.thaiphoon.com

THE INTERIOR CATCHES THE EYE with a window-wrapped dining room up front and cozy booths in the rear painted the colors of lime, cherry and lemon. Stylish amber lights illuminate a menu whose moderate prices encourage frequent visits.

The noodle dishes run greasy and the desserts leave me cold. It took some exploration, but eventually I tasted why there's sometimes a wait for one of Thaiphoon's 80 or so seats. For the most part, this is food that wakes up your mouth, brought to you by servers who manage to slip some graciousness your way every time they stop by your table.

No one in the neighborhood serves a soup brassier than the demure-looking chicken and mushrooms floating in a broth of coconut milk. A bowlful of beige, the soup nevertheless roars with the peppery heat of galangal and a bracing jolt of lime. Fried wonton skins in crisp triangles hide pinches of curry-tinged chicken, onions and potatoes; the sweet-sharp cucumber dipping sauce makes a nice complement. Peanut-sprinkled, citrus-splashed papaya salad is good, but even better is shredded, honey-roasted duck tossed with ginger, chili paste, greens and more. And among the entrees, you'll do just fine with seafood, be it steamed rockfish perfumed by lemon grass or a special of shrimp with pineapple and a tingling tomato sauce.

> ***No one in the neighborhood serves a soup brassier than the demure-looking chicken and mushrooms floating in a broth of coconut milk.***

The best of the vegetables: bright, crisp string beans, delicately batter-fried and enlivened by garlic sauce. It's the stuff of late-night, home-alone junk-food fantasies.

Lunch: DAILY 11:30-3 ***Entrees:*** $6.95-$12.95
Dinner: SUN-TH 3:30-10:30, F-SAT 3:30-11 ***Entrees:*** $7.95-$13.95
Credit Cards: ALL MAJOR ***Reservations:*** RECOMMENDED
Dress: CASUAL ***Cross Street:*** CONNECTICUT AVENUE NW
Parking: STREET ***Metro:*** DUPONT CIRCLE
Second Location: 1301 S. JOYCE ST., ARLINGTON, VA, 703-413-8200

Critic's Pick
☆ ☆ ☆

THAI SQUARE

3217 COLUMBIA PIKE, ARLINGTON, VA 703-685-7040
www.thaisquarerestaurant.com

UNLIKE JUST ABOUT EVERY OTHER THAI SOURCE AROUND, Thai Square isn't much to look at. Indeed, the purveyor's lone attempt at decoration seems to be a red stripe and a few travel posters on otherwise blank white walls.

Judging from the filled seats, however, no one seems to mind, because they're eating some of the finest Thai food to be found in the Washington area. Proof: spice-rubbed pork satays that sit at the head of the class; tender squid sauteed with garlic, basil and chilies; mussels absorbed with lemon grass and Thai basil and served in a clay pot, trailed by a fragrant cloud of steam as they exit the kitchen; and whole fish fired up with red chilies and balanced with tamarind.

Counting specials, there are more than 100 paths to enlightenment on the menu.

Entrees average $9 to $10, and, counting specials, there are more than 100 paths to enlightenment on the menu.

Lunch: M-F 11:30-3 ***Entrees:*** $6.50-$7.75
Dinner: M-TH 5-10:30, F-SAT 5-11, SUN 5-10:30 ***Entrees:*** $7.50-$12.95
Credit Cards: AE, MC, V ***Reservations:*** RECOMMENDED FOR PARTIES OF 5 OR MORE
Dress: CASUAL ***Cross Street:*** S. GLEBE ROAD
Parking: LOT (AFTER 6) ***Metro:*** PENTAGON

★ ★

TOBAGO'S CATERING AND CAFE

1845 SEVENTH ST. NW, WASHINGTON, DC (SHAW) 202-332-1473
www.tobagoscatering.com

THERE ARE ONLY TWO TABLES and four chairs at Tobago's Catering and Cafe, a short walk from the Shaw-Howard University Metro station. But from the small kitchen in the pint-size eatery comes a hearty salute to Caribbean cooking, specifically the flavors of Trinidad and Tobago, which is where chef-owner Antoinette Charles spent her childhood.

Her menu, drawn on a turquoise-and-rose-colored board, brings together such hits as rotisserie jerk chicken, its flesh biting with peppery heat; red snapper, fried to order and draped in a chunky blanket of tomatoes, onion, cilantro and thyme; mustard-laced crab cakes served with a zesty cocktail sauce; and roti, a type of Indian flat bread used to wrap shrimp, chicken or vegetable fillings. (Vegetarians are welcomed with rice and pigeon peas, a toss of cabbage, bell peppers and carrots, and a gravy made without meat products.) The drinking is as memorable as the eating, thanks to the fresh fruit juices made by Charles. They run from the scarlet-hued sorrel, sweet with cloves, to a fire-and-ice blend of fresh ginger and pineapple juice.

The drinking is as memorable as the eating, thanks to the fresh fruit juices made by Charles.

Curious about a dish you've never tried? The personable chef is quick to press a generous taste on you. A former investment professional and real estate agent, Charles has worn a number of hats over the years, but "cooking has always been my passion," she says. Judging from the small crowds that routinely show up in the pale green foyer of her carryout, we think she made the right career move.

Open: TU-TH, SAT 11:30-6, F 11:30-7 *Entrees:* $5.50-$12.50
Closed: SUN, M *Credit Cards:* MC, V *Reservations:* NO
Dress: CASUAL *Cross Street:* T STREET NW
Parking: STREET *Metro:* SHAW-HOWARD U

★ ★ ★

TOSCA

1112 F ST. NW, WASHINGTON, DC (PENN QUARTER) 202-367-1990
www.toscadc.com

NAMED NOT FOR PUCCINI'S OPERA but for the daughter of chef Cesare Lanfranconi, Tosca is my ready response to many dining queries. Where to go for a formal business lunch? A fancy dinner before a show? A special occasion? This northern Italian restaurant comes to the rescue with a spare but stylish interior and equally inviting food.

Not everyone appreciates the cool elegance of the space—a snapshot in beige with splashes of teal—but I find it a soothing environment even when three-quarters of the crowd is rushing through dinner to catch a concert.

Lanfranconi's starches are superb—he previously cooked at Galileo, after all. In fall, the choices lean to pappardelle made with chestnut flour and draped with a sauce of wild boar, and little dumplings featuring squash served with melted fontina cheese. No less interesting are the chef's meat and fish dishes: duck offered in the form of foie gras, breast meat and inside agnolotti—three seductions on a single plate—and simply roasted sea bass lapped with a balsamic vinegar sabayon. Dessert keeps up with the savories: Cannoli are updated with goat cheese, fig sauce and spicy hazelnuts, and a dash of salt lends pizazz to a chocolate tart.

In fall, the choices lean to pappardelle made with chestnut flour and draped with a sauce of wild boar.

All this, plus crisp service and a distinguished Italian wine list and a charming sommelier, Kathy Morgan, to show you around her adopted country.

Lunch: M-F 11:30-2:30 ***Entrees:*** $12-$18
Dinner: SUN-TH 5:30-10:30, F-SAT 5:30-11 ***Entrees:*** $14-$28
Tasting Menus: DAILY 4-COURSE $60, 6-COURSE $95
Chef's Table: M-SAT 10-COURSE $95
Pre-Theater: DAILY 5:30-7 3-COURSE PRIX FIXE $32
Credit Cards: ALL MAJOR ***Reservations:*** RECOMMENDED
Dress: BUSINESS CASUAL ***Cross Street:*** 11TH
Parking: $5 VALET AT DINNER ***Metro:*** METRO CENTER

★ ★

TUTTO BENE

501 N. RANDOLPH ST., ARLINGTON, VA 703-522-1005
www.tuttobeneitalian.com

EVENINGS, THE PLACE COULD PASS for Little Italy USA, with an old-fashioned menu of very nice pizza, thinly cut veal splashed with marsala and the occasional live opera performance.

At a time when every other Italian dining room glows Tuscan yellow, this one looks back, seemingly decades, with dark red walls and paintings of the Leaning Tower of Pisa and the Roman Colosseum. It's all fun and entertaining, one of those rare spots that is as handy for a romantic date as it is for a night out with the bambinos.

Even so, weekend lunches are when I'm most likely to show up. That's when the kitchen pauses from making pasta in favor of baking saltenas, delicious beef- or chicken-filled turnovers the size of small footballs and a staple in Bolivia, which is where the owner of Tutto Bene was born. There's more that summons Bolivia: zesty pork and corn stew, thinly sliced beef tongue over potatoes—and a guitar player whose strumming elicits smiles of recognition from the regulars who flock here for the flavor of home.

It's all fun and entertaining, one of those rare spots that is as handy for a romantic date as for a night out with the bambinos.

Open: M-TH 11:30-10:30, F-SAT 11:30-11, SUN 10:30-9
Entrees: $6.95-$19.95 ***Credit Cards:*** ALL MAJOR
Reservations: RECOMMENDED ***Dress:*** CASUAL ***Cross Street:*** GLEBE ROAD
Parking: COMPLIMENTARY VALET F-SAT DINNER ***Metro:*** BALLSTON-MU

Critic's Pick

☆ ☆ ☆

2941

2941 FAIRVIEW PARK DR., FALLS CHURCH, VA 703-270-1500
www.2941.com

EVEN BEFORE THEY TASTE A MORSEL OF FOOD, people who have never visited this coolly glamorous restaurant are in for a few surprises. First, who could imagine an expense-account restaurant in the base of an office building? Second, the stone walkway that leads from valet attendant to glass entrance is flanked by a pool stocked with lively orange fish. Third, 2941 offers a room with a view—a view of a lake (in Falls Church? who knew?).

The dining room is lovely, all glass windows, warm wood, never-ending ceilings and chairs wrapped in tangerine- or eggplant-colored fabric. Solicitous waiters in elegant suits look after your every whim, and they know the menu as if they had written it themselves.

Jonathan Krinn's food frequently lives up to the grand introduction. The chef's calamari and zucchini tempura is light as air, his steak tartare unites great raw beef with a house-made ketchup infused with brandy. Both appetizers are delicious. Stars among the main courses might include a saffron-perfumed risotto dimpled with sweet clams and a heartier plate of pork loin, lapped with a foamy beige sauce of veal stock —"and brains," a server confides—and offered with pirogi.

Stars among the main courses might include a saffron-perfumed risotto dimpled with sweet clams and a heartier plate of pork loin.

The tab will remind you of New York, but so will the sophistication.

Lunch: M-F 11:30-3 ***Entrees:*** $14-$32
Dinner: M-SAT 5:30-10 SUN NOON-9 ***Entrees:*** $22-$39
Tasting Menus: AVAILABLE AT LUNCH AND DINNER ($75, $130)
Credit Cards: ALL MAJOR ***Reservations:*** RECOMMENDED
Dress: BUSINESS CASUAL ***Cross Street:*** ROUTE 50
Parking: COMPLIMENTARY VALET ***Metro:*** DUNN LORING-MERRIFIELD

★ ★

21P

2100 P ST. NW, WASHINGTON, DC (DUPONT CIRCLE) 202-223-3824
www.21prestaurant.com

NAMED FOR ITS LOCATION in Dupont Circle, 21P sits within a block or two of Al Tiramisu, Johnny's Half Shell, Obelisk, Pizzeria Paradiso and Pesce—restaurants with high standards and legions of fans.

On its best days, the relative newcomer fits right in with the competition. The kitchen is partial to robust flavors and generous presentations, most noticeably in the first-course options. Tender braised veal cheeks are teamed with roasted-garlic custard and draped in a midnight-colored sauce that reverberates with red pepper, garlic and red wine. In another appetizer, a crepe brings together surf and turf (make that lobster and rabbit confit) along with little batons of carrot; a light mango sauce completes the picture. Soups are sure bets, including a seafood gumbo that packs a delicious wollop with pepper. Beyond, whole fried fish with a tingling dipping sauce yields a delight; lamb partnered with lentils is a snooze.

One of the signatures on the dessert list is chocolate diablo, two slender bars of what tastes like fudge punctuated with walnuts and lightened, ever so subtly, by slices of tangerine.

The restaurant's charms extend to a lovely cheese plate, a wine program that offers half-price bottles on Tuesdays and a stylish interior: soft lights, slatted walls and a glass-wrapped front room make for a romantic retreat. Somewhere between fancy and not so, dinner entrees average less than $20, and the diners next to you may be wearing jeans (look to the left) or jackets (look to the right). Service runs smart and attentive.

Chocoholics are in luck at 21P. One of the signatures on the dessert list is chocolate diablo, two slender bars of what tastes like fudge punctuated with walnuts and lightened, ever so subtly, by slices of tangerine. No less dreamy is chocolate pot de creme dressed up with whipped cream. As for the bread pudding, it's a class act, so light it's almost refreshing.

Lunch: M-F 11:30-2:30 ***Entrees:*** $10-$18
Dinner: M-TH 5:30-10, F-SAT 5:30-11, SUN 5:30-10 ***Entrees:*** $16-$28
Brunch Buffet: SUN 11:30-3 ***Price:*** $19.95
Pre-Theater: DAILY 5:30-6:30 3-COURSE PRIX FIXE $30
Credit Cards: AE, D, MC, V ***Reservations:*** RECOMMENDED
Dress: CASUAL ***Cross Street:*** 21ST ***Parking:*** STREET ***Metro:*** DUPONT CIRCLE

Critic's Pick
★ ★ ★

2 AMYS

3715 MACOMB ST. NW, WASHINGTON, DC (CLEVELAND PARK)
202-885-5700

"SEE ANYTHING YOU LIKE?" a bartender asks me as I glance first at the menu and then at the temptations printed on a chalkboard.

Frankly, I always want to order one of everything at this lively Neapolitan pizzeria, whose "little things" include addictive salt cod croquettes and deviled eggs with green sauce, and whose pies could be ordered for their sensational crusts—yeasty, crisp and slightly charred from a wood-burning oven—alone. (But don't. The toppings—fresh mozzarella, prosciutto di parma, sweet cockles—are terrific.)

Parents like 2 Amys because they know they can get a nice glass of Italian wine while they wait.

Parents like 2 Amys because they know they can get a nice glass of Italian wine while they wait; kids are welcomed with plenty of high chairs and crayons and paper. And everyone can relate to food that is made with great ingredients and lavished with attention, be it a glass of fizzy lemonade that tastes of real citrus, an appetizer of fried squash blossoms or dreamy ice creams, almond cake and marsala-laced custard.

Seating in the casual (and LOUD) main dining room spills onto a patio in good weather and a small wine bar, the latter of which finds hanging meats, soft lighting and a *bit* more quiet.

Open: M 5-10, TU-W 11-10, TH-SAT 11-11 ***Entrees:*** $7.95-$13.25
Brunch: SUN NOON-5 ***Entrees:*** $7.95-$10.95
Credit Cards: MC, V ***Reservations:*** NO
Dress: CASUAL ***Cross Street:*** WISCONSIN AVENUE NW
Parking: STREET ***Metro:*** TENLEYTOWN-AU

Critic's Pick

★ ★

URBAN BAR-B-QUE COMPANY

2007 CHAPMAN AVE., ROCKVILLE, MD 240-290-4827
www.urbanbbqco.com

IN SPITE OF ITS NAME AND URBAN SETTING, Urban Bar-B-Que Company comes off as being in the country. The welcoming howdy from whoever's at the counter fuels a laidback spirit, as does the intentionally scruffy interior. "Spitting is positively prohibited" warns a weathered sign. A shelf of cookbooks includes "The Joy of Cooking"—and "Biker Billy Cooks With Fire."

Then there's the real reason for your visit: meaty (and hot!) chicken wings, zippy chili, vinegary pulled pork, and soothing side dishes that span macaroni and cheese and baked beans. Beef brisket was shamefully citified—tame—on a recent pit stop, and collard greens lacked punch. Yet the surprises also embraced "Dave's Almost Famous Crab Cake" (co-owner David Calkins shouldn't be so modest) and a Key lime pie with pitch-perfect tang.

The welcoming howdy from whoever's at the counter fuels a laidback spirit.

Fans used to have to rush for an available stool in this shoebox, which recently added 28 seats—and beer and wine—to its list of draws.

Open: SUN-TH 11-8, F-SAT 11-9 ***Entrees:*** $5-$20
Credit Cards: ALL MAJOR ***Reservations:*** NO
Dress: CASUAL ***Cross Street:*** TWINBROOK PARKWAY
Parking: LOT ***Metro:*** TWINBROOK

★ ★

VEGETABLE GARDEN

11618 ROCKVILLE PIKE, ROCKVILLE, MD 301-468-9301
www.thevegetablegarden.com

THERE ARE NO SURPRISES when your food shows up at Vegetable Garden, because every dish gets a close-up on the menu—and every color photograph mirrors reality. Thus an order of "beef" with pecans looks exactly like it does in its picture (but what looks like beef strips is actually soy protein in a sweet glaze of sauce).

With its light pink walls and sea-green carpet, the small dining room is a modestly attractive place to refuel, and the servers are quick to bring you something refreshing from the juice bar and deliver your food, none of which includes dairy, eggs or MSG. Among the draws are crisp and greaseless spring rolls, each bite bursting with cabbage, carrot and black mushrooms; the gently tingling kung pao tofu, colorful with red and green sweet bell peppers; and soft chunks of eggplant in a delicate black bean sauce.

Among the draws are crisp and greaseless spring rolls, each bite bursting with cabbage, carrot and black mushrooms.

Vegetable Garden isn't as innovative as Sunflower, one of the area's best meatless retreats, and some of its flavors are restrained—tomato and spinach soup is thin, for instance, more spalike than truly satisfying. But the welcome is warm and the small fillips (your water is filtered) add up.

Open: DAILY 11:30-10:30 *Entrees:* $7.49-$16.99
Credit Cards: ALL MAJOR *Reservations:* RECOMMENDED
Dress: CASUAL *Cross Street:* MARINELLI ROAD
Parking: LOT *Metro:* WHITE FLINT

☆ ☆

VERMILION

1120 KING ST., ALEXANDRIA, VA 703-684-9669
www.vermilionrestaurant.com

WHATEVER VIBE YOU'RE AFTER, Vermilion serves it: Downstairs is a red-hued bar and lounge, host to fun cocktails and live entertainment after 9:30 p.m. on Tuesday and Sunday. Upstairs finds walls of brick, an eye-catching wine "cellar" and a bit more quiet with a meal.

The American menu, created by chef Bobby Beard, follows suit. Light eaters can focus on a properly tangy Caesar salad or cilantro-laced scallop seviche, while heartier appetites might home in on cheese-filled risotto cakes, accented with a zippy tomato sauce, or a big pork chop flanked by a scoop of scarily green mashed potatoes (not to worry, they're bright with basil, and delicious).

Light eaters can focus on a properly tangy Caesar salad or cilantro-laced scallop seviche.

Beard's time at Pesce, the very good seafood restaurant in Washington, is recalled in such dishes as linguine tossed with shrimp (and chorizo) and trout served in a nubby coat of cornmeal and bedded on spinach. Gentle twists keep these plates from tasting routine: The pasta is moistened with a saffron-tinged butter sauce and the fish gets a warm vinaigrette of lemon and capers.

If the desserts—second-rate creme brulee and brownies—are mere afterthoughts, the welcome is warm and the setting encourages lingering.

Lunch: M-F 11:30-3 *Entrees:* $7-$13
Dinner: SUN-TH 5:30-10, F-SAT 5:30-11 *Entrees:* $17-$25
Brunch: SAT-SUN 11:30-3 *Entrees:* $7-$13
Credit Cards: ALL MAJOR *Reservations:* RECOMMENDED
Dress: BUSINESS CASUAL *Cross Street:* FAYETTE
Parking: STREET *Metro:* KING STREET

Critic's Pick

★ ★ ★

VIDALIA

1990 M ST. NW, WASHINGTON, DC (DOWNTOWN) 202-659-1990
www.vidaliadc.com

FOLLOWING A MILLION-DOLLAR MAKEOVER in 2003 that helped diners forget they're eating underground, Vidalia took on a new chef, R.J. Cooper. Regulars can still count on finding shrimp and grits and lemon chess pie on the menu, but those Southern staples have been joined by a posse of innovations that demonstrate Cooper's range while retaining the owners' vision. (Jeff and Sallie Buben also own Bistro Bis on the Hill.)

If you haven't been to Vidalia in a while, you owe yourself a look-see. As good as its crab cake remains, a lot of places serve good models. Better to launch with sushi-grade yellowtail, cut into rectangles, lightly dusted with crushed pumpkin seeds and placed atop two little salads of diced squash, apple and almond. One mound glistens with a scooplette of ginger-olive oil sorbet, the other is draped with a frothy curry sabayon dotted with caviar. Both are scrumptious. In another memorable first course, local oysters are showcased in a bowl that also finds room for country ham, swiss chard, soft artichokes and a splash of sparkling wine.

If you haven't been to Vidalia in a while, you owe yourself a look-see.

It's tempting to order the entrees for their plate mates: Swiss chard, buttery carrot puree and candied pecans practically steal the show from sweetbread-stuffed, cornmeal-dusted rabbit. And as much as I appreciate Cooper's carefully cooked slab of wild rockfish, the dish's melting onions, black trumpet mushrooms and fingerling potatoes demand equal time from my fork. Slips—cod cooked a moment too long, smothered greens that need more tang—are infrequent. Tap the expertise of sommelier Doug Mohr, who has assembled a great collection of wines from around the globe, and you'll drink as well as you eat; his commentary on whatever you opt for brings the wine to life.

Vidalia's guiding light—the South—is underscored in gracious service and sweet (but not too sweet) endings, including a model lemon chess pie. Pastry chef Naomi Gallego makes a fetching chocolate-caramel tart, which she lightens with banana "salsa" and a drizzle of lime syrup, and her warm gingerbread is sheer comfort on a cold day. There's more: with the bill comes a blizzard of divine petit fours.

Lunch: M-F 11:30-2:30 ***Entrees:*** $15-$19
Dinner: M-TH 5:30-10, F-SAT 5:30-10:30, SUN 5-9 ***Entrees:*** $25-$34
Credit Cards: ALL MAJOR ***Reservations:*** RECOMMENDED ***Dress:*** BUSINESS CASUAL
Cross Street: 20TH ***Parking:*** $5 VALET AT DINNER ***Metro:*** DUPONT CIRCLE

★ ½

W DOMKU

821 UPSHUR ST. NW (PETWORTH)
202-722-7475

"I DIDN'T KNOW she was opening a restaurant, and she didn't know I was a chef." Eric Evans is recalling how he met his current boss, Kera Carpenter, at a neighborhood gathering a few years back. Carpenter, a former Peace Corps volunteer in Poland, was interested in opening a restaurant in the District's Takoma Park area, and Evans, a stranger, had come to support her request for a liquor license. Months later, the two ended up joining forces, transferring her concept to Petworth and broadening it with some of his input.

For Evans, W Domku, which loosely translates from Polish as "in the little house," is a bit of a homecoming. "I was born in Petworth!" he says with relish. The food he is making these days is pretty familiar to him, too: When Evans was a youngster, his parents sent him on chaperoned trips to Norway, Denmark and Sweden, he explains. "They thought it was a better education." Good call, I think to myself when my order of meatballs is placed before me. Soft, soothing and draped with a light gravy, they get a splash of color from some bright red lingonberries.

For those who choose to drink aquavit, the liquor so potent it brings to mind liquid barbed wire, dinner begins with a bang.

Pow! For those who choose to drink aquavit, the liquor so potent it brings to mind liquid barbed wire, dinner begins with a bang. The clear vodka is infused with the likes of caraway, rose petal, dill, vanilla, red chili or—my favorite—lemon grass and ginger.

Aquavit turns out to be a nice foil to the subtle flavors on the small menu, whether beet soup or a serving of sprats, silvery baby herring eaten with rye crisp, sweet mustard, chopped onions, capers and gherkins. The potato-and-bacon-filled dumplings known as pirogi are tame but tasty, their tops slicked with sour cream. A pink slab of smooth pâté, ringed in gently sweet aspic, would look at home on an elegant buffet; a couple of plump browned sausages on carrot-laced sauerkraut prove homey and strapping.

Domku has the casual feel of a community center, with mismatched sofas and chairs, a small bar, even a game room in the rear. "I wanted a homelike environment," Carpenter says. Her neighbors will find just that.

Breakfast: TH-F 8-11, SAT 8-3, SUN 10-3 ***Entrees:*** $4-$10
Lunch: TU-SAT 11-10, SUN 11-3 ***Entrees:*** $6-$17
Dinner: TU-SAT 11-10 ***Entrees:*** $6-$17
Closed: M ***Credit Cards:*** MC, V ***Reservations:*** RECOMMENDED FOR PARTIES OF 6 MORE
Dress: CASUAL ***Cross Street:*** GEORGIA AVENUE NW
Parking: STREET ***Metro:*** GEORGIA AVE-PETWORTH

★ ★

WILLOW

4301 N. FAIRFAX DRIVE, ARLINGTON, VA 703-465-8800
www.willowva.com

IT'S THE CULINARY EQUIVALENT of the old Mickey Rooney and Judy Garland films, some pals teaming up to put on a show—or in this case, a restaurant. Willow celebrates the friendships and talents of Tracy O'Grady, the former chef at Kinkead's; Kate Jansen, the co-founder of Firehook Bakery; and Brian Wolken, who previously cooked at Butterfield 9 and married O'Grady in their fledgling restaurant—amazingly, the same day it opened to the public.

In her new roost, O'Grady pays tribute to France and Italy while marching to a distinctive American beat. Ten years at the seafood-themed Kinkead's is evident in O'Grady's many fish dishes: halibut stimulated with olives and a sauce of tomato and orange, for instance, and horseradish- and bacon-paved salmon.

But you don't need to trawl among the water-born ingredients to dine well here. Rib-eye with smoked Gouda potatoes and lemony roast chicken are equals on this small and focused script, which is rounded out with excellent flatbreads (try them topped with blue cheese and fresh thyme) and lovely endings. Jansen offers an adorable cookie plate that considers just about every crowd-pleaser you can think of, and, in fall, an elegant pumpkin mousse cake with cranberry jam.

Rib-eye with smoked Gouda potatoes and lemony roast chicken are equals on this small and focused script.

The sprawling space is pleasant enough, but ambience is not the reason to visit. Food—seasonal, simple and enormously satisfying—is what's keeping Willow's seats filled.

Lunch: M-F 11:30-2:30 *Entrees:* $8-$18
Dinner: M-TH 5:30-10, F-SAT 5:30-11 *Entrees:* $18-$32
Chef's Table: M-SAT 5:30-10:30, 5-COURSE $80, 6-COURSE $90, 7-COURSE $100, 8-COURSE $110, 9-COURSE $120
Closed: SUN *Credit Cards:* ALL MAJOR *Reservations:* RECOMMENDED
Dress: BUSINESS CASUAL *Cross Street:* UTAH
Parking: LOT *Metro:* BALLSTON

☆ ☆

YECHON

4121 HUMMER RD., ANNANDALE, VA 703-914-4646
www.yechonrestaurant.com

LOOKS CAN BE MISLEADING. With its low-slung roof, brown wood siding and splash of neon, from the outside this restaurant could pass for a cowboy bar. Open the doors, though, and you'll discover another world: a room bustling with costumed waitresses who are pouring beer and ladling soup, and an SRO crowd of animated diners, many of them hip, young and Korean-American.

Their tables are crowded with little dishes of snacks, salads and condiments, the typical lead-ins to a Korean repast: pickled cucumber, silvery dried fish, sweet shredded radish, bean sprouts, potato salad, fish cake and several kinds of kimchi—as much a staple in Korea as ketchup is in the United States. Everyone around you is ordering soup or barbecue, and you should follow that lead. Out might come a little cauldron of *dae gu mae woon tang*: a simmering broth, fiery with chilies and brimming with chunks of cod and tofu, enoki mushrooms and vegetables. Heady stuff. Or a platter of tender, sweet-edged slices of beef (bulgogi) with sesame seeds and scallions, destined to be rolled up with rice and soybean paste in the crisp lettuce leaves that accompany them. The sushi is ordinary in comparison.

Everyone around you is ordering soup or barbecue, and you should follow that lead.

Service is rushed but helpful, and the hours couldn't be more convenient: Yechon is open 24/7.

Open: DAILY 24 HRS ***Entrees:*** $8.95-$20.95
Credit Cards: AE, D, MC, V ***Reservations:*** RECOMMENDED
Dress: CASUAL ***Cross Street:*** LITTLE RIVER TURNPIKE / ROUTE 236
Parking: LOT ***Metro:*** VIENNA / FAIRFAX-GMU

★ 1/2

YEE HWA

1009 21ST ST. NW, WASHINGTON, DC (DOWNTOWN)
202-833-1244

AS A WORLD CAPITAL, Washington dishes up plenty of global cooking, be it the stews of Ethiopia, the curries of India or the potato dishes made famous by Peru. One cuisine that is abundant in the suburbs of Northern Virginia but pretty much missing from the city is Korean. One of the few exceptions is downtown's Yee Hwa, which offers spicy codfish soup, marinated short ribs, the signature kimchi (pungent pickled vegetables) and even Korean wine, or soju, on its menu.

A weave of hearty and bold flavors, the cooking at Yee Hwa unfolds in a dining room of warm wood, sea-blue carpet and pale-rose booths; glass partitions between the tables are etched with the name of the restaurant in Korean characters. Part of the menu is Japanese, but Japanese food is not the reason to come here. Bibim bap—that lusty marriage of rice, shredded beef and vegetables, served with hot chili paste in a heavy stone bowl—definitely is. At night, the table grills come out, allowing diners the chance to stir-cook their way to a meal of barbecue, Korean-style.

At night, the table grills come out, allowing diners the chance to stir-cook their way to a meal of barbecue, Korean-style.

Lunch: M-F 11:30-3, SAT-SUN NOON-3 *Entrees:* $7.95-$16.95
Dinner: DAILY 3-10 *Entrees:* $10.95-$32.95
Credit Cards: ALL MAJOR *Reservations:* RECOMMENDED
Dress: CASUAL *Cross Street:* K STREET NW
Parking: STREET *Metro:* FOGGY BOTTOM-GWU

★ ½

YOKO

332 ELDEN ST., HERNDON, VA
703-464-7000

HALF A DOZEN MEALS at Yoko have taught me this: To find the restaurant's best assets, all you need to do is use your eyes. Notice how busy the sushi chefs always seem to be? The long, narrow dining room with its display of Japanese masks and its well-trafficked wood floor is pretty in a spare fashion, but it's the dozen or so seats at the sushi bar that connoisseurs seem most interested in (unless they also want to keep up with whatever game is playing on the TV set, mounted in the rear).

A complimentary fillip of custardy tofu slices, animated with red chili and sesame oil, starts a meal off on a hospitable note, and you're wise to continue with something uncooked. All the usual suspects—salmon, flounder, mackerel and sea urchin—can be found on the sushi and sashimi menu, as can baby octopus, pleasantly chewy and subtly sweet from its soy sauce glaze, and raw, sweet shrimp sushi, trailed by an escort of spiky, deep-fried shrimp heads. "Try it, it's very good," one of the helpful waitresses coached my tablemates as she set the plate down. She was right: The heat of the crunchy delicacy is foiled by its cool daikon garnish.

My detours from sushi have been most successful when they've included udon and hamachi kama.

Frying isn't the restaurant's strong suit, though. The pale batter that clings to the tempura dishes, and the mouthful of oil one encounters with every bite of vegetable, shrimp or chicken tempura, indicates fat that's not hot enough to cook them properly; the exceptions are the pan-fried dumplings of beef and vegetables (gyoza) and delicate shrimp (shumai). My detours from sushi have been most successful when they've included udon, its thick wheat noodles filling a big bowl of broth along with wisps of greens, mushrooms and pink-edged fish cake slices, and hamachi kama. The wafer-crisp skin of this broiled, salt-sprinkled yellowtail jaw yields to a delicate interior and a meaty treat. A relaxing jazz soundtrack and a staff that easily juggles soloists, dates and small families add to the dining charms.

Lunch: M-SAT 11:30-2:30 ***Entrees:*** $9-$15
Dinner: M-TH 5:30-10 F-SAT 5:30-10:30 SUN 5:30-9:30
Entrees: $10-$25 ***Credit Cards:*** ALL MAJOR ***Reservations:*** RECOMMENDED
Dress: BUSINESS CASUAL ***Cross Street:*** HERNDON PARKWAY
Parking: LOT ***Metro:*** NO
Second Location: 2946-J CHAIN BRIDGE RD., OAKTON, VA, 703-255-6644

★ ★

YUAN FU

798 ROCKVILLE PIKE, ROCKVILLE, MD
301-762-5937

AN ADMISSION: I'm not generally an advocate of food manipulated to look like something other than what it is. But this vegetarian Chinese kitchen convinces me that there can be delicious exceptions.

The color photographs on the menu look much like crab and duck, for instance, and the smells that follow those dishes are truly fragrant. But the orange-flavored "beef," seemingly caramelized morsels in a citrusy dark sauce, turns out to be soybean protein, while the kung pao "shrimp," tossed with bright green peppers and peanuts, is actually white yams having some fun with your taste buds. That nicely crisped skin on the "fish?" It's seaweed.

That nicely crisped skin on the "fish?" It's seaweed.

As you might expect, actual vegetables are paid great respect; don't miss the sliced, battered eggplant or the crackling spinach pancake, accented with sesame seeds and electrified by some hot mustard sauce. Tucked into a small shopping strip, this dining room is pretty in green and nice enough for toasting a special occasion—although since there's no alcohol, it'll have to be with a soda or tea.

Lunch: DAILY 11-4:30 ***Entrees:*** $5.95-$7.95
Dinner: SUN-TH 4:30-10, F-SAT 4:30-10:30 ***Entrees:*** $7.50-$13.95
Credit Cards: AE, MC, V ***Reservations:*** RECOMMENDED
Dress: CASUAL ***Cross Street:*** WOOTTON PARKWAY
Parking: LOT ***Metro:*** ROCKVILLE

Critic's Pick
★ ★ ★

ZAYTINYA

701 NINTH ST. NW, WASHINGTON, DC (PENN QUARTER) 202-638-0800
www.zaytinya.com

EVER SINCE THIS SPARE, sweeping ode to the flavors of the Mediterranean opened in Washington's Penn Quarter, it has been my response to all sorts of questions. Such as, "What's fun and exciting?" And, "Where can I go with some friends and not spend a ton of money?" And also, simply, "What's really good?"

A big communal table, a soaring grid of shelves set with votive candles and an enthusiastic staff create a convivial party; the kitchen manages to successfully turn out dozens of the appetizers known as mezze, often in creative ways. Tiny lamb meatballs come sweetened with fruit and enhanced by cinnamon oil, for instance, while feta cheese is hooked up with tomato marmalade. Yet Zaytinya does justice to the Greek classics, too: Spinach and cheese pie is fashioned from handmade phyllo, and if there's a better taramasalata (whipped cod roe) around, I've yet to taste it.

Fishermen's stew is tame despite its saffron broth, and so is the chicken kebab, but misses like that are outnumbered on the epic menu, which also features some lovely Greek wines. Among the best reasons to linger is walnut ice cream set off with crisp sails of sheer pastry, tangy yogurt cream and honeyed gelatin. It's called Turkish Delight, and it lives up to its billing.

Tiny lamb meatballs come sweetened with fruit and enhanced by cinnamon oil, while feta cheese is hooked up with tomato marmalade.

Open: SUN-M 11:30-10, T-TH 11:30-11:30, F-SAT 11:30-MIDNIGHT
Entrees: $22 (MEZZE $4.25-$9.95)
Credit Cards: ALL MAJOR ***Reservations:*** RECOMMENDED
Dress: CASUAL ***Cross Street:*** G STREET NW
Parking: $12 VALET AT DINNER M-SAT ***Metro:*** GALLERY PLACE-CHINATOWN

★ ★

ZENGO

781 SEVENTH ST. NW, WASHINGTON, DC (PENN QUARTER) 202-393-2929
www.modernmexican.com

WONTON TACOS, ANYONE? The latest culinary addition to Penn Quarter features a celebrity partner, Placido Domingo, general director of the Washington National Opera, and a veteran New York chef, Richard Sandoval, a native of Mexico who now counts seven restaurants around the country in his domain. In his latest production, the chef fuses the flavors of Asia with those of Latin America, and mostly with good results.

The name explains the concept. Zengo means "give and take" in Japanese. Thus, a sushi roll of salmon is dabbed with a smoked jalapeno mayonnaise—the aptly named "Volcano"—and a plate of coin-size arepas is topped with shredded pork sweetened with hoisin sauce. Broiled black cod swims to the table on a raft of asparagus, while rectangles of fried tofu team with bok choy in a meatless entree enhanced by a delicately sweet ginger sauce. A gaggle of eager but only sometimes efficient servers helps guide you through the many possibilities.

Crafted by Adamstein & Demetriou, the 195-seat Zengo spreads across two floors and includes a seviche bar and lounge. The warm palette evokes fruit and wood colors; outsize windows frame the street action. So far, so good. But the setting is less for the odd brown orbs floating above the grand staircase ("they look like cow patties," I hear one diner remark) and bathrooms that are semi-open to a hall connecting to the kitchen. Let's hope neither is the beginning of a new design trend.

The name explains the concept. Zengo means "give and take" in Japanese.

Lunch: M-F 11:30-2:30 *Entrees:* $15-$21 (SMALL PLATES: $9-$11)
Dinner: DAILY 5-10 *Entrees:* $17-$27 (SMALL PLATES: $9-$11)
Credit Cards: AE, DC, MC, V *Reservations:* RECOMMENDED
Dress: BUSINESS CASUAL *Cross Street:* H STREET NW
Parking: $12 VALET AT DINNER *Metro:* GALLERY PLACE-CHINATOWN

☆ ☆

ZEST

200 S. MARKET ST., FREDERICK, MD 301-620-7480
www.eatatzest.com

HAVING RELOCATED FROM MONROVIA to Frederick, Zest still lives up to its sunny moniker. The airy storefront fairly beams with yellow paint and its shelves bulge with either cookbooks or wine—reminders of how chef-owners David Jones and Keith Sleppy decorated their original place.

And as before, their menu kicks off with "tastings"—six or so hearty hors d'oeuvres to whet one's appetite. Oysters dusted with cornmeal get a kick start from a drizzle of spicy remoulade, tender squid is tossed with basil and garlic, and corn custard trembles atop its lacy doily of fried potatoes. Slightly larger, appetizers run to vegetable "sushi" that is more clever than delicious and a real standout: sweetbreads served like a fancy hamburger, between toasted rounds of brioche and alongside elegant fingerling potato chips.

Entrees are all over the map. Whatever sounds homiest is apt to be best. Fried chicken arranged with shrimp and grits squeezes two all-American hits on one stage, while moist rabbit arrives with a creamy ragout of Brussels sprouts and baby bok choy. Pork shanks, on the other hand, offer none of the punch you'd expect of the promised jerk seasoning, which smacks more of the Midwest than the Caribbean. Better: wasabi-crusted halibut circled with a gingery carrot sauce.

Fried chicken arranged with shrimp and grits squeezes two all-American hits on one stage.

A sense of humor prevails in both the dining room, where Jones frequently plays host, and on the bill of fare, which includes a sampler of salads titled "Yes, A Salad Comes With That" —an in-house joke referring to customers who have asked about what they can expect with their entree.

Lunch: M-SAT 11-3 *Entrees:* $9-$14
Dinner: M-SAT 5-10, SUN 4-8 *Entrees:* $20-$30
Tasting Menus: 5-COURSE $59, 7-COURSE $79
Brunch: SUN 11-3 *Entrees:* $15-$21
Credit Cards: AE, MC, V *Reservations:* RECOMMENDED
Dress: CASUAL *Cross Street:* SOUTH
Parking: STREET *Metro:* NO

★ ★ ½

ZOLA

800 F ST. NW, WASHINGTON, DC (PENN QUARTER) 202-654-0999
www.zoladc.com

WHEN YOUR FOOD is served in a place linked to the International Spy Museum, you can't simply serve what's routine. That explains why chef Frank Morales slips skate into his fish and chips, which he makes even more festive with colorful peppers and three dipping sauces, and why he whips up three kinds of butterscotch pudding, each of which features a different single-malt Scotch—and each of which is so potent, you expect an ID check before ordering. Following a period in which this glam restaurant in Penn Quarter was serving some truly tired cooking, Zola is back on track.

Frustrated with bad service? The staff at Zola reminds us that good attendants are still to be found. The restaurant was among the first in the city to offer black napkins to customers wearing dark clothes and continues to promote the pleasures of the grape: The oval wine displays in the center of each small dining room aren't just handsome props but represent serious collections from around the world. Meanwhile, the look is as fresh and fascinating as ever: Floating glass panels with shadowy portraits of film noir characters separate the three small main dining rooms even as they allow guests to spy on one another from a distance. Tall red velvet booths lend a shock of color to an otherwise sedate interior palette, and the seat backs are punctuated by porthole-size, metal-ringed windows.

Following a period in which this glam restaurant in Penn Quarter was serving some truly tired cooking, Zola is back on track.

Morales likes to tweak familiar dishes. Instead of pizza, he serves a pie (socca), whose thin crust is fashioned from ground chickpeas. Broccoli soup gets a topping of smoked mozzarella and chicken is pounded into submission, brushed with soy sauce and garnished with a hunk of sweet corn. There's even a spin on S'Mores—S'Mores!—for dessert, highlighting house-baked graham crackers and marshmallow and chocolate fondue. (Talk about campy!) Zola is as playful as it is delicious.

Lunch: M-F 11:30-3 *Entrees:* $10-$23
Dinner: M-TH 5-10, F-SAT 5-11, SUN 5-9 *Entrees:* $16-$25
Pre-Theater: DAILY 5-7 3-COURSE PRIX FIXE $28
Credit Cards: ALL MAJOR *Reservations:* RECOMMENDED
Dress: BUSINESS CASUAL *Cross Street:* EIGHTH
Parking: $10 VALET DAILY AT 5 *Metro:* GALLERY PLACE-CHINATOWN

THE ESSENTIAL GUIDE

A roundup of restaurants to help you find the features and food you want, fast

Citrus Cafe, Bryans Road, MD

Listings by Cuisine

AFGHAN

Afghan

AMERICAN / CONTEMPORARY

Addie's
Apartment 2G
Aster
Bob Kinkead's Colvin Run Tavern
Blue Gin
Buck's Fishing & Camping
Carlyle
Cashion's Eat Place
Charleston
Circle Bistro
CityZen
Claire's at the Depot
Coastal Flats
Corduroy
Dahlia
Equinox
Firefly
Foti's
Inn at Little Washington
Jackie's
Komi
Mark and Orlando's
minibar at Cafe Atlantico
Nora
Patowmack Farm
Poste
Restaurant Eve
Rock Creek
Tabard Inn
Tallula
Tasting Room
2941
21P
Vermilion
Vidalia
Willow
Zest
Zola

AMERICAN / TRADITIONAL

Artie's
Bar Pilar
Black Market Bistro
Breadline
Busboys and Poets
Cantler's Riverside Inn
C.F. Folks
Charleston
Charlie Palmer Steak
Colorado Kitchen
DC Coast
Del Merei Grille
The Diner
Harris Crab House
Johnny's Half Shell
Kinkead's
Majestic Cafe
Matchbox
Mimi's American Bistro
Mitsitam Native Foods Cafe
Occidental
Oceanaire Seafood Room
Old Ebbitt Grill
O'Learys
Oval Room
The Palm
Prime Rib
Ray's the Steaks
1789
Sonoma
Sweetwater Tavern
Urban Bar-B-Que Company

ASIAN

Merkado Kitchen
Raku
Spices
Sunflower Vegetarian Restaurant
TenPenh
Zengo

AUSTRALIAN

Inn at Easton

BELGIAN

Belga Cafe
Le Mannequin Pis

BURMESE

Mandalay

CARIBBEAN

Islander Caribbean
Sweet Mango Cafe
Tobago's Catering and Cafe

CHINESE

A & J
Eat First
Fortune
Good Fortune
Hollywood East Cafe
on the Boulevard

Joe's Noodle House
Mr. Chen's Organic Chinese Cuisine
New Fortune
TemptAsian Cafe
Yuan Fu

CONTINENTAL

Citrus Cafe
Patowmack Farm

CUBAN

Cuban Corner

ETHIOPIAN

Dukem
Etete

FRENCH

Bistro d'Oc
Bistro Francais
Bistrot du Coin
Bistrot Lafayette
Bistrot Lepic
Gerard's Place
L'Auberge Chez Francois
Le Paradou
Les Halles
Marcel's
Michel Richard Citronelle
Montmartre

GERMAN

Old Europe

GREEK

Mourayo
Mykonos Grill
Zaytinya

INDIAN

Amma Vegetarian Kitchen
Bombay Club
Bombay Tandoor
Delhi Club
Heritage India
Nirvana

ITALIAN

Al Crostino
Al Tiramisu
Amici Miei
Cafe Milano
Famous Luigi's
Galileo
Laboratorio del Galileo
Maestro
Notti Bianche
Obelisk
Osteria del Galileo
Palena
Pizzeria Paradiso
Sette Osteria
Tosca
Tutto Bene
2 Amys

KOSHER

Eli's

JAPANESE

Kaz Sushi Bistro
Kotobuki
Kuma
Makoto
Matsutake
Sushi Taro
Sushi-Ko
Yoko

KOREAN

Annangol
Gom Ba Woo
Han Sung Oak
Sorak Garden
Yechon
Yee Hwa

LATIN AMERICAN

Cafe Atlantico
Ceiba
Ceviche
Crisp & Juicy
Samantha's
Zengo

MALAYSIAN / SINGAPOREAN

Straits of Malaya

MEDITERRANEAN

Pazo

MIDDLE EASTERN

Amsterdam Falafelshop
Couscous Cafe & Catering
Layalina

Listings by Cuisine

~ CONTINUED ~

MEXICAN

Casa Blanca
Don Lobo's Mexican Grill
Guajillo
Oyamel Cocina Mexicana
Rosa Mexicano
Samantha's
Taqueria Tres Reyes

MOROCCAN

Taste of Morocco

PERUVIAN

Casa Blanca
Costa Verde
El Chalan
La Flor de la Canela

PIZZA

Cafe Milano
Famous Luigi's
Matchbox
Pizzeria Paradiso
2 Amys

PORTUGUESE

Tavira

SCANDINAVIAN / EAST EUROPEAN

W Domku

SEAFOOD

Acadiana
Black Market Bistro
Bonefish Grill
Cantler's Riverside Inn
Coastal Flats
DC Coast
Hank's Oyster Bar
Harris Crab House
Jerry's Seafood
Johnny's Half Shell
Kinkead's
Oceanaire Seafood Room
O'Learys
Pesce
Stoney's Seafood House

SOUTHERN

Charleston
Colorado Kitchen
Vidalia

SPANISH

Cloud Dining Lounge
Jaleo
Taberna del Alabardero

STEAKHOUSES

Capital Grille
Charlie Palmer Steak
Lewnes' Steakhouse
The Palm
Prime Rib
Ray's the Steaks

SUSHI

Kaz Sushi Bistro
Kotobuki
Makoto
Matsutake
Raku
Spices
Sushi Taro
Sushi-Ko
Yechon
Yoko

THAI

Bangkok 54
Crystal Thai
Kanlaya Thai Cuisine
Natta Thai
Regent Thai
Sakoontra
Thai Basil
Thai Coast
Thai Square
Thaiphoon

TURKISH

Tabaq Bistro

VEGETARIAN

Amma Vegetarian Kitchen
Sunflower Vegetarian Restaurant
Vegetable Garden
Yuan Fu

VIETNAMESE

Green Papaya
Huong Que (Four Sisters)
Minh's

Washington, D.C. by Neighborhood

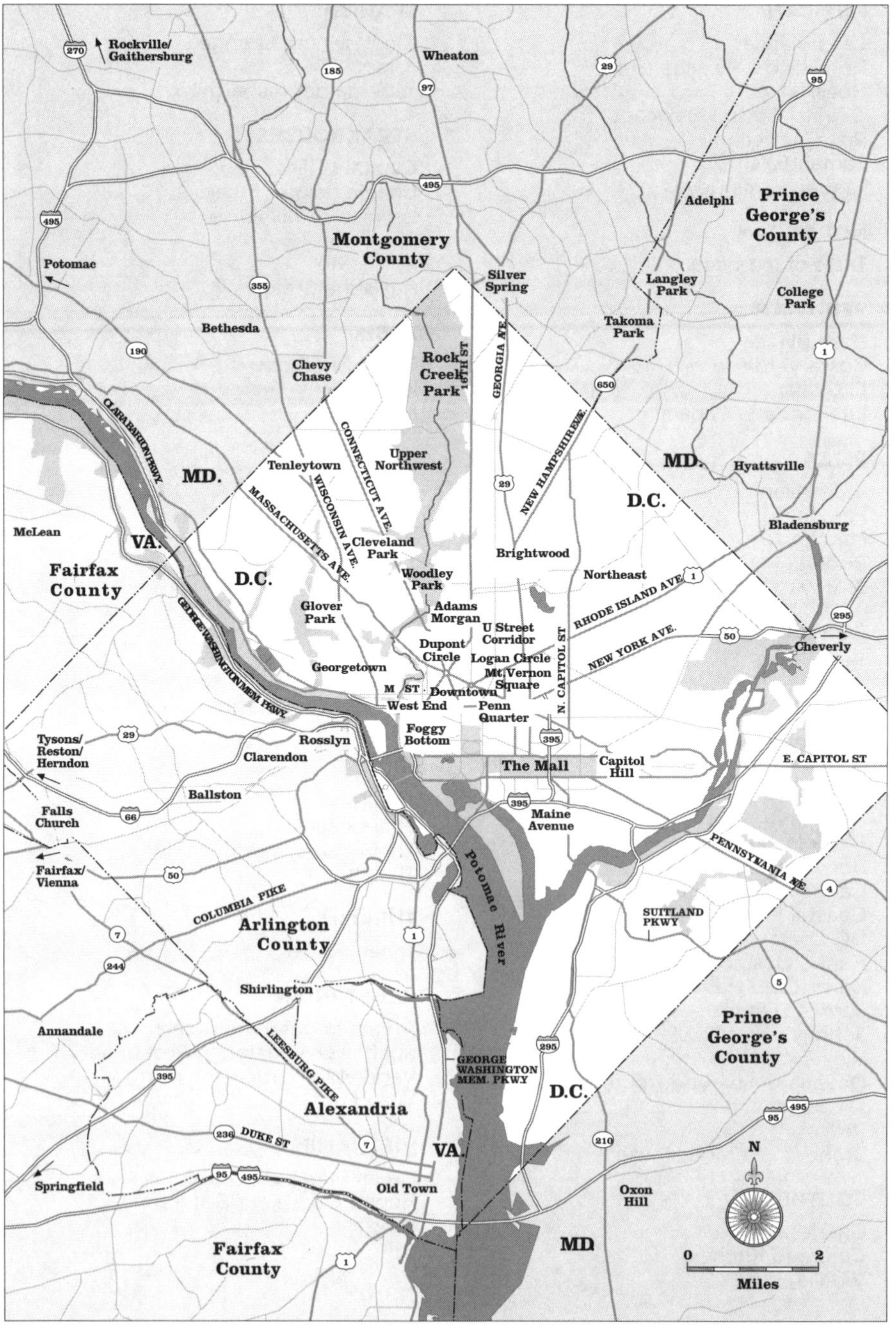

Where They Are

DISTRICT OF COLUMBIA

ADAMS MORGAN

Amsterdam Falafelshop
Cashion's Eat Place
The Diner

BRIGHTWOOD

Colorado Kitchen

CAPITOL HILL

Belga Cafe
Charlie Palmer Steak
Montmartre
Sonoma

CHINATOWN

Eat First
Kanlaya Thai Cuisine
Matchbox

CLEVELAND PARK

Palena
Spices
2 Amys

DOWNTOWN / 16TH STREET AND EAST

Acadiana
Casa Blanca
Ceiba
Corduroy
DC Coast
Gerard's Place
Les Halles
Occidental
Oceanaire Seafood Room
Old Ebbitt Grill
TenPenh

DOWNTOWN / 16TH STREET AND WEST

Bombay Club
Breadline
Couscous Cafe & Catering
El Chalan
Equinox
Famous Luigi's
Galileo
Heritage India
Kaz Sushi Bistro
Laboratorio del Galileo
Nirvana
Osteria del Galileo
Oval Room
Prime Rib
Taberna del Alabardero
Vidalia
Yee Hwa

DUPONT CIRCLE

Al Tiramisu
Bistrot du Coin
C.F. Folks
Cloud Dining Lounge
Eli's
Firefly
Hank's Oyster Bar
Johnny's Half Shell
Komi
Mark and Orlando's
Mimi's American Bistro
Mourayo
Nora
Obelisk
The Palm
Pesce
Pizzeria Paradiso
Raku
Regent Thai Cuisine
Sette Osteria
Straits of Malaya
Sushi Taro
Tabard Inn
Thaiphoon
21P

FOGGY BOTTOM / WEST END

Circle Bistro
Kinkead's
Marcel's
Notti Bianche

GEORGETOWN

Amma Vegetarian Kitchen
Bistro Francais
Bistrot Lepic
Blue Gin
Cafe Milano
Don Lobo's Mexican Grill
Michel Richard Citronelle
Pizzeria Paradiso
1789
Thai Coast

GLOVER PARK

Heritage India
Old Europe
Sushi-Ko

LOGAN CIRCLE

Merkado Kitchen

NATIONAL MALL

Mitsitam Native Foods Cafe

PALISADES

Kotobuki
Makoto

PENN QUARTER

Bistro d'Oc
Capital Grille
Cafe Atlantico
Jaleo
Le Paradou
minibar at Cafe Atlantico
Poste
Rosa Mexicano
Zaytinya
Zola

PETWORTH

W Domku
Sweet Mango Cafe

SHAW

Etete
Tobago's Catering and Cafe

SOUTHWEST WATERFRONT

CityZen

SPRING VALLEY

Dahlia

TENLEYTOWN

Kuma

UPPER NW

Buck's Fishing & Camping

U STREET CORRIDOR

Al Crostino
Bar Pilar
Busboys and Poets
Cafe Saint-Ex
Dukem
Islander Caribbean
Tabaq Bistro

WOODLEY PARK

Mr. Chen's Organic Chinese Cuisine

MARYLAND

ANNAPOLIS

Cantler's Riverside Inn
Lewnes' Steakhouse
O'Learys

BALTIMORE

Charleston
Pazo

BALTIMORE COUNTY

Bonefish Grill

BETHESDA

Green Papaya
Jaleo
Raku
Rock Creek

CALVERT COUNTY

Stoney's Seafood House

CHARLES COUNTY

Citrus Cafe

CHEVY CHASE

Tavira

EASTERN SHORE

Harris Crab House
Inn at Easton

FREDERICK

Tasting Room
Zest

OLNEY

Le Mannequin Pis

PRINCE GEORGE'S COUNTY

Jerry's Seafood
Taqueria Tres Reyes

ROCKVILLE / GAITHERSBURG

A & J
Addie's
Amici Miei
Black Market Bistro
Bonefish Grill
Crisp & Juicy
Cuban Corner
Joe's Noodle House

La Flor de la Canela
Mykonos Grill
New Fortune
Urban Bar-B-Que Company
Vegetable Garden
Yuan Fu

SILVER SPRING / WHEATON

Ceviche
Crisp & Juicy
Good Fortune
Hollywood East Cafe
on the Boulevard
Jackie's
Mandalay
Samantha's

VIRGINIA

ALEXANDRIA

Afghan
Bistrot Lafayette
Del Merei Grille
Majestic Cafe
Restaurant Eve
Vermilion

ANNANDALE / SPRINGFIELD

A & J
Annangol
Gom Ba Woo
Sorak Garden
TemptAsian Cafe
Yechon

ARLINGTON

Bangkok 54
Carlyle
Costa Verde
Crisp & Juicy
Crystal Thai
Delhi Club
Guajillo
Jaleo
Layalina
Matsutake (3 locations)
Minh's
Oyamel Cocina Mexicana
Ray's the Steaks
Tallula
Taste of Morocco
Thai Square
Thaiphoon
Tutto Bene
Willow

CHANTILLY

Bonefish Grill
Sweetwater Tavern
Thai Basil

FAIRFAX / BURKE

Artie's
Bonefish Grill
Coastal Flats
Sakoontra
Sweetwater Tavern

FALLS CHURCH

Crisp & Juicy
Fortune
Han Sung Oak
Huong Que (Four Sisters)
2941

FREDERICKSBURG

Bonefish Grill

GREAT FALLS

L'Auberge Chez Francois

RESTON / HERNDON / STERLING

Fortune
Matsutake
Sweetwater Tavern
Yoko

TYSONS CORNER

Bob Kinkead's Colvin Run Tavern
Maestro
The Palm

VIENNA

Amma Vegetarian Kitchen
Bombay Tandoor
Natta Thai
Sunflower Vegetarian Restaurant

VIRGINIA COUNTRYSIDE

Apartment 2G
Aster
Bonefish Grill
Claire's at the Depot
Foti's
Inn at Little Washington
Pawtomack Farm

The Essential Guide

CHEAP EATS

(DINNER ENTREES STARTING UNDER $10)

A & J
Amma Vegetarian Kitchen
Amsterdam Falafelshop
Annangol
Bangkok 54
Bar Pilar
Busboys and Poets
Carlyle
Cloud Dining Lounge
Coastal Flats
Costa Verde
Crisp & Juicy
Crystal Thai
Cuban Corner
Delhi Club
The Diner
Dukem
Eat First
Green Papaya
Guajillo
Han Sung Oak
Hollywood East Cafe on the Boulevard
Huong Que (Four Sisters)
Joe's Noodle House
La Flor de la Canela
Layalina
Mandalay
Matsutake
Mimi's American Bistro
Minh's
Mr. Chen's Organic Chinese Cuisine
Natta Thai
New Fortune
Nirvana
Notti Bianche
Osteria del Galileo
Oyamel Cocina Mexicana
Pizzeria Paradiso
Rock Creek
Sakoontra
Samantha's
Spices
Sunflower Vegetarian Restaurant
Sweet Mango Cafe
Sweetwater Tavern
TemptAsian Cafe
Thai Basil
Thai Square
Thaiphoon
Tobago's Catering and Cafe
Tutto Bene
2 Amys
Urban Bar-B-Que Company
Vegetable Garden
W Domku
Yechon
Yuan Fu

CHEF'S TABLE AVAILABLE

Galileo
Inn at Little Washington
Laboratorio del Galileo
Le Mannequin Pis
Michel Richard Citronelle
Tosca
Willow

WHERE TO GET BREAKFAST

A & J
Black Market Bistro
Breadline
Busboys and Poets
Casa Blanca
Circle Bistro
Couscous Cafe & Catering
The Diner
Firefly
Gom Ba Woo
Hollywood East Cafe on the Boulevard
Maestro
Michel Richard Citronelle
Notti Bianche
Old Ebbitt Grill
Poste
Tabard Inn
W Domku

OPEN LATE AT NIGHT

24 / 7

The Diner
Yechon

4 AM

Amsterdam Falafelshop (F-Sat)
Bistro Francais (F-Sat)

3 AM

Amsterdam Falafelshop (Th)
Bistro Francais (Sun-Th)
Eat First (F-Sat)
Sette Osteria (F- Sat)

2:30 AM

Amsterdam Falafelshop (Tu-W)

2 AM

Annangol (M - Sat)
Busboys and Poets (F- Sat)
Dukem (F- Sat)
Eat First (Sun-Th)
Good Fortune (F- Sat)
Hollywood East Cafe
on the Boulevard (F-Sat)
New Fortune (F-Sat)
Sette Osteria (M-Th)

1 AM

Bar Pilar
Bistrot du Coin (Th-Sat)
Cafe Milano
Dukem (Sun-Th)
Good Fortune (M - Th, Sun)
Hollywood East Cafe
on the Boulevard (Sun-Th)
New Fortune (Sun-Th)
Sette Osteria (F-Sat)

MIDNIGHT

Al Crostino (F- Sat)
Amsterdam Falafelshop (Sun - M)
Annangol (Sun)
Artie's (F-Sat)
Blue Gin (M-Sat)
Busboys and Poets (Sun-Th)
Carlyle (F-Sat)
Coastal Flats (F-Sat)
Famous Luigi's
Jaleo (F-Sat)
Les Halles
Lewnes' Steakhouse
Old Ebbitt Grill
Pizzeria Paradiso (F-Sat)
Samantha's (F-Sat)
Sette Osteria (Sun)
Tabaq Bistro (F-Sat)

FOR LIVE ENTERTAINMENT OR DANCING (D)

Bombay Club
Bombay Tandoor
Busboys and Poets
Cafe Saint-Ex
Ceviche
Charlie Palmer Steak
Costa Verde
Dukem
El Chalan
Etete
Islander Caribbean
Jaleo
Kinkead's
Les Halles
Marcel's
Mimi's American Bistro
Old Europe
Oyamel Cocina Mexicana
Pazo
Prime Rib
Tabaq Bistro
Taste of Morocco
Tutto Bene
Urban Bar-B-Que Company
Vermilion
W Domku

RESTAURANTS THAT OFFER PRIVATE DINING

Acadiana
Apartment 2G
Artie's
Aster
Bistro d'Oc
Bistro Francais
Bistrot Lafayette
Bistrot Lepic
Blue Gin
Bob Kinkead's Colvin Run Tavern
Bombay Tandoor
Cafe Milano
Capital Grille
Ceiba
Ceviche
Charleston
Charlie Palmer Steak
Circle Bistro
CityZen
Claire's at the Depot
Cloud Dining Lounge
Corduroy
DC Coast
Eat First
Equinox
Famous Luigi's
Firefly
Fortune
Galileo
Harris Crab House
Heritage India
Huong Que (Four Sisters)
Inn at Easton
Inn at Little Washington
Islander Caribbean
Jerry's Seafood
Kanlaya Thai Cuisine

Kinkead's
L'Auberge Chez Francois
Laboratorio del Galileo
Le Paradou
Les Halles
Lewnes' Steakhouse
Maestro
Marcel's
Michel Richard Citronelle
Mitsitam Native Foods Cafe
Mykonos Grill
New Fortune
Nirvana
Nora
Occidental
Oceanaire Seafood Room
Old Ebbitt Grill
Old Europe
Oval Room
Oyamel Cocina Mexicana
Palm
Pazo
Pizzeria Paradiso (Georgetown)
Poste
Prime Rib
Regent Thai Cuisine
Restaurant Eve
1789
Sorak Garden
Stoney's Seafood House
Sushi Taro
Sweet Mango Cafe
Tabard Inn
Tallula
Tasting Room
Tavira
Tosca
Tutto Bene
2941
21P
Vegetable Garden
Vidalia
Willow
Zaytinya
Zest
Zola

FAMILY-FRIENDLY RESTAURANTS

A & J
Addie's
Afghan
Amma Vegetarian Kitchen
Amsterdam Falafelshop
Artie's
Belga Cafe
Bistro d'Oc
Black Market Bistro
Bonefish Grill
Cafe Saint-Ex
Cantler's Riverside Inn
Carlyle
Ceviche
Claire's at the Depot
Cloud Dining Lounge
Coastal Flats
Colorado Kitchen
Costa Verde
Couscous Cafe & Catering
Crystal Thai
Cuban Corner
Dahlia
Del Merei Grille
Delhi Club
The Diner
Eli's
Etete
Famous Luigi's
Fortune
Good Fortune
Guajillo
Hank's Oyster Bar
Harris Crab House
Hollywood East Cafe
on the Boulevard
Huong Que (Four Sisters)
Islander Caribbean
Jackie's
Jerry's Seafood
Joe's Noodle House
Kanlaya Thai Cuisine
La Flor de la Canela
Layalina
Le Mannequin Pis
Les Halles
Lewnes' Steakhouse
Majestic Cafe
Mark and Orlando's
Matchbox
Merkado Kitchen
Mimi's American Bistro
Minh's
Mitsitam Native Foods Cafe
Mr. Chen's Organic Chinese Cuisine
New Fortune
Nirvana
Occidental
Old Ebbitt Grill
Osteria del Galileo
Oyamel Cocina Mexicana
Patowmack Farm

Pazo
Pesce
Pizzeria Paradiso
Raku
Ray's the Steaks
Regent Thai Cuisine
Rock Creek
Sakoontra
Samantha's
Sette Osteria
Sorak Garden
Spices
Stoney's Seafood House
Sunflower Vegetarian Restaurant
Sweet Mango Cafe
Sweetwater Tavern
Tallula
Taste of Morocco
Tasting Room
Tavira
Thai Basil
Thai Coast
Thai Square
Thaiphoon
Tobago's Catering and Cafe
Tutto Bene
21P
2 Amys
Urban Bar-B-Que Company
Vegetable Garden
Vermilion
W Domku
Yechon
Yuan Fu
Zaytinya
Zest

CHILDREN'S MENUS / PORTIONS AVAILABLE

Addie's
Artie's
Black Market Bistro
Bonefish Grill
Cafe Saint-Ex
Cantler's Riverside Inn
Carlyle
Coastal Flats
Cuban Corner
Dahlia
Del Merei Grille
The Diner
Eli's
Etete
Harris Crab House
Les Halles
Matchbox
Mitsitam Native Foods Cafe
Occidental
Old Ebbitt Grill
Old Europe
Oyamel Cocina Mexicana
Stoney's Seafood House
Sweet Mango Cafe
Sweetwater Tavern
Tallula
Tavira
21P
Urban Bar-B-Que Company
Zest

THE BRUNCH BUNCH

A & J (Dim Sum)
Artie's
Bar Pilar
Belga Cafe
Bistro d'Oc
Bistro Francais
Bistrot du Coin
Black Market Bistro
Bombay Club
Bombay Tandoor
Busboys and Poets
Cafe Atlantico
Cafe Saint-Ex
Carlyle
Cashion's Eat Place
Circle Bistro
Citrus Cafe
Claire's at the Depot
Colorado Kitchen
Delhi Club
Firefly
Fortune (Dim Sum)
Guajillo
Hank's Oyster Bar
Jackie's
Jaleo
Kinkead's
Les Halles
Maestro
Majestic Cafe
Merkado Kitchen
Mimi's American Bistro
Montmartre
Nirvana
Old Ebbitt Grill
Oyamel Cocina Mexicana
Patowmack Farm
Poste
Rosa Mexicano

Sette Osteria
Sweet Mango Cafe
Tabaq Bistro
Tabard Inn
Tallula
21P
Vermilion
W Domku
Zaytinya

BUFFETS

(THESE BUFFETS ARE MOSTLY FOR LUNCH OR BRUNCH)

Afghan
Amsterdam Falafelshop
Bombay Club
Bombay Tandoor
Delhi Club
Kuma
Maestro
Nirvana
Tutto Bene
21P

PRE-THEATER BARGAINS

Bistro d'Oc
Bistro Francais
Bombay Club
Cafe Atlantico
Cafe Saint-Ex
Circle Bistro
Le Paradou
Les Halles
Marcel's
Notti Bianche
Poste
1789
Tosca
21P
Zola

OUTDOOR DINING

Acadiana
Addie's
Amici Miei
Amsterdam Falafelshop
Bar Pilar
Belga Cafe
Black Market Bistro
Bombay Club
Breadline
Busboys and Poets
C.F. Folks
Cafe Atlantico
Cafe Milano
Cafe Saint-Ex
Cantler's Riverside Inn
Carlyle
Cashion's Eat Place
Charleston
Circle Bistro
Claire's at the Depot
Cloud Dining Lounge
Coastal Flats
Couscous Cafe & Catering
Crisp & Juicy
Delhi Club
Dukem
Equinox
Famous Luigi's
Galileo
Gerard's Place
Green Papaya
Guajillo
Hank's Oyster Bar
Harris Crab House
Inn at Easton
Islander Caribbean
Jackie's
Jaleo (Arlington and Bethesda)
Kanlaya Thai Cuisine
Kinkead's
L'Auberge Chez Francois
Le Mannequin Pis
Les Halles
Marcel's
Merkado Kitchen
Michel Richard Citronelle
Mimi's American Bistro
Minh's
Montmartre
Mykonos Grill
Notti Bianche
Occidental
Osteria del Galileo
Oval Room
Oyamel Cocina Mexicana
Palena
Patowmack Farm
Poste
Raku
Ray's the Steaks
Regent Thai Cuisine
Restaurant Eve
Sette Osteria
Sonoma
Stoney's Seafood House
Sweet Mango Cafe
Sweetwater Tavern

Tabard Inn
Tallula
TenPenh
Thai Coast
Thaiphoon (Pentagon Row)
2941
21P
2 Amys
Willow
Zaytinya

NONSMOKING RESTAURANTS

A & J
Addie's
Amici Miei
Amma Vegetarian Kitchen
Amsterdam Falafelshop
Annangol
Apartment 2G
Aster
Bangkok 54
Bistro Francais
Bistrot Lafayette
Black Market Bistro
Bob Kinkead's Colvin Run Tavern
Bombay Club
Busboys and Poets
Cafe Saint-Ex
Carlyle
Ceviche
CityZen
Claire's at the Depot
Coastal Flats
Colorado Kitchen
Corduroy
Couscous Cafe & Catering
Crisp & Juicy
Crystal Thai
DC Coast
Delhi Club
El Chalan
Eli's
Equinox
Fortune
Galileo
Gerard's Place
Good Fortune
Green Papaya
Han Sung Oak
Hank's Oyster Bar
Heritage India
Hollywood East Cafe
  on the Boulevard
Inn at Easton
Inn at Little Washington
Jackie's
Jerry's Seafood
Joe's Noodle House
Johnny's Half Shell
Kanlaya Thai Cuisine
Kaz Sushi Bistro
Komi
Kotobuki
Kuma
Laboratorio del Galileo
L'Auberge Chez Francois
La Flor de La Canela
Layalina
Le Paradou
Maestro
Majestic Cafe
Makoto
Mandalay
Matsutake
Mimi's American Bistro
Minh's
Mitsitam Native Foods Cafe
Montmartre
Mr. Chen's Organic Chinese Cuisine
Mykonos Grill
Natta Thai
New Fortune
Nirvana
Nora
Notti Bianche
Obelisk
Old Europe
O'Learys
Oval Room
Palena
Patowmack Farm
Pazo
Pesce
Pizzeria Paradiso
Raku
Ray's the Steaks
Regent Thai Cuisine
Restaurant Eve
Rock Creek
Sakoontra
Samantha's
1789
Spices
Straits of Malaya
Sunflower Vegetarian Restaurant
Sushi-Ko
Sushi Taro
Sweet Mango Cafe
Tabard Inn
Taste of Morocco
Tavira
Thai Coast
Thai Square
Tobago's Catering and Cafe

Tosca
2941
2 Amys
Urban Bar-B-Que Company
Vegetable Garden
Vidalia
Willow
Yee Hwa
Yoko
Yuan Fu
Zest
Zola

RESTAURANTS WITH FIREPLACES

Al Tiramisu
Aster
Bistro d'Oc
Bob Kinkead's Colvin Run Tavern
Charlie Palmer Steak
Circle Bistro
Claire's at the Depot
Dukem
Green Papaya
Inn at Easton
Inn at Little Washington
Kanlaya Thai Cuisine
L'Auberge Chez Francois
Pizzeria Paradiso (Georgetown)
Restaurant Eve
1789
Sonoma
Stoney's Seafood House
Sweet Mango Cafe
Tabard Inn
Tavira
2941
Zaytinya

ROOMS WITH A (SPECIAL) VIEW

Cantler's Riverside Inn
(VIEW OF THE WATER)

Charlie Palmer Steak
(CAPITOL)

Harris Crab House
(VIEW OF THE WATER)

Inn at Easton
(OUTDOOR GARDEN)

Inn at Little Washington
(OUTDOOR GARDEN)

L'Auberge Chez Francois
(OUTDOOR GARDEN)

Patowmack Farm
(VIEW OF WOODS AND WATER)

2941
(TERRACE OVERLOOKING LAKE)

ROMANTIC

Al Tiramisu
Aster
Bob Kinkead's Colvin Run Tavern
Bombay Club
Cafe Atlantico
Cashion's Eat Place
Charleston
Charlie Palmer Steak
CityZen
Claire's at the Depot
Foti's
Green Papaya
Inn at Easton
Inn at Little Washington
Le Paradou
L'Auberge Chez Francois
Layalina
Maestro
Marcel's
Michel Richard Citronelle
Minh's
Nora
Obelisk
O'Learys
Oval Room
Palena
Prime Rib
Restaurant Eve
1789
Taberna del Alabardero
Tosca
2941
21P
Vidalia
Zest
Zola

Ranking by Stars

★ ★ ★ ★

Inn at Little Washington
Laboratorio del Galileo
Maestro
Michel Richard Citronelle

★ ★ ★ 1/2

Restaurant Eve

★ ★ ★

Bangkok 54
Buck's Fishing & Camping
Cashion's Eat Place
Charleston
Charlie Palmer Steak
CityZen
Foti's
Heritage India
Inn at Easton
Jaleo
Johnny's Half Shell
Kaz Sushi Bistro
Komi
Makoto
minibar at Cafe Atlantico
Notti Bianche
Obelisk
Palena
Pazo
Sakoontra
1789
Sushi-Ko
Thai Square
Tosca
2941
2 Amys
Vidalia
Zaytinya

★ ★ 1/2

Addie's
Al Tiramisu
Amici Miei
Artie's
Aster
Bistrot Lepic
Bob Kinkead's Colvin Run Tavern
Bombay Club
Breadline
Capital Grille
Ceiba
Circle Bistro
Corduroy
Dahlia
Delhi Club
Firefly
Galileo
Gerard's Place
Hank's Oyster Bar
Huong Que (Four Sisters)
Jackie's
Kinkead's
Kotobuki
Le Mannequin Pis
Le Paradou
Lewnes' Steakhouse
Majestic Cafe
Marcel's
Minh's
Montmartre
Occidental
Oceanaire Seafood Room
Osteria del Galileo
Oval Room
Oyamel Cocina Mexicana
Pesce
Poste
Ray's the Steaks
Samantha's
Sonoma
Sorak Garden
Spices
Sunflower Vegetarian Restaurant
Tabaq Bistro
Tabard Inn
TemptAsian Cafe
Zola

★ ★

A & J
Acadiana
Annangol
Apartment 2G
Bistro Francais
Bistrot du Coin
Black Market Bistro
Blue Gin
Bombay Tandoor
Busboys and Poets
Cafe Atlantico
Cafe Saint-Ex
Cantler's Riverside Inn
Carlyle
Ceviche

Ranking by Stars

~ CONTINUED ~

C.F. Folks
Claire's at the Depot
Coastal Flats
Colorado Kitchen
Costa Verde
Crisp & Juicy
Crystal Thai
Cuban Corner
DC Coast
Del Merei Grille
Eat First
El Chalan
Equinox
Etete
Fortune
Gom Ba Woo
Good Fortune
Green Papaya
Guajillo
Han Sung Oak
Harris Crab House
Hollywood East Cafe on the Boulevard
Islander Caribbean
Jerry's Seafood
Joe's Noodle House
Kanlaya Thai Cuisine
La Flor de la Canela
L'Auberge Chez Francois
Layalina
Les Halles
Mandalay
Mark and Orlando's
Matchbox
Merkado Kitchen
Mitsitam Native Foods Cafe
Mourayo
Mykonos Grill
New Fortune
Nirvana
Old Ebbitt Grill
O'Learys
The Palm
Patowmack Farm
Pizzeria Paradiso
Prime Rib
Raku
Regent Thai Cuisine
Rock Creek
Sette Osteria
Stoney's Seafood House
Straits of Malaya
Sushi Taro
Sweetwater Tavern
Taberna del Alabardero
Tallula
Taqueria Tres Reyes
Taste of Morocco
Tasting Room
Tavira
Thai Basil
Thaiphoon
Tobago's Catering and Cafe
Tutto Bene
21P
Urban Bar-B-Que Company
Vegetable Garden
Vermilion
Willow
Yechon
Yuan Fu
Zengo
Zest

★ ½

Afghan
Al Crostino
Amma Vegetarian Kitchen
Amsterdam Falafelshop
Bar Pilar
Belga Cafe
Bistro d'Oc
Bistrot Lafayette
Bonefish Grill
Cafe Milano
Casa Blanca
Citrus Cafe
Cloud Dining Lounge
Couscous Cafe & Catering
The Diner
Dukem
Famous Luigi's
Matsutake
Mimi's American Bistro
Mr. Chen's Organic Chinese Cuisine
Natta Thai
Nora
Old Europe
Rosa Mexicano
TenPenh
Thai Coast
W Domku
Yee Hwa
Yoko

★

Don Lobo's Mexican Grill
Eli's
Kuma
Sweet Mango Cafe

Critic's Picks

A & J
Al Tiramisu
Amici Miei
Artie's
Bangkok 54
Bistrot Lepic
Bob Kinkead's Colvin Run Tavern
Bombay Club
Breadline
Buck's Fishing & Camping
Capital Grille
Cashion's Eat Place
C.F. Folks
Charleston
Charlie Palmer Steak
CityZen
Colorado Kitchen
Corduroy
Delhi Club
Del Merei Grille
Etete
Firefly
Foti's
Guajillo
Hank's Oyster Bar
Heritage India
Inn at Easton
Inn at Little Washington
Jackie's
Jaleo
Jerry's Seafood
Johnny's Half Shell
Kaz Sushi Bistro
Komi
Kotobuki
Laboratorio del Galileo
Layalina
Le Mannequin Pis
Lewnes' Steakhouse
Maestro
Majestic Cafe
Makoto
Michel Richard Citronelle
Minh's
minibar at Cafe Atlantico
Mitsitam Native Foods Cafe
Notti Bianche
Obelisk
Oceanaire Seafood Room
Oyamel Cocina Mexicana
Palena
Pazo
Pesce
Ray's the Steaks
Restaurant Eve
Samantha's
1789
Sonoma
Sorak Garden
Sunflower Vegetarian Restaurant
Sushi-Ko
Tabaq Bistro
Tabard Inn
TemptAsian Cafe
Thai Square
2941
2 Amys
Urban Bar-B-Que Company
Vidalia
Zaytinya

About the Author

★

TOM SIETSEMA is the award-winning food critic for The Washington Post, where he writes a weekly dining column for the Sunday Magazine, a weekly restaurant news column for the Wednesday Food section, a monthly report on out-of-town restaurants for the Travel section and an annual dining guide. He previously worked for Microsoft Corp., the Seattle Post-Intelligencer, the San Francisco Chronicle and the Milwaukee Journal. His work has appeared in GQ, Food & Wine, Travel & Leisure and other national publications.